WHAT IS GOOD WRITING?

What Is Good Writing?

Geoffrey J. Huck

OXFORD
UNIVERSITY PRESS

OXFORD
UNIVERSITY PRESS

Oxford University Press is a department of the University of Oxford.
It furthers the University's objective of excellence in research, scholarship,
and education by publishing worldwide.

Oxford New York
Auckland Cape Town Dar es Salaam Hong Kong Karachi
Kuala Lumpur Madrid Melbourne Mexico City Nairobi
New Delhi Shanghai Taipei Toronto

With offices in
Argentina Austria Brazil Chile Czech Republic France Greece
Guatemala Hungary Italy Japan Poland Portugal Singapore
South Korea Switzerland Thailand Turkey Ukraine Vietnam

Oxford is a registered trade mark of Oxford University Press
in the UK and certain other countries.

Published in the United States of America by
Oxford University Press
198 Madison Avenue, New York, NY 10016

Library of Congress Cataloging-in-Publication Data
Huck, Geoffrey J., 1944– author.
 What is good writing? / Geoffery J. Huck.
   p.   cm.
 Includes bibliographical references and index.
 ISBN 978–0–19–021295–7 (hardcover : alk. paper) 1. Fluency (Language learning) 2. Rhetoric—Study and
teaching. 3. Speech acts—Study and teaching. 4. Language and languages—Study and teaching. 5. Writing—
Psychological aspects. 6. Cognitive grammar. 7. Psycholinguistics. I. Title.
 P53.4115.H83 2015
 808—dc23

                              2014041343

9 8 7 6 5 4 3 2 1

Printed in the United States of America on acid-free paper

For Y. N.

Contents

Preface

ALTHOUGH TRAINED IN theoretical linguistics, I found myself a number of years ago teaching in and coordinating a professional writing program in a large public university. As a neophyte writing program administrator, I was intrigued to discover that the teachers and scholars in the program hadn't collectively settled on an answer to the question that serves as the title of this book. Indeed, they seemed surprised that the question should even be asked, the prevailing attitude being that it's natural for people to differ about what the "good" in good writing refers to, since it's inevitably a matter of taste. And at any rate, they felt an educator's professional concern should be more about improving whatever skills students brought to class rather than worrying about something so abstract. There were personal opinions, of course—some quite strongly held—and I was treated to lively discussions about types of pedagogy that might be more or less useful in the writing classroom. I read articles in *College English*, *WPA Journal*, and *College Composition and Communication* (*CCC*) as an outsider, but with interest.

Composition scholars are certainly not the only people in the world interested in writing. Teachers at all levels and in all disciplines inevitably are concerned, directly or indirectly, with the quality of writing of their students. Educational administrators in public and private institutions, journalists, businesspeople, politicians—in sum, you and me and everyone else—all have a stake in writing to one degree or another because so much information in the world is communicated through it. But those who have studied the process of writing in most detail fall generally into two different camps. Composition scholars, along with rhetoricians and literary scholars, make up one of those camps. The other camp consists of those who want to look at writing primarily through the lens of science.

Recently, I was reminded of a retrospective survey of the field from 2005 in *CCC* by the composition scholar Richard Fulkerson in which he identified four issues in composition studies about which he discerned an obvious lack of consensus: "we [in composition studies] differ about what our courses are supposed to achieve, about how effective writing is best produced, about what an effective classroom looks like, and about what it means to make knowledge."[1]

This seems to me now to present a highly accurate picture, as well as a pretty severe indictment, of the current state of composition pedagogy. While vigorous dispute is important in any healthy discipline, the issues here are so fundamental that one might reasonably suspect that there is no solid ground to stand on anywhere in the domain of writing. In fact, Fulkerson reinforced this suspicion by distinguishing various "theories of value" in composition studies that he said might account for these differences of opinion. Reflecting the relativism in the field, Fulkerson implied that one really couldn't choose among these value theories on any privileged principles: the most one could do was to chart the rise and fall of particular theories over time.

Fulkerson's account, and the opinions expressed by my colleagues in our writing program, cut directly against the grain of the research programs that I and others in linguistics and cognitive science have been working in over the past several decades. We in these fields tend toward a much more positivist view of science: we generally believe that the scientific method is the best way to learn about the world, and we carry out experiments to increase our knowledge of it. While some of us (and I count myself happily among them[2]) also believe that social and psychological factors external to a scientific theory can and usually do intrude to affect its reception in the marketplace of ideas, we are for the most part Popperian idealists. We think that a theory whose conclusions from its premises aren't empirically testable isn't much better than no theory at all.

There is, of course, much that linguists, who are often involved in recondite details of theory construction, can learn from writing instructors who every day must closely scrutinize the linguistic performance of real people as they use their language. I suspect most writing instructors have a better grasp of the output of the actual linguistic grammars that reside inside the heads of university students than many linguists do. Compositionists also are in general finely attuned to the role of audience in written expression; linguists and cognitive scientists, often together with sociolinguists, theorize about audience, but composition studies teachers have to attend to audience issues in writing on a daily basis.

Nevertheless, I have also come believe that people in the education community, and in particular in the composition-studies and rhetoric communities, have a great deal to learn from linguists and other cognitive scientists about what competence in writing consists of and how it is achieved. Writing teachers, when informed of research in the cognitive sciences about the representation of grammar in the mind and of the significance and ramifications of conceptions of audience, may say dismissively, "Yeah, we already know all that." And perhaps some of them do know all that. But by and large, the people I meet who study and teach writing seem to me not at all conversant with recent findings of cognitive science that are directly relevant to their field and that imply a rather different perspective from the one they habitually take. As Fulkerson notes, "Even our most empirical journal, *Research in the Teaching of English*, now publishes primarily ethnographic studies." Ethnographic studies may be suggestive, but by their very nature they can't provide a scientific demonstration of any generality.

Similarly, our creative writing community, although thoroughly invested in teaching creative writing, doesn't seem to much believe in its efficacy—or at any rate, doesn't display great concern about it. (The percentage of events classified under the head of teaching at the annual conference of the Association of Writers & Writing Programs rarely reaches double digits.) From my experience, creative writing teachers are mostly unacquainted with cognitive science approaches to writing. There is, no doubt, a feeling that creative writing is concerned with art, and that science is not terribly helpful in this domain. But such a judgment, in order to be tenable, requires actual inspection of the relevant science first.

The public at large is, of course, even less well-informed about the application of cognitive science to writing ability. Although creative and professional writing teachers largely eschew the prescriptions of self-appointed grammar mavens like Lynn Truss, Brian A. Garner, and the late William Safire, the latter still seem to hold sway in public forums (or should I say fora?). There are never-ending cries of alarm from various quarters that people in general and university students in particular are losing the ability to write. The National Commission on Writing in its study "Writing: A Ticket to Work . . . or a Ticket out?" quoted one business leader not long ago as saying, "The [writing] skills of new college graduates are deplorable—across the board; spelling, grammar, sentence structure . . . I can't believe people come out of college now not knowing what a sentence is."[3] This, of course, is either despite or because of the fact that a larger percentage of the population in the English-speaking world now attends university and is more diverse than ever before. What we don't know is whether any plausible change to the curricula in primary, secondary, and post-secondary institutions would, in fact, improve the conditions that have led to the sorts of expressions of horror just quoted. This is not merely of incidental interest, because public opinion affects the disbursement of public funds. Indeed, decision-makers in government and our large writing interest groups appear woefully ignorant of the discoveries of scientists who routinely research the cognitive foundations of language.

This is not to say that there is anything like a single "cognitive science perspective" about writing. Cognitive science is a large and heterogeneous field enlivened by all the usual disagreements and debates about many elements of theory and practice. There are literally hundreds of thousands of scientific articles that could be classified under the rubric of cognitive science. Anyone who works in the field, much less the casual reader, can only hope to become well-acquainted with a small patch in a large landscape.

Moreover, cognitive science as a field, or as a set of subfields (cognitive neuroscience, cognitive linguistics, computational linguistics, artificial intelligence, cognitive psychology, cognitive anthropology, etc.), is still in its infancy. Much is unknown or unresolved about cognitive structure and processing. Nevertheless, there are firm results in some areas and promising lines of research in others, the collective force of which provides a compelling argument for people interested in writing to pay them appropriate heed.

Although I, like most of my colleagues in linguistics, don't hold with some or even many of the propositions about language promulgated in the leading writing journals, especially those that take a postmodernist stance, it's not my purpose in this book to argue against them.[4] Nor is it my purpose to provide a primer for writing teachers or the general public on the empirical results of cognitive science relevant to writing (although such a book would undoubtedly be useful). Here I simply seek to show how people with a strong interest in writing might put the answers to some of their most basic questions about writing—and in particular, the questions of what good writing is and how it is learned—on a more scientific footing than they have hitherto done. No background in cognitive science, linguistics, or composition studies is either assumed or required.

My simple answer to the question "What is good writing?" is that it is the writing typically produced by a writer who is recognized as a good writer by other good writers. That definition of good writing, of course, will pull no weight unless powered by considerably more precision. The terms "good writing" and "good writers" come with broader connotations than I'd prefer, since one might, with reason, pick out both Alice Munro and a random fourth grader as good writers under different conditions. What I'm aiming for is more like the writing equivalent of fluency in speaking. We say that a normal native speaker of English achieves fluency in her language by her teen-aged years—and that's the kind of fluency I mean with respect to writing, a naturally achieved fluency that indicates an ability to converse easily with peers, to convey easily what one wants to convey, and to be easily understood by one's conversational partners. To hold the focus, I will henceforth mostly use the term "fluency" in place of good writing, although by fluency I do more or less mean "good writing" and vice versa. While the concept of fluency in writing does have a history in composition studies, my definition is meant to be operational.[5] That is, it is entirely possible (if rarely done) to canvas fluent writers to determine their judgments of the writing of others. To make this easy, I simply assume that any professional writer is a fluent writer in his language. This may seem either trivial or circular or both, but I also equate fluency with what linguists speak of as competence (a term I'd also rather not use out of concern that readers might supply an implied "mere" before it, even though there's nothing mere about it). The linguistic idea of competence (much simplified) is that the developing child's brain takes a large but unspecified quantity of spoken data as input and, over time and without much explicit instruction, produces general competence (or fluency) in speech as output. That is, we expect a normal child to grow up to be a fluent (competent) speaker of her native language, wherever in the world she comes from, whatever schooling she has. In a like manner, I propose that we should expect the normal developing writer's brain to be able to take in a large but unspecified quantity of written data as input and, over time and without much explicit instruction after the primary grades, produce general fluency (competence) in writing as output. Much of this book will be devoted to showing that this must be the case. The words "competence" and "fluency" are both intended to suggest that there is a level of mental development that all normal humans will ultimately attain given the appropriate input. Lack of appropriate input through reading and the motivation and curiosity to acquire it, I will argue, is the source of many of our students' writing problems.

We generally don't trouble to distinguish levels of ability among fluent native speakers beyond noting that some of them are especially articulate or inarticulate. We also fully anticipate that a child of 3 will not be as fluent as a teenager or adult, so the natural disfluencies of a 3-year-old don't alarm us. Further, we are not particularly bothered by the fact that fluent adult native speakers make frequent speaking errors in normal conversation, which we usually manage to ignore. Of course, fluent writers make mistakes too, which are correctible on revision, so I wouldn't want to imply that all fluent writers effortlessly produce fluent writing at first try. But what is important is that, upon achieving fluency, both writers and speakers command a vocabulary that is generally suitable for everyday interactions in their milieu and typically use grammatical structures that their audiences can efficiently interpret. Thus, a fluent writer, on my understanding, is not simply someone who does not need remedial instruction, nor is she necessarily a writer whom we regard as gifted and who never commits a solecism. Rather, she displays a typical ability with written language that other fluent writers associate with their own productions and those of other fluent writers. That is, I am suggesting something like a concept of "native writer" alongside that of native speaker.

Obviously, there aren't native writers of a language in just the way that there are native speakers. Writing and speech aren't identical in that sense, even if they share many features. In what follows I will talk about some of the features that fluent writing generally displays. These features, though differently formulated, will be familiar to composition studies teachers and scholars in a different guise. However, I maintain that a cognitive science perspective can provide explanations for these features lacking in current compositionist discussions. As a linguist and cognitive scientist, I consider it essential to discuss those features strictly within the context of a coherent theory of language.

The most important reason for taking a cognitive science approach in studying writing is that one can hope to provide empirically based answers to the kind of issues that Fulkerson raises. Because the definition of good writing I offer is operational, any experimental results based on it should be replicable, an essential condition in science. Although we are still far from discovering the precise conditions under which fluent writing is learned, I have no doubt that the appropriate way to approach this problem is through empirical research. It goes without saying among cognitive scientists of all stripes that an appropriate theory of how knowledge is gained (i.e., an epistemological theory) must be driven by empirical results.[6]

I should at this point acknowledge that mine is far from the first work on writing to draw on research in linguistics and the other cognitive sciences. In English, rhetoric, and composition studies, scholars like Linda Flower, James Paul Gee, and Margaret Freeman, among many others, have produced important cross-disciplinary studies in this area.

Joseph M. Williams regularly indicated in his books the debt he owed to linguists and cognitive scientists in increasing his understanding of how writers can improve their writing style.[7] Francis-Noel Thomas and Mark Turner, in their important *Clear and Simple as the Truth: Writing Classic Prose*, show "why learning to write cannot be reduced to acquiring writing skills, why learning to write is inevitably learning styles of writing, and how styles derive from cognitive stands,"[8] a statement with which I almost completely agree. And a myriad of other scholars have over the last century stepped over the boundary between linguistics and writing studies in one direction or another to add to our understanding of writing performance.[9]

In the area of cognitive linguistics and cognitive psychology, following insights of George Lakoff and Charles Fillmore, researchers like Seana Coulson, Todd Oakley, John R. Hayes, Mark Turner, Mark Johnson, and Gilles Fauconnier have shed light on the ways that meaning is constructed from bodily experience. Though more concerned with how meaning is possible at all rather than with the particulars of especially good writing, their work needs to be taken into account by, and linked to, any examination focusing on semantics in language, written or oral. Meanwhile, Flower and Hayes, Thomas and Turner, Williams and his colleague Gregory Colomb, and others have employed findings of linguistics and/or cognitive science in service of discovering principles of good writing in it. The progress that has been made in these areas has been and continues to be impressive, but I will argue that the mental conditions that lead to fluency in both writing and speaking are highly complex and that no explicit system of writing conventions designed to be taught in existing writing programs in high school and college will do much good for average students. My view is that the only writing program that accords with current research and is likely to be successful in developing fluency from normal initial disfluency[10] in writing will be primarily a reading program—one that produces avid independent readers. I don't at all say that there aren't effective strategies that highly accomplished teachers can use to improve students' writing to various degrees—of course there are. But fluency in writing as I conceive it can never be achieved by taking a few courses in writing at the secondary, university, or postgraduate level.

I was not acquainted with Stephen D. Krashen's 1993 book, *The Power of Reading: Insights from the Research* (extensively revised and published in a second edition in 2004), or his many other works, until all the chapters that follow were written, but I am now encouraged to read that his position on the foundational importance to writing of what he calls "free voluntary reading" is very similar to mine.[11] Krashen believes, as I do, that we learn to read and write by reading, that a healthy diet of self-motivated, recreational reading – reading because one wants to – is the key to the development of skill in writing and language achievement in general. Perhaps it is our training in linguistics that convinces us that, as he says, "Language is too vast, too complex to be taught or learned one rule or word at a time."[12] While he focuses more on primary and secondary school students and on ESL learners than I do, his orientation and conclusions are readily transferable to the university context, which most interests me.

Finally, there is another (and more recent) book that is relevant to my work, and that is Steven Pinker's *The Sense of Style: The Thinking Person's Guide to Writing in the 21st Century*.[13] I would recommend this book to anyone interested in writing as not only the best style guide available for competent writers at the moment but also a delightful and entertaining study of language for any avid reader. Like Krashen, Pinker broadly agrees that good writers have most often learned to write through their own avid reading: "[N]o one is born with skills in English composition per se. Those skills may not have come from stylebooks, but they must have come from somewhere. That somewhere is the writing of other writers. Good writers are avid readers. They have absorbed a vast inventory of words, idioms, constructions, tropes, and rhetorical tricks, and with them a sensitivity to how they mesh and how they clash."

In chapter 1, I will briefly discuss previous approaches to good writing that have brought us to our current position. Composition studies teachers and scholars, who undoubtedly know this history well, may safely skip this chapter. After this historical overview, I will introduce in chapter 2 an empirical perspective, the cognitive approach, which appeals to the operational definition of good writing that I mentioned. The material that follows in Part II focuses on the attainment of fluency in writing and reviews the research support for aspects of this alternative as against some of the more familiar approaches. I will also introduce Construction Theory and Relevance Theory, which play an important role in my account. In Part III, I will look at the relationship between ideas and concepts and the language that encodes them, showing how the cognitive approach, and in particular Relevance Theory, is applicable to artistic as well as to the more functional genres of writing.

I would like to thank Robert Chametzky, Schuyler W. Huck, Joseph Fletcher, John Goldsmith, Thomas Kerr, Younghee Na, Ian Colvin, Duncan Koerber, Rosamund Woodhouse, Stephanie Bell, and two anonymous but very insightful reviewers, all of whose good suggestions, ideas, and encouragement I gratefully acknowledge. My excellent research assistants, Mora Ouellet and Lucy Cappiello, provided valuable assistance in tracking down citations. I would also like to thank the many students in my Literary Nonfiction classes at York University for drawing my attention to a variety of interesting and provocative constructions in the English language that I would never have guessed existed. Of course, it shouldn't be concluded that any of these generous people necessarily agree with what I say in this book or is in any way responsible for any errors or omissions in it. Finally, I'm indebted to Hallie Stebbins, my editor at Oxford, for her expert guidance; to Lynn Childress, the book's manuscript editor; and Chakira Lane, the senior production manager, for their highly professional work during the publication process.

Abbreviations

AES	Automated Essay Scoring
CCC	*College Composition and Communication*
CCS	Critical/Cultural Studies
CG	Construction Grammar
CWPA	Council of Writing Program Administrators
NCTE	National Council of Teachers of English
NWP	National Writing Project
PIR	Professional Intuitive Rating
TBI	Traumatic Brain Injury

WHAT IS GOOD WRITING?

Prologue

OBVIOUSLY, THOSE OF us who have a professional interest in writing need to be clear about what we mean when we say a piece of writing is good. But even among people whose business it is to identify good writing there is a conspicuous lack of agreement about what the "good" in good writing is.

Take a particularly striking example from the education literature: in 1992, the researcher Daniel Koretz and his colleagues at UCLA undertook a routine study of the writing skills of fourth- and eighth-graders in the state of Vermont.[1] In this study, each student completed a writing sample which was graded twice—once each by two different teachers—over several dimensions of writing ability. To determine whether the teachers had graded the papers consistently according to the same criteria, Koretz compared the two sets of grades using a common statistical technique. If the two teachers mostly agreed with each other, then the grades would be considered a reliable indicator of the students' writing abilities. To Koretz's surprise, however, it turned out that the graders in this study actually disagreed with each other more than half the time.[2] In fact, the disagreements about what was good writing and what was not in these graders' eyes were so pervasive that the researchers concluded the scores were useless for any administrative purpose.

To ensure against error, Koretz hopefully repeated his study the following year, but with only trivial improvement in score reliability. Reviewing his results, he suggested that a different scoring system and more intensive training of the graders might have delivered better results, but he himself undertook no further tests.[3] In fact, over two decades later, reliability remains a persistent problem in essay scoring not only in the primary grades, but at every level in which essay tests are administered. Indeed, the low reliability scores that Koretz found are almost identical to those at the professional academic level that have measured agreement between ratings by peer reviewers of articles submitted to academic journals, where quality of written argument is obviously a paramount criterion for acceptance.[4] If educators at every level can't decide what good writing is, what does that say about their efforts to instill good writing practices in their students?

Looking at the problem from a different perspective, consider the popular conclusion of many a teacher of creative writing that "writing cannot be taught."[5] Flannery O'Connor, a certifiably good writer and beneficiary of an education at the Iowa Writer's Workshop, undoubtedly the most prestigious school for writers in North America, agreed, with one qualification: "I believe the teacher's work should be largely negative.... We can learn how not to write."[6] Whatever she meant by that, Iowa itself has taken a guarded position in its recent promotional material about the extent to which good writing is teachable: "If one can 'learn' to play the violin or to paint," they say on their website, "one can 'learn' to write, though no processes of externally induced training can ensure that one will do it well."[7]

Implicit in the Iowa statement, I think, is acceptance of a distinction between what we usually think of as art, on the one hand, and craft, on the other. Writing well (producing art, literature) is considered high, but merely writing proficiently (producing craft, journalism) is low. You can insult a writer of high aspiration by asserting that his product does not rise above craft to the more exalted level of literature, as John Updike apparently intended to insult Tom Wolfe by writing the following: "*A Man in Full* [Wolfe's novel] still amounts to entertainment, not literature, even literature in a modest aspirant form."[8] By contrast, however, the *Wall Street Journal*'s reviewer called *A Man in Full* "a masterpiece," while *Newsweek* said of it that "Right now, no writer"— presumably including John Updike at that time—"is getting it on paper better than Tom Wolfe." Tom Wolfe's near name-sake, Thomas Wolfe, the author of *Look Homeward, Angel*, which the *New York Times* hailed as being "as interesting and powerful a book as has ever been made out of the drab circumstances of provincial American life" and which the writer Malcolm Cowley in *The New Republic* compared to the work of Dickens and Dostoyevsky, was excoriated by the critic Bernard DeVoto for displaying neither art nor craft: "[he has] mastered neither the psychic material out of which a novel is made nor the technique of writing fiction."[9] Similarly, Truman Capote once said about the novels of Jack Kerouac, "It's not writing; it's only typing," though John Updike (whom Tom Wolfe likened to one of the Three Stooges) evidently admired Kerouac.[10] And so it goes. Such examples of conflicting opinion about the quality of the work of this or that writer could be multiplied ad nauseam. Even allowing for professional bias, jealousy, and the general sniping for which writers and critics are well known, one is hard-put to find even a modicum of reasoned argument about the qualities of good writing in these differing reviews: When personal taste is subtracted, not much of consequence is left to hang a hat on.

As mentioned earlier, we do set different standards for essays about their pets by fourth- and eighth-graders and for novels by well-known professional authors. What counts as good writing in the context of a high school assignment on citizenship and of a *New Yorker* short story will not be the same. But within any genre, no matter how widely or narrowly defined, there are certain to be differences of opinion among readers about what rises to the level of "good." Does this mean that what makes for good writing is merely a creature of fashion? There must be very few, if any, in the writing business who are willing to say that it is. The evidence notwithstanding, those of us who teach and write are compelled, not only by what we see but also by what seems to amount to an article of faith, to believe that there really is such a thing as good writing, that it exists independently of personal taste, and that it is provably different from bad writing. But if we are going to insist on this distinction, then we really ought to justify it—as well as to explain why any usable concept of good writing is so frustratingly difficult to pin down.

Conceptual Introduction

Historical Background

THERE WAS A time when good writing would invariably be defined by adverting to the literary classics. Prior to the nineteenth century, for example, it was customary to identify good writing with the achievements of the ancient Greek and Roman poets and orators, which constituted a central part of the curriculum,[1] and by the early eighteen-hundreds, an English-language canon had been established that schoolboys would regularly be referred to for composition instruction. But these days, now that inquiry in educational settings has become considerably more free-wheeling, the canonical answer no longer suffices. In fact, the idea of a discreet canon is itself no longer widely accepted, and in any case, if you say that good writing is to be found in the classics, then aspiring writers will demand all the particulars, so that, if required, they will be able to reproduce it in their next assignment.

But how are we to say, precisely, what makes the writing in *Pride and Prejudice* and *Moby-Dick* so wonderfully good, other than it obviously is? We could apply the traditional tools of literary criticism to it and haul out notions of plot, character, organization, voice, and so on. But that, from the perspective of the student, would be just begging the question. And anyway, at least since the rise of the New Criticism in the 1940s, the interests of literary critics have been more focused on the consumption of literature than on its creation. Indeed, the move to so-called Theory initiated by French postmodern critics in the 1950s and 1960s has pretty much shoved authorial intention out the window and accepted the text as given.[2] This has left contemporary theorists little to talk about with students who are simply looking for concrete advice about how to become good writers.

It is true that, alongside the classics, classically oriented writing instructors have always had an arsenal of epigrams about the practice of good writing to fire off in their classes, as if these might possibly clarify what good writers were about. The history of writing instruction is replete with flowery injunctions that sound quite sensible to the ear but then, in the application, have a tendency to wither away in the hand:

> The perfection of style is to be clear without being mean. The clearest style is that which uses only current or proper words. (Aristotle)

> Unless I am mistaken, the force and charm of arrangement will be found in this: to say at once what ought at once to be said, deferring many points, and waving them for the moment. (Horace)

> An acceptable sentence (*sermo congruus et perfectus*) arises from four principles . . . material, the words as members of grammatical classes; formal, their union in various constructions; efficient, the grammatical relations between different parts of speech expressed in the inflexional forms . . . final, the expression of a complete thought. (Thomas of Erfurt)

> For a man to write well, there are required three necessaries: to read the best authors, observe the best speakers, and much exercise of his own style. (Ben Jonson)

> Proper Words in proper Places, makes the true Definition of a Style. (Jonathan Swift)[3]

These are fine sentiments, but by themselves will they actually help anyone anxious to improve his or her writing? For example, how is one to know that one's words are the proper ones and that they are put in the proper places? Isn't that pretty much the whole ballgame? To say the very least, as Jack Lynch, an English professor and historian of lexicography, notes, a formulation like the one from Dean Swift is "rather cryptic."[4]

The community at large of writing teachers must have felt much the same way, because by the time Austen and Melville were writing their novels, composition texts had begun to lay out a smorgasbord of more particular admonitions and urgings, often focusing on punctuation.[5] Samuel Phillips Newman's *A Practical System of Rhetoric, Or, The Principles and Rules of Style Inferred from Examples of Writing: To Which is Added a Historical Dissertation of English Style* (1837) was an early entrant, but to my mind the epitome of this type of text is William Strunk and E. B. White's brief and beloved *Elements of Style* (original edition, by Strunk alone, prepared 1918 or earlier; current ["Fourth"] edition, edited and with an introduction by White's stepson, Roger Angell, published 2000), which contains several dozen useful rules and principles designed to "cut the tangle of English rhetoric down to size."[6] Among Strunk and White's precepts are the following: "Enclose parenthetic expressions between commas"; "Do not join independent clauses by a comma"; "A participial phrase at the beginning of a sentence must refer to the grammatical subject"; "Omit needless words"; and (my personal favorite) "Be clear." I've used Strunk and White in the classroom and have found it elegantly written and ultimately frustrating. While most of the rules are straightforward and can be memorized and applied to some effect in student assignments, a few of them, like "Omit needless words" and "Be clear," often seem to puzzle aspiring writers, especially those who always thought they were, in fact, doing so and being so. Students certainly can learn the approved places to use a comma, but as a definition of good writing, adherence to rules in the Strunk and White fashion has two obvious flaws which should be plain to even the most fervent fan: (1) good writers don't always observe those rules, and (2) you can rigorously follow all of them without producing anything close to what literary people usually have in mind when they speak of good writing.[7] The first objection inflicts serious damage to the equation of conscious rule-following and good writing, but the second provides the coup de grace. Together, they serve to reinforce the message of the creative writing community that, however you conceive of it, good writing simply can't be taught.

At any rate, during the twentieth century the Strunk and White approach, which had never sat very comfortably in the university curriculum, ultimately suffered the consequences of its inflexibility. Those who adhered tightly to it—generally known these days as prescriptivists—succeeded in marginalizing themselves in the academy with their resistance to developments in linguistic science and the new scholarship of writing assessment, which was sweeping the academy in the 1920s and 1930s. Moreover, while prescriptivists were worshipping at the altar of H. W. Fowler's *Modern English Usage* (1926) and George Orwell's "Politics and the English Language" (1946), the apostates were replacing classical and current-traditional rhetorics with new ideas in pragmatism and behaviorism that were designed to address the increasingly difficult problem of teaching writing to, and assessing the writing of, a rapidly growing middle-class school population. By the 1940s, quantification and measurement had become de rigueur in English departments, as in the humanities generally. Where once students were required to write the stodgy essay, they now answered multiple-choice questions that could be mechanically graded.[8] The benefits to the teacher were manifold: there could be no question of grader bias, answers were unambiguously right or wrong, students were less able to question their marks, time spent grading was reduced, etc.—one can see how the process was immediately attractive to the schoolmaster who had up till then been drowning in student essays.

Aligned with forward-looking composition teachers on the other side of the fence from the prescriptivists were ranks of educational psychologists, statisticians, and test developers who promised to bring to the writing vocation the sort of respectability that scientists had enjoyed. Rhetoricians, whose influence had been waning with the decline of classical education in the late 1800s, and structural linguists, whose field was suddenly blossoming, were happy to join in, seeing in the new scientific approach to composition an important role for their own brand of academic inquiry, which they too wished to think of as "scientific."

Another of the significant influences on the drift of writing instruction in the twentieth century was pressure from public education's various constituencies—not only teachers and researchers but also parents, politicians, businesses, the military, etc.—who were demanding that teaching outcomes be accurately assessed and reported. This demand for accountability was easily answered by the statisticians, who could of course measure the results of standardized tests with great precision and authority. As standardized tests proliferated, and companies and organizations like the College Entrance Examination Board, the American College Testing program, and the Educational Testing Service developed and perfected their psychometric products, writing teachers became more accustomed to measuring writing skills with multiple-choice-type tests. No one may have felt that they were unquestionably the very best substitute for the essay assignment, but they certainly were an expedient one.

The institutionalization of standardized testing brought with it two concepts seemingly essential to its effectiveness: reliability and validity. We have earlier met with reliability in connection with Daniel Koretz's Vermont study. As suggested there, a test is said to provide reliable scores to the extent that different graders will give the same score to any particular student's performance on that test. The more reliable the test scores are, the less they can be questioned as having been affected by the personal whims and fancies of the grader. (Technically, statisticians refer to this as *interrater reliability* to distinguish it from other kinds of reliability; henceforth, when I use the term I mean it in just this sense.) By contrast, a test is said to provide valid scores to the extent that they measure exactly the constructs that they purport to measure. For example, the crease in your palm that palm readers call the "life line" is claimed (by them) to predict the length of your life, though there has never been a scientifically satisfying demonstration that it is a valid measure. It may nevertheless be a completely reliable measure if all palm readers deliver exactly the same verdict on any particular palm. One always wants reliability, of course, though not if it has to come at the expense of validity. Obviously, in "objective" or multiple-choice testing, reliability will always border on perfection as long as the graders are machines supplied with the same template answer sheet.

The question that has always dogged multiple-choice testing as a measure of writing ability is whether the scores it provides are valid. In other words, do we really want to say that the very definition of good writing is a high grade on a standardized test? Although the multiple-choice tests used in writing assessment—often called indirect tests of writing—can deliver scores for spelling, punctuation, capitalization, vocabulary, and grammaticality, unfortunately they don't at this point have much to contribute toward measuring style. The problem is just one of trying to correlate something that can be easily quantified (i.e., what the indirect tests measure) with something that, at least at present, can't (i.e., style). Just because a student's spelling and punctuation are off, it doesn't necessarily mean that he or she isn't an excellent writer in all other respects. With this in mind, classroom teachers, who, after considerable experience with standardized tests, began to see writing as something that doesn't reduce to the dimensions measurable on them, pressured test designers to add a direct measure, an actual writing component, to their tests. But while grading a writing sample the good old-fashioned way may provide a relatively valid measure of writing ability, it is open to serious objection concerning its reliability, as we saw in the Koretz study. This is the toothpaste tube problem: to get the toothpaste fully into one end of the tube, you have to squeeze it out of the other.

To achieve reliability in direct tests of writing while holding validity relatively constant, test designers have tried to impose consistency on graders with a three-pronged strategy of providing them with a precise grading rubric, a graded sample using the rubric, and regular monitoring during the grading process. This is occasionally characterized as grading to the instruction. In addition, composition instructors have learned to teach their students specific features that the tests will address—often characterized as teaching to the test. With these additions, test designers have often claimed both reasonably high reliability and reasonably high validity for their direct writing tests, even though these tests emphatically do not measure anything so subjective as quality. In fact, teaching to the test and grading to the instruction entirely undermine validity if the tests are meant to be taken as measuring anything more than the specifics of what has been taught and graded.[9] Consequently, although reliability has long been assumed to be a necessary but not sufficient condition for validity, some researchers today, recognizing this problem as intractable, would like to ditch reliability as a criterion altogether.[10] But, of course, that puts us right back where we started.

Writing rubrics today generally come in two varieties. A holistic rubric yields a single score for the entire piece or portfolio, while an analytic score yields subscores for individual traits or criteria (spelling, grammar, continuity, organization, etc.). In either case, the scores remain the subjective assessment of the grader. For comparison purposes, table 1.1 shows a holistic rubric and table 1.2 an analytic rubric.

The feature of rubrics like these that stands out is their generality. The criteria "displays consistent ability in the use of language," "command of language," and "consistent, appropriate use of conventions of Standard English for grammar, usage [etc.] for the grade level" are no less open to subjective interpretation than are the classic epigrams of Horace and Swift. One would have to be more precise about what these rubrics mean to ensure consistency and, hence, reliability, especially in the upper grades where the language structures used by students become more complex and the purposes to which the structures are being put more subtle. But where guidance to the scorer becomes more precise there is the danger of grading to the instruction, where the scorer is tipped as to what the test designer considers quality in written productions and what the students have been explicitly taught.

In this sense, grading to the instruction turns the exercise into just another indirect test of quality—which is therefore not a test of quality at all. An essay that, in the grader's mind, displays a logical sequence of ideas and/or events may exemplify good writing—or it may not. Although many show dogs have brown hair, having brown hair

TABLE 1.1

Pennsylvania System of School Assessment Writing Scoring Guidelines (Narrative)
WRITING
PSSA NARRATIVE SCORING GUIDELINE

4		
	FOCUS	Sharp, distinct controlling point or theme with evident awarness of the narrative
	CONTENT DEVELOPMENT	Strong story line with illustrative details that addresses a complex idea or examines a complex experience. Throughly elaborated narrative sequence that employs narrative elements as appropriate
	ORGANIZATION	Skillful narrative pattern with clear and consistent sequencing of events, employing a beginning, a middle, and an end. Minor interruptions to the sequence may occur.
	STYLE	Precise control of language, literary devices, and sentence structures that creates a consistent and effective point of view and tone.

3		
	FOCUS	Clear controlling point or theme with general awareness of the narrative.
	CONTENT DEVELOPMENT	Story line with details that addresses an idea or examines an experience. Sufficiently elaborated narrative sequence that employs narrative elements as appropriate.
	ORGANIZATION	Narrative pattern with generally consistent sequencing of events, employing a beginning, a middle, and an end. Interruptions to the sequence may occur.
	STYLE	Appropriate control of language, literary, and sentence structures that creates a consistent point of view and tone.

2		
	FOCUS	Vague evidence of a controlling point or theme with inconsistent awareness of the narrative.
	CONTENT DEVELOPMENT	Inconsistent story line that inadequately addresses an idea or examines an experience. Insufficiently elaborated narrative sequence that may employ narrative elements.
	ORGANIZATION	Narrative pattern with generally inconsistent sequencing of events that may employ a beginning, a middle, and an end. Interruptions to the sequence may interfere with meaning.
	STYLE	Limited control of language and sentence structures that creates interference with point of view and tone.

1		
	FOCUS	Little or no evidence of a controlling point or theme with minimal awareness of the narrative.
	CONTENT DEVELOPMENT	Insufficient story line that minimally addresses an idea or examines an experience. Unelaborated narrative that may employ narrative elements.
	ORGANIZATION	Narrative pattern with little or no sequencing of events. Interruptions to the sequence interfere with meaning.
	STYLE	Minimal control of language and sentence structures that creates an inconsistent point of view and tone.

Source: <http://www.portal.state.pa.us/portal/server.pt/community/state_assessment_system/20965/pennsylvania_system_of_school_assessment_(pssa)/1190526>.

isn't and can't be a criterion for being a show dog. Similarly, a feature that is detected in some (much? most?) of what an examiner or constructor of rubrics considers good writing can't determine good writing. This is the problem with trying to break good writing down into what are supposedly its component parts: try as you might to find them, all good writing isn't put together from exactly the same set of elements susceptible to either direct or indirect testing. As the philosopher Ludwig Wittgenstein observed, when it comes to "family resemblances" (which is what we are dealing with when we talk about pieces of good writing), any two members of the family may have exactly no features in common. Wittgenstein gave the example of the family of games: while the game of

TABLE 1.2

Michigan Educational Assessment Program Rubric/Scoring Guide (Analytic)

Narrative Writing: Grades 4 and 7

IDEAS

o points: Ideas are not focused on the task and/or are undeveloped.

2 points: Tells a story with ideas that are minimally focused on the topic and developed with limited and/or general details.

4 points: Tells a story with ideas that are somewhat focused on the topic and are developed with a mix of specific and/or general details.

6 points: Tells a story with ideas that are clearly focused on the topic and are thoroughly developed with specific, relevant details.

ORGANIZATION

o points: No organization evident.

1 point: Organization and connections between ideas and/or events are weak.

2 points: Organization and connections between ideas and/or events are logically sequenced.

3 points: Organization and connections between ideas and/or events are clear and logically sequenced.

STYLE

o points: Ineffective use of language for the writer's purpose and audience.

1 point: Limited use of language, including lack of variety in word choice and sentences, may hinder support for the writer's purpose and audience.

2 points: Adequate command of language, including effective word choice and clear sentences, supports the writer's purpose and audience.

3 points: Command of language, including effective and compelling word choice and varied sentence structure, clearly supports the writer's purpose and audience.

CONVENTIONS

o points: Ineffective use of conventions of Standard English for grammar, usage, spelling, capitalization, and punctuation.

1 point: Limited use of conventions of Standard English for grammar, usage, spelling, capitalization, and punctuation for the grade level.

2 points: Adequate use of conventions of Standard English for grammar, usage, spelling, capitalization, and punctuation for the grade level.

3 points: Consistent, appropriate use of conventions of Standard English for grammar, usage, spelling, capitalization, and punctuation for the grade level.

Source: <http://www.michigan.gov/documents/mde/Informational__Rubric_332528_7.pdf.>

bridge may share some features with canasta, and the game of baseball may share some features with cricket, there are no features common to canasta and baseball, except that we consider them games. The same applies to the family of good writing. There is no set of proxies (ignoring the tautologous "control" or "command of language") that are both necessary and sufficient in the determination of good writing.

Recently, writing teachers have adopted several different strategies that, while not explicitly intended to rescue their discipline from this particular dilemma, have shifted attention away from it to other issues. In his surveys of the composition-studies field from the 1980s through the first few years of the new century, Richard Fulkerson identified several distinct theories of writing that could claim adherents during this period and that tended to downplay the significance of traditional rubrics: Expressivism, Mimeticism, Rhetoricism,[11] and Critical/Cultural Studies (CCS), each with its own particular variants. As Fulkerson points out, Expressivists focus their attention on the writer, valuing "openness, honesty, sincerity, originality, authentic voice, and personal topics for writing." Mimeticists are interested in the representation of external reality, valuing accuracy, soundness, and truth. Rhetoricists are interested in the reader and value the effectiveness of the communication with a particular audience.[12] Finally, CCS teachers are interested in cultural artifacts and value cultural analysis and interpretation. One could, of course, be both a mimeticist and a CCSist, seeing cultural critique as leading to larger truths. Or one could combine rhetorical and expressive interests by claiming that a student's openness, honesty, etc., are most likely to engage the reader.[13]

The different values attached to these theories ensure that there will be different conceptions of what constitutes good writing. Moreover, cutting across the four theories are different ideas about the process of literary creation and the best way to teach it. For example, on one view there are three stages in the writing process, usually characterized as pre-writing, writing, and rewriting.[14] A teacher who emphasizes process may wish to liberate students from the shackles of rule-following and to stimulate self-expression by focusing on procedures that are likely, in his or her view, to lead eventually to success, rather than on the success of the final product itself. Meanwhile, CCS advocates may encourage aspiring writers to assault the ramparts—to do what they can in their writing to subvert existing power structures and to challenge traditional forms of argument.[15] In this way, they hope aspiring writers will find their true voices instead of merely acceding to stultifying norms.[16]

One exemplary program that combines the interests of the theories is outlined in the "Framework for Success in Postsecondary Writing," jointly developed by the Council of Writing Program Administrators (CWPA), the National Council of Teachers of English (NCTE), and the National Writing Project (NWP).[17] This program urges teachers to develop "habits of mind" in their students that include curiosity, openness, engagement, creativity, persistence, responsibility, flexibility, and "metacognitive" abilities. This roster of positive habits is to be fostered by "experiences" meant to "enhance students' rhetorical knowledge, critical thinking, writing processes, knowledge of conventions, [and] ability to compose in multiple environments." The authors of the Framework call rhetorical knowledge "the basis of good writing" and urge teachers to develop it in their students by, among other things, helping them to "learn and practice [*sic*] key rhetorical concepts such as audience, purpose, context, and genre through writing and analysis of a variety of types of texts." As for "knowledge of conventions," the authors say, "Conventions are the formal rules and informal guidelines that define what is considered to be correct (or appropriate) and incorrect (or inappropriate) in a piece of writing. Conventions include the surface features of a text such as mechanics, spelling, and attribution of sources, as well as more global concerns such as content, tone, style, organization, and evidence."

I think at this point it would be worthwhile to note that although the composition-studies community these days almost unanimously eschews prescriptivism in both form and practice, and has done so for decades, the impulse to regulate usually finds its way into the classroom. (Observe the words "correct (or appropriate) and incorrect (or inappropriate)" in the Framework.[18]) In composition classes, even in expressivist and CCS classes, ideas of cohesion, coherence, clarity, precision, and concision are rarely completely ignored. To the extent that such ideas express the virtues of good writing implicitly held by these composition teachers, no matter how anti-prescriptivist they may feel themselves to be, their motivation may well be prescriptivist in character. When a person says that good writing consists of such-and-such, that person is not simply making an observation; he or she means that if you want to write well, you had better do such-and-such: you should follow the rules that doing such-and-such entails. The prescription is inherent in the valuation.[19] And, indeed, that goes for me as well. When I say that good writing is fluent writing, I definitely do mean that if you wish to write well, you must attain fluency in your writing. Where I depart from many in the writing community is that I don't pretend that I can enumerate all or even the main rules of fluent writing (any more than I can enumerate all or even the main rules of fluent speaking). Nor, I should emphasize, do I believe that anyone else can at this juncture. When I speak of prescriptivists henceforth, I include such nominal anti-prescriptivists among them. To urge that a student attend to his audience, that he try to organize his essay more logically, etc., is, in the school setting, to prescribe. And even as I preach the anti-prescriptivist canon in my approach to good writing, I admit that I occasionally find myself in their company.

Prior to the promulgation of the Framework, the CWPA had drafted a statement that elaborates on the desired outcomes of the first-year composition course (see table 1.3). In evaluating this, the reader might want to refer back to the venerable distinction between the structure (grammar, syntax) of a string of words, its meaning (sense, semantics), and its function (use, pragmatics). All three of these, of course, are integral to the string: one cannot exist without the others. And this holds true of sentences, passages, chapters, essays, whole books. You cannot logically say, "The structure is good, but the function is poor," or treat function independently of structure and meaning. You don't get the structure of a passive sentence without its function. We will look at this in more detail in chapter 3. But it is notable that in the Framework and the WPA Statement, as well as

TABLE 1.3

WPA Outcomes Statement for First-Year Composition

RHETORICAL KNOWLEDGE

By the end of first-year composition, students should

- Focus on a purpose
- Respond to the needs of different audiences
- Respond appropriately to different kinds of rhetorical situations
- Use conventions of format and structure appropriate to the rhetorical situation
- Adopt appropriate voice, tone, and level of formality
- Understand how genres shape reading and writing
- Write in several genres

Faculty in all programs and departments can build on this preparation by helping students learn

- The main features of writing in their fields
- The main uses of writing in their fields
- The expectations of readers in their fields

CRITICAL THINKING, READING, AND WRITING

By the end of first year composition, students should

- Use writing and reading for inquiry, learning, thinking, and communicating
- Understand a writing assignment as a series of tasks, including finding, evaluating, analyzing, and synthesizing appropriate primary and secondary sources
- Integrate their own ideas with those of others
- Understand the relationships among language, knowledge, and power

Faculty in all programs and departments can build on this preparation by helping students learn

- The uses of writing as a critical thinking method
- The interactions among critical thinking, critical reading, and writing
- The relationships among language, knowledge, and power in their fields

PROCESSES

By the end of first-year composition, students should

- Be aware that it usually takes multiple drafts to create and complete a successful text
- Develop flexible strategies for generating, revising, editing, and proof-reading
- Understand writing as an open process that permits writers to use later invention and rethinking to revise their work
- Understand the collaborative and social aspects of writing processes
- Learn to critique their own and others' works
- Learn to balance the advantages of relying on others with the responsibility of doing their part
- Use a variety of technologies to address a range of audiences

Faculty in all programs and departments can build on this preparation by helping students learn

- To build final results in stages
- To review work-in-progress in collaborative peer groups for purposes other than editing

TABLE 1.3 (*CONTINUED*)

- To save extensive editing for later parts of the writing process
- To apply the technologies commonly used to research and communicate within their fields

KNOWLEDGE OF CONVENTIONS

By the end of first year composition, students should

- Learn common formats for different kinds of texts
- Develop knowledge of genre conventions ranging from structure and paragraphing to tone and mechanics
- Practice appropriate means of documenting their work
- Control such surface features as syntax, grammar, punctuation, and spelling

Faculty in all programs and departments can build on this preparation by helping students learn

- The conventions of usage, specialized vocabulary, format, and documentation in their fields
- Strategies through which better control of conventions can be achieved

COMPOSING IN ELECTRONIC ENVIRONMENTS

By the end of first-year composition, students should:

- Use electronic environments for drafting, reviewing, revising, editing, and sharing texts
- Locate, evaluate, organize, and use research material collected from electronic sources, including scholarly library databases; other official databases (e.g., federal government databases); and informal electronic networks and Internet sources
- Understand and exploit the differences in the rhetorical strategies and in the affordances available for both print and electronic composing processes and texts

Faculty in all programs and departments can build on this preparation by helping students learn

- How to engage in the electronic research and composing processes common in their fields
- How to disseminate texts in both print and electronic forms in their fields

Source: "WPA Outcomes Statement for First-Year Composition, Adopted by the Council of Writing Program Administrators (WPA), April 2000; amended July 2008." Available online at <http://wpacouncil.org/files/wpa-outcomes-statement.pdf>. Creative Commons Attribution—NoDerivs 3.0 Unported License.

in the Michigan rubric, grammatical structure is separated from meaning and function, tucked into a formalist grab bag that includes how to attribute sources and how to format a chemistry lab report.

What the Framework and the WPA Statement are not able to provide is a way to extract reliable and valid scores from tests composed under its desiderata. Assessment of rhetorical knowledge, critical thinking, and writing processes will have to be by subjective rubric, and the reference to "formal rules," "better control of conventions," and what is "correct (or appropriate) and incorrect (or inappropriate)" suggests a re-encounter with the deficiencies of prescriptive rubrics. (I will have more to say about this in chapter 2.) However, this is not to say that some rubrics may not assist the experienced teacher in identifying conceptual and strategic defects in a student's work; undoubtedly they can help. However, independently of their problems with reliability and validity, they may well have the unfortunate effect of throwing the inexperienced teacher, much less the aspiring writer, considerably off-course.[20] For one thing, they aren't meant to be used in every circumstance. To take some extreme examples, what would happen if one were to apply the rubrics in tables 1.1, 1.2, and 1.3 to the following extracts from the works of three well-known and highly accomplished and influential writers?

(1.1) Hernia, hernia, hernia, hernia, hernia, hernia, hernia, hernia, hernia, hernia, hernia, hernia, hernia, HERNia; hernia, HERNia, hernia, hernia, hernia, hernia, HERNia, HERNia, HERNia; hernia, hernia, hernia, hernia, hernia, hernia, hernia, eight is the point, the point is eight; hernia, hernia, HERNia; hernia, hernia, hernia, hernia, all right, hernia, hernia, hernia, hernia, hard eight, hernia, hernia, hernia, HERNia, hernia, hernia, hernia, HERNia, hernia, hernia, hernia, HERNia, hernia, hernia, hernia, hernia.

(1.2) Dew falling. Bad for you, dear, to sit on that stone. Brings on white fluxions. Never have little baby then less he was big strong fight his way up through. Might get piles myself. Sticks too like a summer cold, sore on the mouth. Cut with grass or paper worst. Friction of the position. Like to be that rock she sat on. O sweet little, you don't know how nice you looked. I begin to like them at that age. Green apples. Grab at all that offer. Suppose it's the only time we cross legs, seated. Also the library today: those girl graduates. Happy chairs under them. But it's the evening influence. They feel all that. Open like flowers, know their hours, sunflowers, Jerusalem artichokes, in ballrooms, chandeliers, avenues under the lamps. Nightstock in Mat Dillon's garden where I kissed her shoulder. Wish I had a full length oilpainting of her then. June that was too I wooed. The year returns. History repeats itself. Ye crags and peaks I'm with you once again. Life, love, voyage round your own little world. And now? Sad about her lame of course but must be on your guard not to feel too much pity. They take advantage.

(1.3) Nickel, what is nickel, it is originally rid of a cover. The change in that is that red weakens an hour. The change has come. There is no search. But there is, there is that hope and that interpretation and sometime, surely any is unwelcome, sometime there is breath and there will be a sinecure and charming very charming is that clean and cleansing. Certainly glittering is handsome and convincing. There is no gratitude in mercy and in medicine. There can be breakages in Japanese. That is no programme. That is no color chosen. It was chosen yesterday, that showed spitting and perhaps washing and polishing. It certainly showed no obligation and perhaps if borrowing is not natural there is some use in giving.

The first extract consists of the first sentence of Tom Wolfe's nonfiction article, "Las Vegas (What?) Las Vegas (Can't hear you! Too noisy) Las Vegas!!!!,"[21] the second extract is from James Joyce's *Ulysses*,[22] and the third is from Gertrude Stein's *Tender Buttons*.[23] We can guess what E. B. White and Will Strunk would have thought of these experimental authors.[24] Expressivists might grant them points for willingness to experiment with genre or style, and all three extracts definitely challenge conventions as a CCSist may prefer, but the rubrics in tables 1.1, 1.2, and 1.3 would not tell us what we really want to know about the quality of the writing here.

The point is that as the definition of good writing has shifted over the years from the work of the classic authors to rule-following to scores on indirect tests to categorization via rubric, it has been accompanied by the deliberate walling off of school and university students from professional writers. As we've seen, prior to the nineteenth century, there was a single standard that was (profitably or not) accepted for all forms of writing. But a literary critic today would not use the rubrics in tables 1.1, 1.2, and 1.3 to evaluate the work of writers like Tom Wolfe, James Joyce, or Gertrude Stein, though comparison with the novels of John Updike, Joseph Conrad, or Ernest Hemingway would not be out of place. We appear now to need at least two different definitions of good writing, one for courses on literature and the other for courses on writing. Some may even argue that separate standards are required for every age group and every genre. This suggests to me a serious problem in determining what the essence of good writing is and how it is achieved that standard approaches are not well-equipped to solve.

The remainder of this book is designed to confront this problem directly. Chapter 2 contains an introduction to a cognitive approach to writing that underlies most of what follows. In chapter 3, I will introduce a Constructionist theory of language whose ultimate goal is to formulate a coherent set of templates for the word patterns found in English, their meanings, and their functions in spoken and written discourse. The point of this chapter is not to extract templates for use in teaching writing but to show that there are so many of them and their interactions are so complex that any attempt to do so would be bound to fail. For example, the common observation that old information generally precedes new information in discourse is often true, but it is not a satisfactory rule of good writing because the situation is far more complicated than the rule suggests. There is simply too much else going on, as the chapter will demonstrate.

In chapters 4 through 6, I will discuss aspects of Relevance Theory, which addresses at least some of the situational and contextual issues raised by rhetoricists and other adherents of process and post-process strategies. One advantage of Relevance Theory is that it is an empirical theory of the mind just as a theory of language is, and, furthermore, it is consistent with the Constructionist Theory that I will be using. But again, the point is that the complexity of the theory is such that, at present, no conclusions can justifiably be drawn about how writing pedagogy might benefit, if at all, by isolating a handful of its discoveries about grammatical processes for instruction.

Chapters 7 through 9, which make up the final part of the book, look at a type of fluency that plays a role in the creation of literary works. We might call this "superfluency," because it is a sort of powering-up of fluency for certain literary ends. In addition to considering the familiar topics of figurative language, surprise, and repetition, I will also consider the general relationship between form and content in writing.

Some Preliminary Distinctions: Literacy, Dialect, and Register

I imagine there are some who would prefer to use the term "literacy" to describe what I am calling fluency, especially in the context of writing and reading, but I want to distinguish these words for the purposes of my argument not in terms of the medium of communication but in terms of facility with language. On my particular interpretation (which I think accords with the common understanding), all fluent writers are literate, but not all literate writers are fluent. It may be said that there are several kinds of literacies, each one of them differing in various sociocultural respects from the others, and that individuals may display differences in their mastery of them.[25] I would say that fluencies have a variety of dimensions too and that these go beyond the sociocultural. But I will reserve the term "literacy" for the basic reading and writing skills that are necessary to fulfill the obligations of citizenship in contemporary society as well as to reap at least some of the central benefits thereof. In general, literacy has been the concern of elementary and secondary schools, writing fluency that of universities.

By putting fluency in writing on the same footing with fluency in speaking, I don't mean to suggest that there aren't marked and systematic differences between spontaneous spoken speech and planned and edited writing.[26] There are, and it would be a mistake to think that fluent writing is simply fluent speech written down. For example, here is a transcript of fluent speech from a press conference conducted by Dee Dee Myers, President George W. Bush's press secretary. The topic is the president's agenda for that week:

(1.4) MYERS: This is Russia week. Ten o'clock a.m., he speaks to the American Hospital Association. Then at 11:30 a.m., he speaks—
VOICE: Here at the White House?
MYERS: No, these are—I'm not sure what that is—it's off—both these events are off-campus. At 11:30 a.m. he speaks to the National Governors Association—I believe that's at the Omni, and the subject of that is welfare and health care.
VOICE: Will he go from one place to the other?
MYERS: Probably. Then Wednesday—that's it for public events on Tuesday. On Wednesday, he'll have a meeting with the joint congressional leaders in the morning. Then he will—

VOICE: When you say "joint congressional," what does that mean?
MYERS: Members of both Houses.
VOICE: Does it mean bipartisan, or does it mean just—
VOICE: What time is it?
MYERS: I think it's bipartisan, yes. As opposed to—it's at 10:00. I think it's bipartisan, but it could be committee chairs. So I'll have to double-check that. Which will be from both houses—the House and Senate, but not necessarily bipartisan.[27]

You'll notice that Myers employs a number of linguistic conventions that are usually not found in planned and edited writing. She backtracks ("Then Wednesday—that's it for public events on Tuesday"), fails to complete thoughts ("As opposed to—"), and uses sentence fragments ("Probably"; "Members of both Houses"). Typical elements of dialogue are also in evidence, including turn-taking, question-and-answer protocols, pressing for more detail, attempts to answer more than one question within a single sentence, and so forth. Not in evidence in this transcript are body gestures, facial expressions, and indications of vocal tone, stress, and quality, all of which mark spoken English and assist in the conveyance of meaning. (Thus, when Myers says "I'm not sure what that is," the audience at the press conference would most likely have cues to tell them what "that" refers to; it's also possible that the transcript contains an error and that what Myers actually said—or wished to say—was "I'm not sure where that is." The reader is not in a position to know.)

And yet, Myers would usually be regarded as a highly fluent speaker of English (which is no doubt in part why she was chosen for the job), and the excerpt appears to be a typical example of fluent spontaneous speech.[28] The essential difference between fluent spontaneous speech and fluent planned and editing writing is that in the case of the latter the writer can revise and rearrange and satisfy herself that she has done her utmost to convey exactly what she meant to convey and hasn't made a hash of it. But, as it turns out, fluent formal writing engages for the most part the same fluencies in language found in the formal register of fluent spontaneous speech, with these differences: (1) writing allows for systematic revision in principle over an indefinite period, whereas speech usually allows for only instantaneous correction or restatement; (2) formal writing may range over a larger vocabulary and a more complex grammar than formal speech, in large measure because with the former there is usually ample opportunity for reflection; (3) there are aspects of fluent writing, such as punctuation and spelling conventions, not found in fluent speech; and (4) there are aspects of fluent speech, such as intonation and gesture, that are not found in fluent writing. However, except where the distinction has significant consequences for them, in what follows I will often use results from studies of speech behavior to inform my conclusions about good writing.

It is also important to understand that when we talk about fluency in either speaking or writing we are not necessarily talking about a standard. There are similarities between speaking a standard dialect and being fluent in a dialect, in that both do suggest levels of achievement. But one may be entirely fluent in a nonstandard dialect. Samuel Clemens appears to have been fully fluent in several nonstandard dialects of the English of Missouri of his time and expressed this fluency delightfully in writing in *Adventures of Huckleberry Finn*.[29]

A standard dialect (for example, the somewhat unctuous dialect fluently spoken by the anchors of national television news broadcasts) is not necessarily the target of speakers attempting to achieve fluency in the language that that standard is a dialect of. An immigrant to Houston, Texas, may well wish to become fluent in the East Texas dialect of English of that region rather than (or in addition to) the dialect sometimes called Standard American English. If in London "BBC English" is the dialect accepted as standard, in New York and Atlanta and Rapid City it is most assuredly not.

There's a common misconception that nonstandard dialects are corruptions or degradations of standard dialects and that, as such, they are not as well formed or as fully grammatical as standard dialects. There may be social or literary consequences to speaking or writing in a nonstandard dialect, but linguistically every dialect is a fully formed language. As the linguist Max Weinreich was fond of repeating, a language is just a dialect with an army and navy.

For example, in African American Vernacular English (AAVE), the verb "ask" is regularly pronounced as if it were spelled "ax." This is sometimes described as a "mispronunciation"[30] and is often associated, in the United States at least, with an African American identity.[31] Some call it "sloppy" and imply that it is used because it is easier to pronounce than the standard alternative. However, this slur ignores the fact that the ax pronunciation has been extant in English for well over a thousand years and was regularly used by one of the great writers of Middle English, Geoffrey Chaucer. It is entirely by historical accident, not linguistic destiny, that the dialect of English that became standard was not one in which the ax pronunciation was dominant. From a linguistic perspective, the ax pronunciation could just as easily have become the standard, with the ask variety heard only in provincial areas.

Nor should dialect be confused with what linguists call register. A dialect generally comprises several different registers or levels of speech, from high (formal) to low (colloquial), each of which is used in a particular social situation. When the language a teen uses varies according to audience (for example, when she or he uses different language conventions when speaking with classmates, on the one hand, and with parents or teachers, on the other, all of whom nevertheless speak the same regional and sociocultural dialect), we would say she or he is using different registers. Achieving fluency in a dialect usually entails becoming fluent in more than one register, as parents can readily attest. And in a sense, fluency in writing can be considered fluency in a particular register of a dialect, with the differences between spoken and written language noted earlier.

The written equivalent of the standard dialect spoken by newscasters is plausibly the language of national newspapers, printed and online, but many nonstandard written dialects are not broadly published. Thus, one can logically be a deceptively fluent writer—that is, fluent in a dialect that is not necessarily widely shared. It only takes two people to share a dialect, spoken and/or written, and to be provably fluent in it. Many (and I could include myself with them) would say that the following opening lines of chapter 19 of *Adventures of Huckleberry Finn* constitute a brilliant example of good writing, even though they are written in an approximation of a nonstandard dialect:

(1.5)   Two or three days and nights went by; I reckon I might say they swum by, they slid along so quiet and smooth and lovely. Here is the way we put in the time. It was a monstrous big river down there—sometimes a mile and a half wide; we run nights, and laid up and hid daytimes; soon as night was most gone we stopped navigating and tied up—nearly always in the dead water under a towhead; and then cut young cottonwoods and willows, and hid the raft with them. Then we set out the lines. Next we slid into the river and had a swim, so as to freshen up and cool off; then we set down on the sandy bottom where the water was about knee deep, and watched the daylight come. Not a sound anywheres—perfectly still—just like the whole world was asleep, only sometimes the bullfrogs a-cluttering, maybe. The first thing to see, looking away over the water, was a kind of dull line—that was the woods on t'other side; you couldn't make nothing else out; then a pale place in the sky; then more paleness spreading around; then the river softened up away off, and warn't black any more, but gray; you could see little dark spots drifting along ever so far away—trading scows, and such things; and long black streaks—rafts; sometimes you could hear a sweep screaking; or jumbled up voices, it was so still, and sounds come so far; and by and by you could see a streak on the water which you know by the look of the streak that there's a snag there in a swift current which breaks on it and makes that streak look that way; and you see the mist curl up off of the water, and the east reddens up, and the river, and you make out a log-cabin in the edge of the woods, away on the bank on t'other side of the river, being a woodyard, likely, and piled by them cheats so you can throw a dog through it anywheres; then the nice breeze springs up, and comes fanning you from over there, so cool and fresh and sweet to smell on account of the woods and the flowers; but sometimes not that way, because they've left dead fish laying around, gars and such, and they do get pretty rank; and next you've got the full day, and everything smiling in the sun, and the song-birds just going it![32]

The dialectal features here are of a piece with the import of the paragraph and serve to make vivid for us the character of Huck Finn, who is the narrator. Notably, we don't even have to speak this dialect ourselves to appreciate what Twain has done with it.

At this point the developing writer may want to interject: OK. But so what if good writing is fluent writing? Where does all this get me? How precisely am I supposed to become fluent?

Becoming fluent in written language is a process, just as becoming fluent in spoken language is. As I've said, you learn by massive exposure and a minimal amount of explicit correction in contexts where you are highly motivated to acquire and exchange information via that language. One is at a severe disadvantage if one lacks the exposure and/or the motivation, which is why many people without organic brain disorders have difficulty reading and writing—or, for that matter, becoming a great orator. This, by the way, in no way demonstrates a deficiency in intelligence. You can be highly intelligent by almost any standard and still not write well or be able to deliver moving speeches. And without the exposure and motivation, you almost certainly never will.

2

A Cognitive Approach to Good Writing

Validity and Reliability Revisited

The approach to answering the question in my title that I adopt will, I hope, impress the reader as more intuitively plausible than the alternatives, though I recognize that its plausibility is not in itself a decisive strike in its favor. The judgment should rightly rest on whether it delivers results for those who aspire to be good writers. However, results over the short term may be difficult to discern, since, as I will argue, building writing fluency in one's brain is not a short-term enterprise. As for the longer term, I know of nothing in the way of current research that provides a persuasive basis for choosing any one of the several common pedagogies over another, much less one that establishes a reasonable criterion for success that any new approach must meet. Although there have been many well-designed experiments that attempt to provide empirical proof of the effectiveness of one or another compositionist strategy, the evidence is not very compelling. If gains are observed in an experiment that demonstrates students have learned to write to specific standards involving proxies for good writing—such as evidence of adherence to certain rules of spelling, punctuation, grammar, structure, or argument, or of having written for multiple purposes and audiences or having explored the concept of intellectual property and evaluated sources for credibility, etc.—in which they have been instructed, then the strategies used to teach the procedures may be considered effective for those particular standards, though it has not been demonstrated that the strategies promote anything so broad and subjective as, say, good writing. This problem is general in the expressive arts where assessment that is claimed or assumed to be reliable and valid almost always involves scoring proxies, teaching to the test, and grading to the instruction. In such cases validity is inevitably compromised in the attempt to achieve reliability.

You might think that the more proxies you can design into a grading rubric, the closer you'll be to specifying the character of good writing, especially if you believe that these proxies in fact closely describe what good writing consists of and you have the support of your community in this belief. But as we've seen with respect to the Pennsylvania and Michigan rubrics discussed in chapter 1, there is no set of proxies that is both necessary and sufficient for the task. Yes, an essay that displays conventional spelling *in addition to* transparent organization may be well written. But then again it may not be. If you add to your rubric the production of a "strong story line with illustrative details that addresses a complex idea," you may be closer to giving your graders something they can grade reliably, but only if you elaborate on exactly what "strong story line" and "complex idea" mean to you. But by doing this you are still grading proxies rather than something so subjective as good writing. Even if you gather ten or a hundred composition teachers in a room all of whom insist that they know what a "strong story line" is, they may not all agree which particular writing samples demonstrate one unless they're coached. Moreover, they will almost certainly not all agree with a hundred professional people drawn randomly from the general public about the meaning of "good writing" or "strong story line" or "complex idea," or about what sort of writing instantiates these terms. You yourself may be content with your several or many proxies, but you are still no closer to persuasively demonstrating validity than you were before.

One common justification for such proxies and the type of writing that they encourage is that young writers must first master the basics before moving on from there. There is some virtue in this argument, but it is questionable whether rubrics of the sort that we've been discussing actually get anywhere close to the cognitive foundations of good writing. From the perspective of a linguist examining the development of linguistic skills in children and young adults, these rubrics look nothing like the building blocks upon which fluency is understood to be constructed, except for their tautologous appeal to "control" or "command of language." Of course, having command of language is having the ability to successfully deploy "proper words in proper places" for an appropriate communicative purpose. But how does that come about? For many of the students who file through our composition courses, understanding process and technique will do them as little good as mastering the Oxford comma, because they haven't yet internalized the syntax, semantics, and pragmatics of sufficiently many constructions of their language to make them fluent in writing it.

If teachers could devise objective criteria to assess exactly the neurological conditions leading to deficiencies in each student's writing and had proven strategies that would succeed in motivating each student to do what was necessary to correct those deficiencies in such a way that the result was what we all would agree is good writing, then there might be some hope of implementing a valid and reliable program that also worked. But we are at present still far from arriving at that pedagogical utopia.

Given the state of our current knowledge, the attempt to move from subjective to objective in writing assessment is destined to be derailed by arbitrariness. When there is no one-to-one correspondence between the desiderata expressed in proxies and a precise specification of a communicative event that is relevant, effective, and suitable for each person and each occasion as all would understand it, then choices have to be made, and those choices can't help but be arbitrary. To the extent that you are able to narrow down the choices with objective criteria, you have to rely on a subjective process to do so—"You can use the spelling conventions in *The American Heritage Dictionary* or *The Oxford English Dictionary* but not *Dictionary.com* or *YourDictionary.com*." Or "You can use any spelling you find on the Google Books Ngram Viewer with a frequency consistently above .001% between 1980 and 2000." Or "Your essay must begin with a concrete example and end with a general concluding statement." A teacher may have defensible reasons for adopting one or another of these kinds of requirements for his or her assignments, but another teacher could just as confidently defend a different set of requirements.

A nice example from the research literature of an influential paper with the kind of validity problem that I've been discussing is Steve Graham's 2006 meta-analysis of studies of a cognitively oriented process model for writing known as Strategy Instruction (SI). (In a meta-analysis, a usually large set of experimental studies is statistically analyzed to determine whether any conclusions can be drawn from the set as a whole.) After analyzing the results of thirty-nine separate studies published between 1981 and 2006, Graham concluded that "[f]or all groups of students, the impact of Strategy Instruction on quality [of writing] was large."[1] In subsequent meta-analyses with Delores Perin[2] and Karin Sandmel,[3] Graham compared the effect size of process models generally to other writing approaches and used slightly more muted language to report evidence for impact on quality: "When studies were conducted in general education classrooms, students receiving process writing instruction were better writers at the end of the experiment than were students in the control condition."[4]

Graham's analyses are exceptionally well-constructed, statistically sophisticated, and thorough. He also is careful to admit that extraneous issues connected with his analyses may have confounded his results, such as type and age of student population surveyed, variability in the composition of control groups, the statistical quality of the individual studies considered, as well as so-called Hawthorne effects, where teachers given special instruction consequently "feel special," which may influence the quality of their teaching. He also points out that the studies included in his meta-analysis did not all use the same measure of writing quality—"this variability included not only the attributes assessed, but the number of points on the scales and how these points were operationalized."[5] In his meta-analysis with Sandmel, he also included studies where scoring reliability had not been established, acknowledging that "assessment of writing quality involves some degree of subjectivity."[6] Since he found that, where scoring reliability was established in a study, it was not associated with an effect on student performance, he felt justified in including these additional studies. Interestingly, where he was able to find evidence of "professional development" involving instructing teachers and graders, he did not find a statistically significant relationship with quality of writing.

Does this mean that process models, and in particular Strategy Instruction, validly improve quality of writing? Well, no. As Jonsson and Svingby have argued,[7] "[j]ust by providing a rubric there is no evidence for content representativeness, fidelity of scoring structure to the construct domain or generalizability. Nor does it give any convergent or discriminant evidence to other measures." In translation, this means that rubrics don't necessarily test what it's claimed they test when the content tested is different from the content taught, when the scoring is not consistent with the content taught, and when the scores do not generalize to anything outside the test.

Good test designers know this and try to develop their testing instruments accordingly, and Graham did make an effort to evaluate the quality of the studies before entering them in the meta-analysis. However, Graham did not consider control for teaching to the test or grading to the instruction in weighing any of the scores derived from traditional holistic scoring systems in the thirty-nine studies. As he pointed out in his paper with Perin: "we doubt that most of the instructional procedures . . . especially the more complex ones like strategy instruction, can be widely and effectively implemented without a considerable amount of teacher preparation."[8] Most significantly, Graham's measure of the quality of a study was related to evidence that interrater reliability was high "and/or that trainers were taught how to score compositions,"[9] which may amount to the same thing but at any rate magnifies the grading-to-the-instruction problem. But the more confidence we place on high interrater reliability scores associated with teacher and rater training, the less confidence we should have in the validity of the scores as actually providing a meaningful measure of quality of writing.

Consider the following scenario. Let us say that you are a school administrator and are thinking about implementing a new program of writing instruction whose effectiveness you would like to test. We'll call it the "WX" program, and it focuses on conventions involving commas, apostrophes, colons, semicolons, and periods. You have ten schools in your district in which you may implement the program. You choose five as the experimental schools and the remaining five as control schools. For the purposes of this example, we'll say that the ten schools are demographically identical and that there are no significant differences among them in faculty or administration. In the experimental schools teachers are pre-trained in teaching the WX program. The teachers in the control schools receive no instruction and teach the writing course as they have been used to doing. Two teachers teaching writing classes in each of the schools grade each student's test written in that school. Let's also say that the grading rubric for the writing test is the Michigan holistic test in table 1.1. Since the WX program stresses punctuation, then punctuation will almost certainly be given more weight than the other criteria in both instruction and grading in the experimental condition. Moreover, because the students in the experimental condition have been explicitly taught punctuation conventions, they would be expected to do better on this part of the test than students in the control group, who have not. Even if students in the experimental treatment do more poorly on other aspects of the test (e.g., grammar, style, vocabulary, precision) than those in the control group, their raters would tend to give more weight to their higher scores in punctuation, since that's what WX prioritizes. But because the rubric is holistic, this will not be explicitly coded, and the WX students may receive higher scores overall without the sort of breakdown that an analytic rubric would provide. These higher overall scores may be easily interpreted as confirming that WX improves the general quality of student writing, though actually all the tests have shown is that certain elements of punctuation are teachable.

Teachers and researchers can, of course, decide to simply live with the fact that whichever pedagogical strategy they champion at the moment is technically unsupported by solid empirical proof of its effectiveness in doing what the outside world thinks it's doing. But taking such a position strikes me as misguided and, ultimately, counterproductive. Proxies need to be labeled as such. Thus, Graham's assured conclusion that "[f]or all groups of students, the impact of Strategy Instruction on quality was large" should probably have been recast as "[f]or all groups of students, the impact of Strategy Instruction on what the researchers considered to be proxies for quality of writing was large." But it could have been large for reasons having nothing to do with quality of writing as measured by anything other than the construction of the testing instruments, the focus of instruction, and the bias of the raters.

Defining Good Writing

In this book I want to suggest a different approach from the one commonly taken in composition studies. My point is that if we can arrive at a definition of good writing that works well for our purposes, if we can identify writers who have produced such good writing, and if we can distinguish their experiences from those of others who have not, then we are in a good position to hypothesize about how that condition was achieved. Since we also have a solid foundation of empirical results in the areas of neuroscience, language acquisition, and cognitive linguistic theory to rest our approach on, we can be more confident of our conclusions. If we accept this, then any inquiry into teaching methodologies for writing will have to start with the question in our title.

In brief, I will argue that the most useful definition of good writing is fluency in language put on paper, board, or screen and that style and content, in both pedagogical and literary contexts, are difficult, if not impossible, to separate. Moreover, just as fluency in a spoken language or a dialect can be acquired through learning,[10] I will argue that fluency in writing can be too. However, the evidence that fluency in writing can be routinely learned through classroom teaching that focuses on writing process and technique is, as suggested earlier, very thin. Despite the enormous effort that has gone into writing instruction at all levels in our educational system, the only empirically supported route to good writing I know of that doesn't resort to teaching to the test or grading to the instruction is through frequent, avid reading. This does not mean that instruction in writing can't facilitate the acquisition of certain writing skills in a limited way among some students. But acquiring fluency in writing must necessarily involve massive exposure to written language, just as acquiring fluency in spoken language necessarily requires massive exposure to speech. Children naturally learn to speak their native language as a result of such exposure, and the empirical data support something quite similar with writing, as we'll see.

This approach may be seen to be in conflict with others that are more widely approved of in the field of composition studies. For example, the distinguished compositionist Peter Elbow, in his article "Write First: Putting Writing Before Reading Is an Effective Approach to Teaching and Learning,"[11] considers what he calls "the unexamined dominance of reading" and argues that "writing helps children comprehend written language," concluding that "weakness in reading often stems from neglect of writing. Students will put more care and attention into reading when they've had more of a chance to write what's on their minds." Consequently, he advocates a program of teaching that puts writing ahead of reading from the very start.[12] Elbow does qualify his idea by granting that "reading is 'really writing' (actively creating meaning)," but he still proposes that "writing promotes more psychological and physical engagement than reading."

From a scientific perspective, Elbow provides little for the empirically minded to chew on: he offers no precise research hypotheses for testing or experimental evidence to support his claims. His statement that "weakness in reading often stems from neglect of writing," like many others in this article, could be interpreted to mean any number of different things. At most, his idea suggests an unspecified program in which gains or losses in writing skill might perhaps be measured by looking at time spent practicing writing as compared with that spent practicing reading. But at this point there is no particular scientific reason to believe that reducing time spent reading relative to practicing writing will improve writing fluency. In contrast, as I will show in what follows, there is a solid grounding of research that indicates that it is avid independent reading that is essential.

Certainly, we do know that there must be interconnections between writing and reading while skills in both are developing in children. At the limits, it's obvious. A capable writer with no organic deficits who has never learned to read is unimaginable. At the other extreme, our greatest writers past and present have inevitably presented themselves as having read copiously from childhood onward. An intriguing suggestion, complementary to Elbow's, is contained in this reflection by the writer E. L. Doctorow, who claimed he began to think of himself as a writer, at the age of 9, before had written anything:

Whenever I read anything I seemed to identify as much with the act of composition as with the story. You're imagining the words, the sounds of the words. . . . So it's very hard to make any distinction between reader and writer at this ontological level.[13]

I will discuss this issue in more detail in chapter 3.

Any approach that defines good writing as fluent writing would obviously be useless or worse if reading-acquired fluency in writing were defined circularly as good writing and could not be assessed according to some external, objective criteria. I will suggest that evaluating fluency in writing should not be much different from evaluating fluency in speaking, though for our purposes, I don't think the bread needs to be sliced so thinly as it is, say, in the Educational Testing Service's TOEIC and TOEFL tests in the second-language context (for example, a score of 874 out of 990 on TOEIC betokens "Proficiency in English," while an additional two points bumps one up to "Professional Proficiency"). I would prefer to say that speakers are generally fluent in a spoken language or a dialect when they can engage in an ordinary conversation with mature native speakers of that language or dialect at what the native speakers regard as an essentially equivalent level of effectiveness and efficiency (i.e., the effectiveness and efficiency of their own speech and that of their peers). A person who is perceived by native speakers to approximate their own linguistic ability in diverse conversational situations is, in this respect, a generally fluent speaker of that language. Native speakers have an excellent ear for fluency: it's not at all difficult for a native speaker to identify another native speaker (even independently of accent) or to detect dysfluency in the speech of someone else.

If we had a concept of native writer parallel to that of native speaker, we should similarly be able to pick out those who have developed the normal capacity for written language from those who have not. But since in normal circumstances we humans do not acquire writing skills in the same way that we acquire speaking skills,[14] there is—and probably can be—no concept of native writer that is exactly equivalent to that of native speaker. However, there are important parallels, and if we look closely at the conditions under which speech is acquired, we will also find some answers to our questions about the acquisition of writing.

There are those, like Ronald T. Kellogg, who dispute that acquiring speech and writing are similar enough to draw any significant conclusions about the latter from the former. He likens learning writing skills to learning to type or learning how to play chess.[15] Although there are some parts of Kellogg's position with which I agree, I will argue that the critical foundations of writing ability are to be found in the same mechanism that accounts for the acquisition of fluent spoken language and that what is specific to writing skill (beyond the standard motor, visual, and associational complexes) are refinements built on those foundations. If learning to write fluently is like learning to speak fluently, then it's not practicing writing that primarily matters; more broadly, it's recognizing and gaining facility with patterns that occur in written language through avid independent reading.

The Role of Motivation

At the age of about 12 months, and before they have developed speech, most infants begin to point as a way of communicating. By analyzing instances of these preverbal pointing actions and their contexts, the psychologist Michael Tomasello and his colleagues have identified three kinds of motivations that underlie them.[16] One obvious kind of pointing indicates a request or demand—the infant wants help in satisfying a need or interest, so she'll point at a cookie jar she can't reach. A second type of pointing involves sharing emotions or responses with others, such as something or someone the infant finds funny or unpleasant. And the third type is informational: the infant wants to direct the attention of others to important things when those others have seemed not to notice and when their attention is important to the infant. All of these motivations are ultimately self-serving, even those, like sharing and informing, that may at first glance seem altruistic but that ultimately involve satisfying a desire to interact with others socially for reasons of personal satisfaction.

As children begin to learn language during their second year, pointing begins to be supplanted by the utterance of words. However, the fundamental communicative motivations remain the same—as Tomasello says, they share the same "information structure."[17] What these children continue to do is to use communication skills when they have desires that can only be satisfied by social interaction. Tomasello's conclusion is that these motivations are a prerequisite to learning language.

Children of primary school age generally do not need instruction or exercises to help motivate them to learn how to speak their language. The motivation is there in the circumstances in which they find themselves. They need to communicate, for their own requesting, sharing, and informing purposes. But contrast this now with the child learning to write. Virtually all of her primary motivations for communicating have already found appropriate expression in speech, while writing serves few if any of them. It may be that the child discovers in school that by performing writing activities she can receive certain social rewards that she wants, but if she has no particular interest in those types of rewards, then the conditions for learning writing won't be met.

The more that students read, the more stimulation they should be able to find in their reading. By the time they have reached college, the advantages of being able to participate fully in written as well as spoken discourse have already begun to assert themselves forcefully. But for those who have not experienced much motivation before, the problems mount, since they are in the position of having to catch up to the rest. The negative feedback they get from their attempts overwhelms the benefits. But if they don't read widely, they won't be exposed to the wide range of constructions, expressions, and conventions used in writing their language. A plausible reason, then, why college students fail in their writing activities is not that they haven't received appropriate instruction in writing. As with spoken language, instruction in writing or lack of it might have little to do with the development of their writing skills. Students who don't see how they can satisfy their needs by participating in a wide and diverse range of written interactions are unlikely to read widely and avidly. And if they don't read widely and avidly, they won't learn those aspects of language that are essential in writing culture.

Of course, there is an abundant literature in composition studies proposing ways to motivate students to write, but little of it directly pertains to the particular actuating forces Tomasello has identified. For example, a useful summary of recent composition studies research can be found in "Motivation Research in Writing: Theoretical and Empirical Considerations," by Gary A. Troia, Rebecca K. Shankland, and Kimberly A. Wolbers.[18] The authors of this paper focus on four components of achievement motivation in writing, three of which (confidence in one's abilities and skills, orientation toward goals, and perceived causes of success or failure) play no role in the normal acquisition of speech except in the most abstract way—and therefore are of little significance in this context (whether or not they happen to be useful in advancing performance specific to the classroom). The fourth component, which consists of what the authors style "interest and value," is of significance, but it appears to subsume Tomasello's three fundamental motivations for communication.

Consider a writing teacher who asks her students to write an essay on William Gladstone, or William Dean Howells, or William Harvey. Her students usually won't have a clue either as to why they should want to participate in such a written conversation (other than for a grade) or, on the remote chance that actually they do want to participate, as to what they would have to do in order to complete the task successfully. The teacher and scholar Lad Tobin quotes one of his students as saying that writing is "doing errands when you're not sure why you have to do them and you're not even sure where the stores are,"[19] a nicely executed metaphor which I think captures just about exactly the dilemma of the unmotivated writer. An "errand"—an unpleasant task imposed from without—is by definition not something one would do if he had his druthers, and what makes it worse is that "you're not sure why you have to do" it or even how to go about doing it.

Teaching students the canonical essay form or the four stages of apprenticeship toward membership in a disciplinary discourse community[20] will do nothing to solve that problem for them, since their real interests lie elsewhere. This brings us to the personal essay, which expressivists sometimes see as a panacea for lack of interest. But writing a personal essay, unless doing so taps into the set of personal motivations we've discussed, brings a student no closer to avid participation in a discourse community of her choice. The student still has to get past the problem of "you're asking me to do something that I have no interest in." Yes, sometimes we have to do things for education's sake that we don't want to do, but that's not why or how we become fluent in language.

Because the motivations Tomasello identifies are about communication broadly, they apply to any language, dialect, or mode of delivery—English spoken and written, Spanish, British Sign Language, Latin, Pig-Latin, Valley Girl Speech, bureaucratese, academese, etc. An infant's desire to participate in a conversation (or dialogue or discourse, if you prefer) with others from whom something is wanted is evidenced as soon as she or he begins to babble. It is well established that young people before the age of 14 or 15 pick up certain dialectal features (including vocabulary, pronunciation, and syntax) primarily from others who are their age or slightly older, sometimes emphasizing these features in their speech as a way to identify with a favored group.[21] Thus, children of immigrants who are in their pre-teens at immigration usually don't speak the accented variety of their adopted language that their parents do.

Fluency and Professional Writers

If we are to extend the concept of native speaker fluency to the achievement of writing fluency, the fluencies must have the same or similar ontogenetic (developmental) sources. Tomasello's three fundamental motivations—requesting, sharing, informing—etiolate during development in predictable ways. The urge to engage with and be accepted by a favored group manifests most obviously in the formation of cliques and participation in extracurricular activities in high school. Young people who receive pleasure from their reading and come to admire the authors of the articles, stories, and books they read will be motivated to try to communicate in the language of those authors, just as they are to imitate the language of their favored peers. If, through reading, they come to form their own ideas about aspects of the world relevant to them, they will want to share those ideas and demonstrate their alliance with the authors they admire. Those who receive rewards (in the form of recognition and grades), will be further motivated to develop and express their reading and writing skills in just that way.

If the grammars of spoken and written language are cognitively equivalent (as we will see later), then we should be able to equate the experience of normal speakers with that of writers whose motivations for writing align with the ones they have for speaking. There is, in fact, a readily identifiable group of writers who have a powerful need to use writing for requesting, sharing, and informing purposes, and these are, naturally, writers who write for a living. Such professional writers, whose income derives in substantial part from their skill in writing, clearly must be competent writers and clearly must have had all the prerequisites necessary to learn to express themselves in writing at that level; otherwise, they would not have been hired for the writing that they do. While there are people who write fluently who are not professional writers, we can be reasonably confident in saying that professional writers are, by definition, fluent writers, or at least they are so in the same way that normal adult native speakers of English are fluent speakers of English. Experienced professional writers, such as community and trade newspaper reporters, advertising copywriters, public-relations specialists, freelance writers, lawyers, bloggers, newsletter writers, teachers, business executives and managers, administrators, and so on, must generally be able to recognize immediately and without coaching the writing of other appropriately skilled professional writers for the purposes of hiring, task

A Cognitive Approach to Good Writing 35

assignments, subcontracting, referral, etc. If they are successful in their profession, their own skill and familiarity with writing practice in their milieu should have equipped them to make intuitive judgments about the skills of younger writers looking for a professional career, just as professional tennis coaches, for example, can usually identify whether a young tennis player has the skills to break into the professional ranks (see, e.g., Rose et al. 1990). Although such judgments are undoubtedly subjective, they differ from typical aesthetic or other tastes derived from happenstance, habit, or idiosyncratic experience, since they entail recognition of a developed ability over a practically infinite domain as a predictor of future performance. In the assessment of writing fluency, the substance of the professional writer's intuitions typically won't be reducible to the checklists of standard writing rubrics that focus on the demonstration of received notions of process and technique because those intitions don't break down into the familiar hierarchies but are scattered in a highly particularized, distributed, and interconnected network, so that a small adjustment in a novice's writing here may be seen by the professional to have the potential to make a large difference there.

Because fluency is a matter of competence rather than performance, it has nothing to do with what Bitzer (1968) called "exigence" ("a [rhetorical] situation which strongly invites utterance"): a writer's fluency is not dependent on the actual exercise of that skill on any particular occasion, during which irrelevant external conditions may intrude to affect it. In the same way, a judgment of fluency has little to do with the "outcomes" often mandated for first-year composition students – e.g., that those students be able to show understanding of "the relationships among language, knowledge, and power," "how genres shape reading and writing," "how a writing assignment is a series of tasks" and so on (WPA Outcomes Statement for First-Year Composition). The fluent writer may or may not have explicit, declarative knowledge (as opposed to tacit knowledge) of these desiderata without effect on her or his inherent ability.

Another important difference between the professional intuitive rating approach sketched here (the PIR approach, for short) and the standard approach using rubrics is that no decision a professional grader makes about a writing sample requires, or even allows for, logical justification, because the decision simply records the grader's intuition, which is not rebuttable: *De intuitibus non est disputandum.* The PIR grader has no answer to the question, "Why did your intuitions lead you to say that this sample is an example of fluent writing?," other than that those intuitions did. By contrast, a decision made according to rubric can be logically interrogated and defended: "Why did you give this sample a 3 when the rubric indicates that for a sample to receive a 3 the sequencing of ideas should make the writer's points easy to follow?"

The judgment of professionals that we look for in a PIR exercise is just thumbs up or thumbs down—nothing in between. Would you say that *X* is a fluent writer of English? Yes or no. Either *X* reaches that standard of writing that you consider fluency according to your own lights or *X* doesn't. Just as a fluent speaker of English can detect lack of fluency in speech when it presents itself, a fluent writer should be able to identify those other writers who are not as fluent in their writing . But if you are perceived by professional writers as communicating at least as effectively and efficiently as they think they and their colleagues generally do, then you yourself must be a generally good (fluent) writer as well, whether or not you are a professional. Of course, the money words in that sentence are "effectively" and "efficiently." What is effective and efficient to you may not be so to me. But that's exactly the point: A fluent writer has only one vote concerning whether a particular text demonstrates fluency with the language. If the professional writer thinks it does, no one can dispute her right to hold the opinion she does, although others may of course hold a different one.

Remember that the purpose of a PIR assessment is to identify fluent writing, not to taxonomize the ills of writing that isn't fluent. We should expect PIR graders to differ among themselves in their assessments of the samples they've read. In this respect, the PIR approach might be thought no less unreliable than the practice of rating by standard rubrics when the raters are uncoached. But to look at the PIR approach that way would be to make a kind of category error, for two reasons. Of course, the PIR graders are not scoring to template or rubric, so they aren't focusing on the particular criteria a rubric would direct them to. But equally, determining whether different raters agree to a predetermined extent on *all* ratings using our definition of good writing is, usually, irrelevant to the PIR exercise. What we're primarily interested in, assuming we have a sufficient number of raters of the appropriate type, are the samples concerning which there is uniform or near-uniform agreement, either positive or negative. These are the clear cases, and at the university level they should provide convincing evidence that each sample so rated is (or isn't) well written according to the PIR definition. About the intermediate cases, the PIR approach allows no firm conclusions to be drawn.

Obviously, it would be a practical impossibility to canvass the judgments of all fluent writers about a particular specimen of writing. But it is sufficient to know that it remains a theoretical possibility. Of course, we can sample the pool of fluent writers, though I don't think anyone has ever tried in any meaningful way to do that. There is also a tool we can use to inform us about the grammatical preferences of a particular audience: one of the signal contributions of the field of corpus linguistics has been to provide great data banks of language as it is actually used, so that we might investigate computationally, for example, exactly how often an infinitive split by an *–ly* adverbial occurs in reporting in the *New York Times* during a particular time period. This could give us some idea of the status of that construction among at least one important group of fluent writers during that period. And, depending on the corpus, we may be able to expand or narrow our search as we please.

But a data bank is neither a substitute for nor a perfect predictor of personal judgment. And our definition of writing fluency depends on the judgments of fluent writers, not on their actual behavior. It isn't that we shouldn't trust the behavior of fluent writers; it's rather that it's beside the point in this case. As with speech fluency, it doesn't really matter whether you commit disfluencies yourself here and there: if you, as a native speaker are judging whether someone else is fluent in the sense that you consider yourself fluent, then it's that judgment that matters. The judgment is essential because it's a cognitive recognition of similarity of skill, and that's really what we're trying to get at.

Fluency and Patterns

One of the most powerful mental tools we humans have is our prodigious ability to recognize patterns. It is this ability on which our ear or eye for fluency in our language rests; indeed, it's what our linguistic skills in general rest on. We can decide very quickly that someone is speaking with a "foreign accent" or that a child has got something wrong when she says "I goeded to the store." Fluent writers make similar judgments in discriminating between those who write as they think they do and those who don't. However, although we can and often do make discriminations concerning individual sentences or even words or punctuation (which is, in fact, exactly what teachers do when they correct the sentences of their students), good writing isn't something that can usually be captured in a single sentence; it is wholly discursive, consisting of a package of communicative tokens. The more tokens we have, the more confident we will be in our judgments.

The value of these judgments does not lie in their statistical quantity—or even in their quality. Rather, it lies in their potential as markers of the community's reaction to the effectiveness of a particular style of communication, which the writer sporadically gets inklings of, both in and out of school. The judgment of any single judge is, tautologously, relative to that judge. Thus, the value of any judgment or group of judgments of a given writer's fluency must in practice be symbolic, but the symbol conferred represents what we might think of as the attainment (or the failure to attain) a certain level of development of the human capacity for writing. Here, obviously, we are talking about biological, or, better, neurological development, but the argument applies to artistic or game-playing development as well.

So, when the publishers of the *American Heritage Dictionary of the English Language* assemble, as they regularly do, a "Usage Panel" comprised of a "group of some 200 distinguished educators, writers, and public speakers" to "pass judgment on both new and longstanding usage problems" and to issue "[t]rustworthy advice on controversies and conundrums in English usage,"[22] they are not taking a step toward defining good writing in a way that I would endorse. The purpose of judging fluency in service of determining the contours of good writing is not to issue advice (though a writer who is told her or his writing isn't "good" may well take that as an incentive to work on improving it). Moreover, the panel's goal evidently remains the prescriptive one of legislating at the margins rather than discovering what constitutes the center. In any case, what we are looking for is something much more capacious than a small group of hand-picked experts.

It's a telling fact that in the educational environment we try to make very fine distinctions between writers of different abilities, but we largely ignore speech distinctions in first language performance except where there seems to be either pathology or exceptional articulateness. It is accepted that by their early teens most speakers have almost fully developed their linguistic capacity for native speech. Of course, training in forensics or oratory may help them develop specific skills, but typically we don't devote anywhere near the resources to speaking that we do to writing. Looking at writing through the lens of cognitive science as a modality of language in general, we begin to see that, with the appropriate level and type of input, a normal level of attainment will normally be reached as a result of normal biological processes.

The Cognitive Approach

A cognitive approach to writing has a large stake in experimental results from the study of both normal and damaged brains but also relies on theoretical models where conclusions deduced from initial hypothesis can be empirically confirmed or rejected. There are, these days, two competing models of cognition that we'll need to consider. The first, usually called a connectionist or neural-network model, envisions the brain as a network of neural nodes that can receive and transmit electrical impulses. Imagine a chessboard with a node in each square that is connected by wires to all (or at least many of) the other nodes. In this model, any particular thought or idea or concept or emotion can be associated with a specific pathway through the network—say, starting at the lower left, going up one square, then to the right two squares, then up three squares, and so on. The more times any particular pathway is traversed by electrical impulses, the more entrenched the idea, thought, etc., associated with it becomes. You can think of it as the pathway getting wider or as conductivity being improved. In the actual human brain, since there are many billions of neurons and many trillions of connections among them, the number of possible pathways (and hence ideas, thoughts, etc.) will evidently be enormous.

A computer that instantiates a connectionist model can learn just as a human can from the input it receives. In fact, since the 1980s, a great deal of research involving the modeling of language learning and language disorders has employed connectionist models. For example, a connectionist model can take the noun "watches" and associate with it the concept of more than one watch. The more often that "watches" is presented to the network, the more entrenched will that word become as the plural form of "watch." Similarly, the more often that "parks" and "spas" are associated with the concepts of more than one park and more than one spa, respectively, the more entrenched will those words become as appropriate plural forms. What the network is learning is that the plural of a word that ends in a vowel or a stop consonant is formed by adding *-s* to the singular form, but if the word ends in an affricate like *-ch*, it takes *-es* instead. However, no rules of this sort are actually encoded in the model.

The second type of cognitive model explicitly recognizes rules like the morphological one for plural formation just suggested. Such a model, usually called an algorithmic or symbolic model, operates by implementing directions: Take a noun stem and add *-es* to it if it ends in the affricate *-ch* but *-s* otherwise. These directions can be "hard-wired" in the model or can be learned by processing large amounts of data, but in either case the directions are or come to be explicitly coded in the model. In this model, plurals like "oxen," "alumni," and "seraphim" are learned as exceptions to the general rule.

Algorithmic models don't make claims about exactly how such directions are realized in the biological human brain, only that the directions represent what the adult actually knows about language. Thus, an algorithmic model and a connectionist model might amount to the same theory about language if the connectionist model ends up in a state in which you could capture the essence of its operations by using the shorthand of directions. But the two models may also diverge on significant issues. For our purposes, we will distinguish them as similar models with different emphases, one that focuses on real-time learning (connectionist) and the other that focuses on the hard-wired or beginning-state directions and the end-state directions that result from learning (algorithmic).

Connectionist and algorithmic theories, considered purely as theories of brain organization, will naturally divide over issues of localization (i.e., whether and, if so, how the brain is divided geographically into regions or clusters of cells, each with its particular function and each visually identifiable via one of the brain imaging techniques), specialization (whether any neurons, individually or in networks, are or become specialized for a particular function), and modularity (whether networks of neurons, independently of localization, are organized for a particular function and are for the most part informationally encapsulated, so that only certain information is transmitted outside the module). A modular theory of language postulates that in the mature human brain there is a module specialized for language which interacts with other modules only at their interfaces, where only a limited amount of information is allowed to pass. There are currently different views among modularists as to whether the brain is pre-programmed for such specialization at birth or whether specialization arises naturally through learning, about how fine-grained the modularity is (different modules for, say, syntax and pragmatics), and about exactly what information can pass from one module to another.

A connectionist theory, in contrast, posits that the brain is an initially undifferentiated network of neurons which are capable of organizing themselves into well-delineated functional units over time given appropriate input. Connectionist theory is usually modeled on massively parallel distributed processors which may be supervised (i.e., given hints or rules) or unsupervised (left to their own devices). Even here, connectionist and modular theories of cognition are not necessarily incompatible: if the brain begins life as a connectionist organ but develops modules (or module-like units) during maturation, a sort of hybrid model can be maintained, though with possibly some information leakage between modules.[23] However, those researchers doing connectionist modeling are currently much more concerned to accommodate the different stages of development leading to maturity than are those building modular models. What this means is that many of the characteristics that a modularist can claim to be confined to a particular module can be attributed by a connectionist to the effects of the operation of many independent units in the network during development. The arguments are technical and I will not go into them here.[24]

On a modularist account of language, there is the obvious question as to whether speech production and interpretation can be said to occupy different modules separate from reading and writing, at least in the mature brain, and whether reading and writing are themselves separate submodules. The traditional test for modularity in the cognitive neuropsychology framework is known as "double dissociation"—if two different brain functions can be seen to be differently affected by different brain lesions in patients who have suffered illness or accident, then there is evidence for modularity.[25] For example, if a certain brain lesion affects speaking but not reading or anything else, and another brain lesion affects reading but not speaking or anything else, then the double-dissociation test is satisfied and there is evidence that speaking and reading reside in different modules. There has been criticism of the double-dissociation test from connectionists as being subject to bias and as ignoring brain plasticity.[26] Nevertheless, double dissociation remains a useful tool in hypothesizing different brain functions.

Neuroscientists use two primary tools to investigate the workings of the brain. First, functional Magnetic Resonance Imaging (fMRI) traces patterns of neuronal activity in the live brain: with this tool it is possible to see exactly where and when in the brain various areas or modules or networks of neurons are activated during the production and processing of speech and writing. Second, studies of the behavior of patients who are deaf or who have sustained various types of brain injuries are also important in determining brain functioning during language activities. In addition to various aphasias, three types of dyslexia—surface dyslexia, phonological dyslexia, and deep dyslexia—are particularly important for what they reveal about the reading process. A patient with surface dyslexia displays difficulty in reading words whose spellings can't be predicted from their sounds (e.g., "neighbor," "laugh," "gauge," "island"). Phonological dyslexia presents as a difficulty in reading novel or non-words ("blick," "nemorades," "foganther"). Those with deep dyslexia confuse written words with other similar words ("read"~"dear," "depth"~"deep"). Using fMRI and/or connectionist modeling with patient studies, a neuroscientist can determine how a localized neural lesion and behavior are related.

Keeping to generalities, there are several results from this research that are of interest:

1. Deaf children learn sign language pretty much on the same schedule as that on which hearing students learn spoken language,[27] so there's no doubt that a visual language system that has all the complexity of the spoken language system can be learned just as a spoken language is learned. A study of British Sign Language users along with normal hearing, non-signing speakers has shown that language use in both displays similar localization patterns in the left hemisphere of the brain and, in particular, in the regions known as Broca's area and Wernicke's area.[28]

2. Both hearing and signing aphasics with damage to Broca's area have difficulty producing speech (or signing) but not comprehending speech (or comprehending signing). Similarly, both hearing and signing aphasics with damage to Wernicke's area can speak (sign) fluently but have difficulty comprehending speech (signing).[29]

3. Producing and comprehending speech activate overlapping areas of the brain,[30] as does comprehending speech and comprehending written language (reading).[31] Similarly, although both reading and writing activate a variety of distinct brain areas and involve a number of different physical and cognitive activities,[32] the same overlap is found in the left cerebral cortex.[33] The overlap areas exclude regions that are implicated in visual processing and hand movement for writing, vocal tract movement and auditory processing for speaking, and visual processing again for reading. Acquired dysgraphia (a writing disorder) and dyslexia (a reading disorder) may occur independently, although they are often found together, just as acquired auditory agnosia (inability to appropriately process speech sounds) and speech dyspraxia (inability to appropriately articulate speech sounds), which also often occur together, may present separately. Nevertheless, various studies confirm that the receptive and productive processes in both speech and writing are integrated cross-modally. The widely accepted conclusion is that the regions around and including Broca's and Wernicke's areas constitute a general multimodal language processing area.[34]

4. Neural networks involved in the processing of reading are normally established by the time children are 7 years old and pattern similarly with the local reading networks of older children and adults.[35] Neural networks involved in producing writing are normally established by age 8 and also pattern similarly with the local writing networks of older children and adults.[36]

A significant conclusion that follows from this work is that reading and writing are parasitic on the speech system. Whether the language system is itself a module as properly understood or a specialized network, reading and writing employ general cognitive strategies like symbol recognition that interface with the speech system. Further, there must be some mechanism that takes visual (or, in the case of the blind, tactile) input and associates it with the phonological representation of a word stored in memory. After the two are associated, the syntactic and semantic/pragmatic parts of the system function in reading and writing pretty much exactly as they do in the processing of verbal speech. What this means is that achieving fluency in writing should follow the same path as achieving fluency in speech, which we know involves learning from input. Although we've noted that the input for speech is spoken language and the input for writing is written language, in the association areas the input from reading can be used to construct a spoken output, just as input from heard speech can be used to construct a written output (i.e., you can add a word to your vocabulary whether the input was written or spoken, even if in the former case you may not have the conventional phonological representation and in the latter you may not have the conventional graphemic representation).

Although the empirical research cited earlier is not conclusive in respect of the position on the learning of writing that I take, it is entirely consistent with it.[37] At the same time, it is inconsistent with the following propositions:

- ⊘ Writing involves a completely separate cognitive process from reading.
- ⊘ One learns the skill of writing primarily through the exercise of writing.
- ⊘ One learns the skill of writing primarily through being taught writing techniques.

The empirical support for this from the cognitive sciences is quite clear. Although obviously different neural processes are involved in the brain during reading, writing, speaking, and processing speech, there is persuasive evidence that these processes all map onto common, mode-independent representations in higher association regions of the brain. So if writing skill is poorly developed in a student, in the absence of pathology the logical place to look for its cause is in the quantity and quality of input to the language mechanism, which is overwhelmingly through reading and speech. I'll elaborate on this in chapter 3.

I anticipate there may be concerns that by hypothesizing a paradigmatically normal brain when referring to the learning conditions I'm interested in (as I did in the last paragraph), as opposed to brains with various lesions or perhaps just different biochemistry, I am preparing to ignore individual differences in how and how much students in the average classroom learn. These differences undoubtedly exist and are important in the classroom, but I believe the first order of business should be to understand the paradigmatic cases of language learning, postponing fine differences until we have a firmer grasp of general species capacity.

Testing for Fluency

The concept of fluency we're using is grounded in cognitive theories of language and mind rather than in instructional strategies, theories of testing, or prejudices of style. I'll have more to say about theories of language and mind later, but at this point I wish to point out only that a systematic theory about how language works, about how a person's brain subconsciously discriminates among possible alternative wordings or phrases, can illuminate why one or another of them might be preferred in a certain context. This is significant because we want our pronouncements about language to be not only coherent and consistent among themselves but also consistent with what we know about the cognitive processes at work in both the writer and the reader. A rule that a teacher insists on that actually has either a deleterious or no effect on ease and accuracy of mental processing is not a good candidate for a rubric for good writing. And an explicit, conscious prejudice in favor of a particular phrasing may or may not reflect anything at all about the way the language is encoded in the writer's brain. Over the larger population of mature writers, such prejudices will tend to wash out. Yes, consciously learned conventions do occasionally play an important role in written language (most particularly in relation to its graphical realization); but one needs to consider whether, without any supporting theory, they are crucial in the identification of good writing.

These differences between testing with rubrics in the Michigan or Pennsylvania style or usage panels in the American Heritage style, on the one hand, and identifying good writing by registering recognition of like skills, on the other, go together with different approaches to teaching writing. Nobody expects a native speaker of English to become a fluent speaker of Russian by taking a few years of college instruction in that language. The most that can be expected is that those courses will provide a foundation on which students can build in order to learn the language fluently on their own, usually by traveling to places where the language is spoken and immersing themselves in the culture of native speakers for a considerable period. The courses are, in fact, dispensable. You can become a fluent speaker of a foreign language without ever having taken a course in it. Just so with writing, obviously. The crucial elements are motivation and subsequent immersion in the culture of mature writers through avid reading and then through writing in order to communicate in that culture.

Fluency

3

Constructional Fluency

I EXPECT GRAMMAR is one of the more feared subjects in the curriculum not only because it can be oftentimes dull and boring but also because it's hard and in general thoroughly foreign to a person's natural store of conscious knowledge about his or her language. The special vocabulary is unenlightening if not downright frightening ("island violation," "split antecedent," "stripped constituent," "double-headed relative"), the concepts opaque ("antecedent-contained deletion," "empty category principle," "lexico-semantic rule"), and the application to problems of writing prose difficult to see. The irony, though, is that students who are native speakers of English already know implicitly, without ever having been told, almost everything about English grammar in the grammar texts they're required to read; they just don't know it in the somewhat strange form in which it's presented. Another bit of irony is that, although knowledge of grammar is essential to good writing, where aspiring writers commonly have trouble is in areas that are rarely if ever taught in school, except perhaps in graduate seminars in linguistic theory. You can forgive the aspiring writer for feeling that grammar is useless, since writing teachers and theorists seem often to feel exactly the same way.[1]

However, there is no possibility of adequately answering the question "What is good writing?" without getting a little bit into grammar, because being fluent in a language means being fluent in respect of (among a limited number of other things) its grammar. And to understand what gives rise to fluency in grammar, one has to know what the grammar is that we're talking about.

As linguists use the term, grammar can mean either (1) the unconscious knowledge of his or her language that a native speaker has in some way stored in the brain and that should allow him or her in principle to communicate fluently with others in that language, or (2) the linguist's speculations about what that knowledge consists of. Since we do not as yet have instruments so sensitive and finely calibrated that we can determine the exact contours of a person's internalized knowledge of language, we are left to speculate—i.e., to create theories of grammar.

Constructions and Construction Grammar

There are many grammatical theories—some more popular among linguists than others—though none has a monopoly on accounting for the facts. The one I will use here is Construction Grammar (CG), and it is called this because central to that theory is the idea of a construction, which is the learned pairing of a particular linguistic pattern with its meaning and function in discourse.[2] The idea of a construction has a long and distinguished history in linguistics, philosophy, and rhetoric, going back at least to the time of the Stoics in Ancient Greece. In recent years, researchers in CG have been incorporating results in cognitive science, language acquisition, and linguistic theory, so that CG today reflects many of the leading ideas in current research on language. In this book I will not venture far beyond the rudiments of CG, which should be sufficient for the limited purpose of discussing good writing.

As indicated earlier, humans are very good at recognizing patterns, linguistic patterns among them. A linguistic pattern can be a particular configuration of sounds or letters (a word, or meaningful parts of a word) or of types of words or even types of patterns. A pattern is a construction if its meaning is not predictable from its component parts (and therefore has to be learned). Here follow some examples of construction patterns:

(3.1) Construction Patterns
  Morpheme: pre-, post- (as in "prenuptial agreement")
  Word: "avocado"
  Complex Word: "daredevil"
  Idiom: "going great guns," "give the Devil his due"
  Go Verb-ing ("Don't go sticking your nose in other people's business")
  Noun will be Noun ("Boys will be boys")
  The Xer the Yer ("The bigger they come, the harder they fall")
  What's X doing in Y? ("What's a nice girl like you doing in a place like this?")
  Intransitive Pattern: Subject Verb ("She's crying")
  Transitive Pattern: Subj Verb Object ("Sam bought beets")
  Caused Motion Pattern: Subj Verb Obj Location ("She hit the ball to David")
  Ditransitive Pattern: Subj Verb Obj Obj ("He gave her a taco")

Passive Pattern: Subj be V-ed (by Prepositional Phrase) ("The cat was hit by a car")

Resultative Pattern: Subj Verb Obj Result ("She knocked him unconscious")[3]

In the first four of these examples, constructions are created by associating a particular meaning with a specific part of a word, a specific word itself, or a specific combination of words, something that's accomplished in the main for nonspecialized vocabulary within the first two decades of a person's life, with piecemeal additions thereafter. The last six examples involve learning the meaning of complex linguistic patterns composed of simpler constructions, and that too is accomplished mainly before the age of maturity. For example, the ditransitive pattern, which begins to emerge in children as young as 16 months,[4] consists of a subject followed by a verb followed by two objects; the meaning associated with such a pattern in the ditransitive construction is that the individual indicated by the subject undertook whatever action is indicated by the verb with the intention of transferring the second object to the first object. Now, it is extremely important to understand that this learning does not involve anything like memorizing the description of the ditransitive I have just given. There is no need even to know the term "ditransitive" or for intensive study of the pattern, in the way perhaps that a student studies a biology textbook. On the contrary, the knowledge involved is gained in childhood merely by exposure to a variety of instances of the construction in situations where its meaning can be determined from context. If Billy knows the words "Mommy," "give," "you," and "cookie" and Mommy gives Billy a cookie after saying, "Mommy will give you a cookie," Billy then has all the information he needs to determine what the ditransitive construction means here. (Note that if Mommy has been at the bottle and says "Cookie … give … Mommy … you," the intended information about the ditransitive pattern will not have been communicated.)

Once language learners have learned a complex construction like the ditransitive, they are free to substitute in the pattern other words they know—"Daddy give Billy a train," "Billy give Mommy a snake," and so on. In time, after exposure to many other instances of the ditransitive in different contexts, learners apprehend that the central meaning can be extended with some slight alteration to fit different situations, especially with different verbs. So we have not only "Mommy will bake Billy a cake" and "Daddy will toss Billy the ball" with the central meaning intact but also instances like "Mommy will blow Billy a kiss," "Daddy will teach Billy French," and "Billy will make Daddy a happy dude," where the intended transfer involves something other than a physical object. Further extensions are easily accommodated: "Sam e-mailed me his crazy idea," "Joe crunched me some outstanding numbers," etc.

One thing that makes learning constructions fairly easy is that their meanings often conform to familiar scenes or scenarios which are common to human experience. We give things to others and take things from others, we ride and propel ourselves (and other things) in various directions, we engage in commercial and legal and criminal transactions (buying, selling, borrowing, loaning, bequeathing, inheriting, suing, stealing) and in social ceremonies (getting married, ordained, divorced, elected Grand Poobah), etc. In all these cases, we have mental images of the situations in which we know who does what with what or whom and for what reason. For example, in the prototypical sales trans- action there is a buyer, a seller, a piece of property, and an amount of money to be exchanged ("Daddy buys a hyena from Billy for a dollar," or "Billy sells Daddy a refrigerator for a penny"). We all have an image of the standard scenario, and once we have learned to asso- ciate it with the appropriate constructions, we understand the meaning of the sentences using those constructions, with particular words stuck into their intended places.

There are, as they've been defined earlier, a huge number of constructions in any lan- guage, all of which have to be learned. Most of those constructions are simple vocabulary items and idioms, but there are also many sentence patterns. In primary and secondary school you may have been taught in class to identify perhaps a dozen of the patterns, but you had already learned on your own far more than that. In (3.2) I've listed a few sentences in- volving different sentence patterns in which the verb "kick" can comfortably participate:

(3.2) Pat kicked the wall.
    Pat kicked Bob black and blue.
    Pat kicked the football into the stadium.
    Pat kicked at the football.
    Pat kicked his foot against the chair.
    Pat kicked Bob the football.
    Pat kicked his way out of the operating room.[5]

A significant problem for the learner of English is determining which patterns any particular verb fits. For example, while you can say "Bill froze the pumpkin," meaning that Bill caused the pumpkin to freeze, you wouldn't say "Bill kicked the pumpkin" if you mean that Bill caused the pumpkin to kick. One of the greatest difficulties in formu- lating a theory of grammar is accounting not only for the types of sentences that we know everyone uses but also for the infinite number of types that they don't use. A sen- tence like the one in (3.3) is not English; and anyone who speaks English fluently would know that something has gone horribly wrong in the constructing of that sentence if it's meant to be English.

(3.3) *Rays moldovan thoughtful fall motor-pool neuroma forewoman bundled-up babblement tau hesperornis birthmark barillet horticulturist crateva pyroleic.[6]

A linguist proposing a theory like CG therefore has to account for the fact that Eng- lish speakers not only use and know how to interpret sentences like (3.2) but also know immediately that (3.3) does not instantiate a pattern that is usable in English. Note that (3.3) is not a sentence that a developing writer would probably ever write (unless, perhaps, a cat walked over the keyboard in the midst of its composition)—or would ever need to be corrected for writing—in an essay or a story. It would be strange to say that it is bad writing. It doesn't seem to have been created by a developing writer's mishandling of familiar English phrases. It is just not even close to being English at all.

In the Constructionist approach I'm advocating here, it certainly isn't the case that language is a free-for-all. Languages do operate according to the cognitive principles that govern the forming and combining of constructions. You might call these principles "rules," but in attempting to distinguish them from the rules that prescriptivists generally allude to, I'll continue to refer to what governs constructional combination as conventions, because I want to emphasize that following prescriptivist rules is for the most part pointless in the teaching of writing.[7] I don't mean to say that a prescriptive perspective is useless for any purpose: in fact, some prescriptive preferences are very helpful when taken as suggestions about clarifying a stretch of prose, and I will discuss these later at various points.

Competence and Performance

In his early work, the linguist Noam Chomsky liked to distinguish between the notions of competence and performance in the production of language. Competence consisted in a person's inherent ability to produce and understand language. By contrast, a person's actual performance could be affected by distractions, memory lapses, temporary or permanent physical impairments, etc. If a performance factor got in the way of producing a perfectly acceptable, grammatical sentence, the speaker of the sentence, given sufficient time and perhaps enhanced memory and articulatory equipment, should be able to recognize the problem and to correct it. The ability to reflect on and revise a stretch of written prose that is assumed in the production of formal writing is exactly equivalent.

The challenge that those working in the Chomskyan framework immediately confronted was whether they could logically distinguish a sentence displaying a performance error from one that was deviant relative to a person's competence. That is, rather than merely declaring by fiat that a sentence like (3.3) is different in kind from the sentences of (3.2) spoken by someone with the hiccups, they had to provide a reasoned argument not only for making such a distinction in the first place but also for assigning the sentences to their respective categories once the distinction was made. The solution they offered was to let the overall theory of grammar decide. The theory would mark certain sentences as grammatical because they comported with the algorithms or rules of the hypothesized grammar. One would then look at the way the grammatical theory handles various sentences and decide whether that is satisfying. (In the philosophy of science, this venerable strategy is called the "hypothetico-deductive" method.) A theory that divides up sentences in a way that seems wrong on its face would be jettisoned.

The importance of looking at language this way is that it made a linguistic theory both explanatory and predictive – explanatory in the sense that if the theory is correct it explains what principles underlie the mechanisms in the brain that make communication possible, and predictive in the sense that the theory predicts that any sentence composed according to its algorithms or rules should be judged grammatical by native speakers.[8] (Note, importantly, that the theory does not claim to predict actual behavior by a speaker or writer.) If the predictions turn out to be consistently wrong, then, well, it's back to the drawing board with the theory.

The competence/performance distinction has been accepted by many (but not all) linguists today and will be taken for granted in this book. The weak point of this approach is that it assumes, but has not really delivered, a theory of performance to accompany its theory of competence.[9] Instead, it relies on the fluent writer or speaker to be able upon reflection to identify a performance error. "I'm sorry," the speaker might say. "You're right, I meant antediluvian, not antebellum." If the speaker cannot, then it becomes a question of competence—or, in our terminology, fluency. The benefit of thinking about at least some of the prescriptivist rules as suggestions (sometimes apt, sometimes not, as suggestions are wont to be) for improving a particular performance is that it avoids the trap (which one would otherwise fall into by taking them as belonging to the conventions of grammar) of being neither necessary nor sufficient for good writing. What exasperates descriptive linguists about prescriptive rules is not that when held up for view they don't hold water (although they often don't); it's that the prescriber generally evidences no awareness that language is a system and that its parts are massively interconnected with each other. To make a claim about whether a certain sentence is "grammatical" without reference to that system—and especially without a grounded argument in support of that claim—has value only as one person's idiosyncratic and perhaps uninformed opinion and nothing more. Context is essential. The linguist Jerry Morgan illustrated this in an important study entitled "Sentence Fragments and the Notion 'Sentence.'" As paraphrased by James D. McCawley, Morgan's point was that "the sentence 'Bush conjectures poached' is interpretable only by providing a context relative to which 'poached' can be taken as an elliptical form of a subordinate clause (e.g., it could be an answer to the question 'Does anyone know how Reagan likes his eggs?')."[10] Out of context, the sentence seems incoherent: one would be tempted to insist that "conjectures," if used as a verb rather than a noun, must take a clause as a complement, as in "Bush conjectures that Iraq has weapons of mass destruction."

It is interesting in this connection that many accomplished writers do not consult style guides for tips on style. For example, as the writer John Updike has said, "The fact seems to be that while writing I rarely consult Fowler or any other guide to usage; I would rather trust my ear and unconsciously acquired sense of the language." John O'Hara put it more bluntly: "Don't cite dictionaries to me.... Dictionary people cite me, not I them."[11] On the other side of the fence, hard-core prescriptivists are not impressed by a demonstration that good writers haven't followed their prescriptions. Simon Heffer, in his book *Strictly English: The Correct Way to Write . . . And Why It Matters*, has countered Updike and O'Hara with this: "I happen to believe that the 'evidence' of how I see English written by others, including some other professional writers, is not something by which I wish to be influenced"; and "English grammar shouldn't be a matter for debate."[12] This reminds one of the Pope and the Archbishop of Canterbury after the English Reformation: Both maintained that they spoke directly with God but would speak with each other only through intermediaries.

The *New York Times* currently has a column entitled "After Deadline," in which it returns to and endeavors to correct what it sees as solecisms recently published in its pages. The irony is that the solecisms were committed by some of the best journalists in the country—journalists who as a group of professional writers must be counted among the most fluent and accomplished that anyone could assemble—and yet they are still in for a whipping behind the shed. (As the Roman poet Horace famously said, one gets offended when even the great Homer nods.) But if they have let slip a dangling modifier or used a word according to an inexact definition, it's not because they aren't fluent in the language. Their problems are most often problems of performance.

For example, think for a moment about the dangling modifier. The proscriptions against using a dangler are many and varied, and often misguided. Strunk and White phrase their rule (as noted earlier) thusly: "A participial phrase at the beginning of a sentence must refer to the grammatical subject." Other texts, like Simon & Schuster's *Handbook for Writers*, acknowledge that initial modifiers of any form must describe another word in the sentence. Ignoring for the moment the conflict between the two formulations, what exactly does it mean for a phrase or modifier to refer to or describe a subject or another word in the sentence? Consider the following sentences:

(3.4i) Remembering how the legs of the normal ones twinkle as they dash up and down the beach, it was amazing to see how fast this little fellow got about just hopping.

(3.4ii) Having stood, waiting for her, in the cold rain outside the restaurant for over an hour, with no result other than his surrender to the chill that penetrated to his bones, there finally seemed to John no reason at all that he should have expected her to come in the first place.

(3.4iii) Without detracting from Fowler's point, aren't some Anglo-Saxon verbs overused?

(3.4iv) Bearing in mind the competitive environment, this is a creditable result.

(3.4v) Considering that no one had a map, it's a miracle that the group reached its destination.

(3.4vi)   Soaring high above the mountain, their wings outspread like great feathered canopies, we caught a final glimpse of our eagle and his mate before they disappeared into the mists.

(3.4vii)   Having just seen his own face reflected brightly in the glass, but with the mole on his left cheek naturally appearing to be on the right, the solution came to John immediately.

(3.4viii)   Rudolph gave a sharp cry and ran in a panic from the house—while the collapsed man lay there quite still, filling his room, filling it with voices and faces until it was crowded with echolalia, and rang loud with a steady, shrill note of laughter.

(3.4ix)   As a Member of Parliament, your job, like mine, requires you from time to time to stay at one of Canada's nearly 400,000 hotel rooms.[13]

I would say that these sentences are examples of fluent written English, though I know there are many who would disagree. But as a theorist, it seems to me that the issue is not whether a modifier dangles, but whether the conventions of English grammar allow these constructions, and if so, whether performance or other criteria need to be invoked to account for them. The issue is more general, and more complex, than the proscription against dangling indicates. Clearly, the sentences in (3.4) contrast with (3.5i), which seems decidedly off-kilter:

(3.5i)   *Lying awake, the floor creaked

But is it really impossible? This is actually the first clause of a multiply compound sentence from Virginia Woolf's *Mrs. Dalloway*. The entire sentence reads as follows:

(3.5ii)   Lying awake, the floor creaked; the lit house was suddenly darkened, and if she raised her head she could just hear the click of the handle released as gently as possible by Richard, who slipped upstairs in his socks and then, as often as not, dropped his hot-water bottle and swore.[14]

There is no question that (3.5i) constitutes a clausal unit in (3.5ii) and, out of context, seems to suggest that the floor was lying awake. So, did Virginia Woolf, one of the great writers of the twentieth century, commit a horrendous grammatical gaffe here? Some might think so, but I would be hesitant to say that she did. The issue, I would argue, is ease of relevant interpretation, in context, given the conventional meanings of the constructions that have been joined together, "Lying awake" and "the floor creaked." The prescriptivist who tries to salvage Strunk and White's dangler rule by saying that "Lying awake" is a contraction of "She was lying awake" (and that the comma in (3.5i) simply separates two short, complete sentences) is in fact denying the rule and admitting to just this. Again, I am not at all saying that anything goes in the construction of an English sentence, only that the rules that determine what is fluent English are considerably more complex than is often assumed—and this complexity is driven by the interaction of a variety of principles that aren't obvious to the casual observer. I will have much more to say about relevant interpretation in context and complexity in what follows.

For the moment, though, consider a slightly different case, involving the reference of pronouns.

(3.6i) Near him, Dan saw a snake.

(3.6ii) Near Dan, he saw a snake.

Here we have two very similar sentences with an initial adverbial modifier, both unexceptional, both constructed using essentially the same words. However, their meanings differ sharply. In (3.6i), the person who saw the snake is Dan and the location of the snake can be near either Dan or some third male party. By contrast, in (3.6ii), the person who saw the snake cannot be Dan but must be some male third party.[15] The conventions which permit combining a modifier with a clause determine the possibilities for associating a pronoun with another noun in the sentence or discourse, but it is obviously not so simple as insisting that the modifier "refer to" or "describe" the grammatical subject. I will not go into the explanations that linguists have come up with to account for these facts—they can be complicated[16]—but suffice it to say that the Strunk and White formulation won't do as anything more than a not terribly useful approximation.

Of course, it would be silly to insist that exactly the same grammatical mechanism that accounts for the sentences of (3.4) and (3.5) must also account for the sentences of (3.6). Depending on what else is in your theory of grammar, they might—or they might not. What are prized in science are explanations that cover the widest possible terrain, so if your explanation for (3.4) and (3.5) also accounts for other phenomena (such as (3.6)), then that is an advantage. By Occam's Razor, the fewer grammatical conventions your theory requires in order to explain the linguistic facts, the better your theory is. This is why linguists can be dismissive of rules like Strunk and White's prohibition against participial phrases at the beginning of a sentence that don't refer to their subjects. As a hypothesis about the sentences that professional writers find acceptable, it ultimately fails. But even if it were entirely accurate, one would prefer an explanation for the prohibition that fits well with other facts about the language that we are aware of. In that case, you might say that there is a generalization about the phenomena to be made. By contrast, if all you do is provide a list of good sentences and bad sentences without attempting to explain what sort of mechanism could account for the distribution, then it's hard to know what to make of it. Since the sets of good sentences in English and bad sentences in English are both potentially infinite, who's to say that the sentences you've arrayed are representative of anything?

The Intentional Stance

A different approach to the problem that the distinction between competence and performance is designed to address has been proposed by philosophers concerned with questions of mind. Daniel Dennett coined the phrase "the intentional stance" to denote a particular assumption about communicators: "we must treat a [communicator] as an agent, indeed a rational agent, who harbors beliefs and desires and other mental states that exhibit intentionality or 'aboutness,' and whose actions can be explained (or predicted) on the basis of the content of those states."[17] That is, we assume that a person has a rational reason for saying or writing something, and even if it doesn't fit a particular pattern that we are familiar with, we try to make sense of it using our rational tools. We attribute to the communicator the same sort of mind that we have.

For this to work, we all must come equipped with a logical mechanism to interpret what Chomsky would call the grammatical sentences of the language. But we also must have a logical mechanism to interpret sentences with performance errors as long as we assume the communicator is acting rationally. If I say, "I'd like, OK, could you just, you see that radish over there on the counter, please," where in fact the object is a small beet, you are able to make the adjustment and say, "You want me to bring you this beet?" This requires a fairly powerful logical apparatus, but one, as we will see in chapter 4 in the section on Relevance Theory, that can be simply described. Nevertheless, there are limits to this interpretive strategy, as we will see in chapter 7.

Constructional Conflation

A good deal of the theoretical work in CG has investigated how native speakers know (or can learn) the difference between a purported sentence like (3.3) and sentences like (3.2), and an account of some of this work can be found later on in this chapter. However, what I want to focus on at the moment, in order to make my point about conscious rule-following in answering the question "What is good writing?," are the sorts of problems you see in developing writers all the time. What is at issue here is usually a writer's lack of fluency in handling the constructions he or she is using, and no style book that I'm aware of provides the kind of instruction that will help writers to avoid these problems.

Consider the constructions in (3.7i) and (3.7ii), both ordinary English phrases with very similar but not quite identical meaning:

(3.7i) on a personal note
(3.7ii) in a personal vein

One might use (3.7i) to inject a personal opinion, sentiment, or anecdote into a story that has heretofore been about someone or something else: "On a personal note, I should say that I myself have a family member with elephantiasis." The meaning of (3.7ii) is quite similar, but it may suggest a shift of mood or style: "In a more personal vein, let me tell you a humorous story about my brother, who has elephantiasis." Now, someone who does not have a firm grip on the two constructions and the difference between them might produce either (3.8i) or (3.8ii):

(3.8i) *in a personal note
(3.8ii) *on a personal vein

I call the process that produces (3.8i) or (3.8ii) *Constructional Conflation*.[18] Although traditional writers' handbooks might mark (3.8i) and (3.8ii) as containing errors in choice of preposition, a linguist working with CG would be likely to conclude that the two similar constructions in (3.7i) and (3.7ii) have been confused and conflated, with the result that a preposition appropriate to one has been inserted in the other. The traditional view is unenlightening about the source of the error; on that view the writer could just as well have substituted the preposition "to" or "with" for "on" in (3.7i). But if Constructional Conflation has produced the error, there would be no possibility of substituting "to" or "with". The possibility of a developing writer writing, "To a personal note..." is close to nil.

Here is another example.

(3.9i) We should let it be known to him that we don't allow caterwauling in here.
(3.9ii) We should let him know that we don't allow caterwauling in here.

The construction in (3.9i) has a somewhat antiquated flavor but should still be within the native speaker's competence;[19] sentence (3.9ii) is similar to but not quite synonymous with (3.9i),[20] and it is more colloquial. Constructional Conflation explains the production of (3.10):

(3.10) *We should let him be known that we don't allow caterwauling in here.

Again, we can see that conflation of two similar constructions has resulted in a third construction that is unconventional in English with the intended meaning. It's not that (3.10) is, strictly speaking, ungrammatical—for example, (3.11) is a perfectly acceptable sentence of English although it is built on the same constructional pattern as (3.10):

(3.11) We should let the news be broadcast that we don't allow caterwauling in here.

The problem with (3.10) is that the meaning that the writer of that sentence evidently had in mind (namely something like the meaning of (3.9ii)) is not conventionally derivable from it in the way that the meaning of (3.11) is derivable from the sentence pattern that it instantiates. That's why it seems garbled. Somehow (3.10) suggests that the person indicated by "him" is to be made known rather than the proscription against caterwauling. If the teacher follows standard practice and indicates to the writer that the error in (3.10) is faulty use of a pronoun, it would be not only unhelpful, but misleading.

A more complex example of Constructional Conflation can be found in (3.12).

> (3.12)   *This style preference characterizes her novel as an innovative and unusual read.

In (3.12), the writer has mashed together what appear to be three different constructions that would be legitimate on their own—"(Someone) characterizes her novel as innovative," and "This style preference characterizes her novel," and "This style makes her novel an innovative and unusual read." The result is again a sentence whose intended meaning(s) cannot be conventionally derived from the constructional patterns within it, because the mashing has produced a construction that isn't one of those conventionally associated with a particular meaning in English. The verb "characterize" fits into two constructions, one of which could be instantiated as "This style characterizes her novel" and the other of which could be instantiated as "I would characterize her novel as innovative." In the first construction, the one without "as," the meaning of characterize is something like "be characteristic of" and requires, in order to make sense, a quality that can serve as a characteristic as its subject. In the second construction, with "as," characterize means something like "describe" and requires an agent capable of describing as its subject. There is then no way to make sense of a sentence like "This style preference characterizes her novel as innovative," which mixes the two constructions together. Notice that the traditional approach would entirely fail to capture this fact.

Rather than drag the reader through further examples of this sort, I will simply list in (3.13) five more instances of Constructional Conflation and leave it to him or her as an exercise to decide which patterns each has been derived from.[21]

> (3.13i)   *I learned the art of parking cars from a young age.
> (3.13ii)   *I'm grateful to know you're coming.
> (3.13iii) *I hope to capitalize from its potential.
> (3.13iv)   *You have expressed very eloquently what goes on through students' minds these days.
> (3.13v)   *I'm going to dispense of this problem in the next section.

Constructional Conflict

A different—and more pervasive—problem that developing writers have is one I call *Constructional Conflict*, which arises when two or more legitimate constructions appear in different places in a legitimate sentence pattern but conflict in interpretation.

An example should help to differentiate this sort of problem from that of Constructional Conflation.

(3.14) *By this time I had known Ramona since I was young, throughout which we had talked about her wonderful success in sports.

Here we have four perfectly formed and interpretable constructions—"By this time"; "I had known Ramona"; "since I was young"; and "throughout which we had talked about her wonderful success with sports." None has been distorted by conflation or mixing with another. The first is an adverbial prepositional phrase that requires the main clause to be an accomplishment, an action that is completed before the time of the action of a previous sentence. It says, roughly, "You know the time we were just talking about? Well, prior to that time, the following had happened." The main clause could of course stand by itself—I had known Ramona since I was young. But when modified by "By this time," it means "Prior to the time I've just been talking about, I had been acquainted with Ramona." But now there is a conflict in the interpretation of the constructions "By this time" and "since I was young." It would be fine to say, "By this time I had known Ramona for over four years." Or you could say "I had been acquainted with Ramona since I was young." But "By this time" and "since I was young" don't comfortably go together: the first stands at a point in time nearer the present and looks backward into the past while the second stands at a point in the past and looks forward toward the present. Basically the writer is trying to stand in two different places at once, in the same clause, and you can't do that without confusing the reader mightily. You can see what the writer was trying to do—she wanted to cram into the sentence the fact that she had known Ramona since she was young. But the cramming doesn't work.

The last construction in (3.14)—"throughout which we talked about her wonderful success in sports"—is a subordinate or dependent relative clause, which qualifies the meaning of a noun that precedes it by indicating the activity that occurred during the span of time indicated by the noun. You might say, for example, "I met Ramona at a five-minute speed-dating session, throughout which she talked of her wonderful success in sports." In that sentence, "throughout which . . ." qualifies or modifies the noun "session"; the word "which" refers directly to "session." But in (3.14), "throughout which . . ." follows an adjective, "young," and has no noun to attach to. What I assume the writer really meant was something like "I had known Ramona since I was young. Ever since we were first acquainted, she had talked of her wonderful success in sports." And it would have been better for the reader if she had said just that.

Let's look at another example of Constructional Conflict.

(3.15) *We should not overly depend on prescription drugs for fear of becoming habituated.

In (3.15) we have two perfectly formed and interpretable constructions—"We should not overly depend on prescription drugs" and "for fear of becoming habituated." The first is a main or independent clause and could stand by itself. The second is a construction beginning with "for fear of," which provides the reason that the subject of the main clause did not take, is not taking, or will not take the action indicated in that main clause. A typical sentence involving the second construction is "Ben won't go outside without a hat for fear of catching a cold." It's Ben's fear of catching a cold that causes him not to go outside without a hat. For this construction to work, it requires that the main clause contain an action that the subject of that clause did not take, is not taking, or will not take. Note, however, that (3.15) doesn't contain such an action, because it uses, along with the negative "not," the modal "should." That "should" takes the "not" following it into its bosom and doesn't let go, which is to say that the main clause doesn't say what "We" don't do; it says what (the writer believes) "We" shouldn't do. The main clause then does not satisfy a requirement of the "for fear of" construction in order to make sense. If (3.15) is interpretable at all, it suggests that what people shouldn't do is allow their fear of building up a tolerance to cause them to overly rely on medications, which is nonsensical. It is difficult to see how a traditional rules analysis could handle either (3.14) or (3.15), though both are naturally accommodated as examples of Constructional Conflict.

For one last example in this section, which involves both Constructional Conflation and Constructional Conflict, see (3.16):

(3.16) *Using the metaphor of disliking cilantro as a comparison to why some men do not like women bears truth and is also quite funny.

Here we have a truly screwed up sentence. What the writer means, I think, is that the author of the work she's discussing used cilantro as a metaphor to illuminate why some men do not like women. The writer found this metaphor not only enlightening, but also funny.

To figure out what in the world is going on in this sentence, let's take it apart phrase by phrase:

(3.17) Using the metaphor of disliking cilantro
(3.18) as a comparison to
(3.19) why some men do not like women
(3.20) bears truth
(3.21) and is also quite funny.

The sentence starts off well—there's nothing terribly wrong with (3.17)—but then it goes right off the rails in (3.18). The phrase as "a comparison to" is a constructional conflation of "in comparison with/to" and (probably) "as a metaphor for." But neither works with (3.17), and the mash-up doesn't either. Since the writer has already introduced the idea that disliking cilantro is a metaphor, she can't use that word again but apparently still wants to fit the idea of comparison in; she might have more economically begun as in (3.22) or (3.23):

(3.22) Using the metaphor of disliking cilantro to illuminate why some men do not like women . . .

(3.23) Disliking cilantro is a metaphor the author uses to illuminate why some men do not like women.

Now we come to (3.20), "bears truth," a verb-phrase construction which requires as its subject something that can be truthful. The phrase (3.17) "Using the metaphor of disliking cilantro" has no truth-value in itself. A description or a statement or a story might bear truth, but not the activity of using something. (Whether a metaphor per se can be truthful I'll leave to the more metaphysically inclined.) There is a similar problem with (3.21). The writer probably doesn't mean that it's the *use* of the metaphor that she finds funny, although it's possible that she does. But I think it more likely that she finds the metaphor itself funny.

In some rules-based approaches, the combination of (3.20) with (3.17) would fall under the rubric of "faulty alignment," which refers to a situation in which two elements in the sentence are illogically aligned with each other.[22] Faulty alignment includes "faulty predication," where what is predicated of the subject is illogical.

There are, however, numerous instances where the idea of faulty alignment is either too broad or too narrow to cover the facts. We have seen in (3.14), (3.15), and (3.16) cases in which *structural* alignment, rather than logical alignment, is the source of the problem. Another (perhaps clearer) case of what I take to be structural alignment is in (3.24), which is acceptable in Canadian English, but would be odd in American English.

(3.24) As well, we went for a swim in the creek.

The issue here is the placement of the sentence modifier "As well," which does not usually appear sentence initially in American English. Although it doesn't mean none exists, I can't see any reason to ascribe this behavior to logical principles.

Although the question of whether structure or function or meaning determines the acceptability or naturalness of a given sentence has been long debated in linguistics,[23] there is little doubt that there is no sense in talking about meaning or function independently of structure. You might say that (3.3) is a case of faulty alignment, but where to begin? From a constructionist perspective, you would simply note the lack of recognizable sentence patterns to be interpreted and stop there.[24]

More problematical for rules-based approaches are what linguists, following John R. Ross, have called "Island Constraints." We form relative clauses in English by moving a noun phrase to the front of the sentence if necessary and then placing a relative pronoun (who, that, which) after it. For example, we can form the relative clause in (3.26) from the sentence in (3.25).

(3.25)   The shortstop went to the movies.
(3.26)   The shortstop who went to the movies . . .

In (3.26), the relative pronoun "who" substitutes for "the shortstop" inside the relative clause and explicitly refers to the head noun preceding the relative clause, which is "shortstop." This works so long as the relative pronoun doesn't substitute for a noun inside a so-called island, which is a construction that is incompatible with the process. In (3.27) "Billy and the shortstop" is an island. You can't substitute a relative pronoun for one of the two constructions it contains in the subject (either "Billy" or "the shortstop") and place that relative pronoun at the front, yielding (3.28).[25]

(3.27)   Billy and the shortstop went to the movies.
(3.28)   *The shortstop who Billy and went to the movies . . .

Another case where rules-based approaches fail involves what are sometimes called "purpose constructions," which provide a reason for doing something and come in either the infinitival form "to do X" or the gerundive form "for doing X." For example, (3.29) and (3.30) contain purpose constructions that give the reason for asking a person whether he or she has clean shirt and solvent, respectively.

(3.29)   Do you have a clean shirt to wear to the party tonight?
(3.30)   Do you have any solvent for removing marine enamel from wood surfaces?

However, the constructions are not interchangeable.[26]

(3.31)   *Do you have a clean shirt for wearing to the party tonight?
(3.32)   *Do you have any solvent to remove marine enamel from wood surfaces?

The difference between infinitival purpose constructions (like "to wear to the party tonight") and gerundive purpose constructions (like "for removing marine enamel from wood surfaces") is that the infinitival is taken to indicate the specific use to which the head noun is to be put, while the gerundive restricts the head noun to the kind designated for the purpose indicated—a very subtle semantic difference, to be sure, but one that a good writer will be sensitive to. Simply because a clean shirt can be put to a number of different uses and because there are many different kinds of solvents, (3.31) and (3.32) naturally sound odd.

Constructional Complexity

There are evidently hundreds or thousands of constructions like this in English, and you can see that it would be folly to try to explicitly teach them in a composition class. Even though you may now agree that there is a distinction between (3.29) and (3.30), on the one hand, and (3.31) and (3.32), on the other, you probably have never before this been aware that there is such a distinction to be made.

Indeed, the exquisite complexity of English is hardly indicated even by the standard analyses in introductory linguistics textbooks, although you can catch a glimpse of it in the 1,860 pages of the *Cambridge Grammar of the English Language*. The difficulty for the learner of English is not simply in memorizing these constructions but in learning how they interact with each other. It's of course not the case that any construction type can be put together with any other construction type to form a coherent sentence. But even those constructions that are happily joined syntactically may conflict in meaning or usage (as (3.31) and (3.32) indicate). It is the possibility of infelicitous interaction when constructions are joined that makes language complex, even if the general combinatorial principles are straightforward. The linguist Noam Chomsky has consistently pointed out a fact that becomes obvious on a little reflection: native speakers of English cannot possibly have learned all the rules of their language through explicit instruction.[27] Thus, trying to teach aspiring writers even just a small subset of these, as rules-based instructional materials do, is guaranteed to have little effect on their overall command of the language. While it might teach students to avoid a few of their teacher's pet peeves, as a pedagogy for good writing it can't possibly suffice.

When a person learns a language fluently, she or he learns the way various constructions combine through exposure to their usage in various contexts. The more exposure and the more contexts, the more entrenched that person's understanding of the constructions becomes. Because written language, and especially academic prose, generally employs a wider variety of constructions in a wider variety of contexts than you'll find in the colloquial speech of the average adolescent, students who haven't read voraciously can have trouble fitting together constructions whose features they haven't fully grasped. University students in particular may find themselves challenged for the first time to put together and express highly complex ideas. Through their course reading they have become aware that the writers their teachers favor and evidently want them to emulate often express themselves in sentences composed of constructions put together in complicated if not entirely unfamiliar ways. When they try out this style themselves, they may stumble.

Overlap

In a compelling study from 1981, Colette Daiute analyzed 215 placement exam essays written by first-year university students from the New York area for grammatical errors.[28]

One of the more common sorts of error she found she called *Overlap*,[29] which is similar to what I've called Constructional Conflict. Here are three examples she provides:

(3.33) *This waste of two intelligent women I know + would still be active if this boss never had such policies at work.

(3.34) *This category of high school students + are bored with disco.

(3.35) *They were too busy with being attractive + than taking time off and studying the mind's riches.

In (3.33) there are two linguistic constructions that have been overlapped: "This waste of two intelligent women I know" and "two intelligent women I know would still be active if this boss never had such policies at work." In (3.34), the overlap involves "This category of high school students is bored with disco" and "These students are bored with disco." The overlap in (3.35) is a result of mixing two different types of constructions: "They were too busy being attractive to take time off and study the mind's riches" and "They were more interested in being attractive than in taking time off and studying the mind's riches." Daiute identified a position in the error sentence where things began to go awry, which she called the error onset. (This position is indicated by a superscript plus sign in (3.33) to (3.35).) The error onset position overwhelmingly occurred after six words, and a majority of errors included a phrase or clause that contained several clause elements (subject, verb, direct object, object of preposition, etc.) immediately before the error onset. Daiute hypothesized that these errors resulted from an impoverished or overburdened short-term memory, which allowed the structure of the first part to fade before the second could be syntactically coded. If this is the case, we would predict that students who have difficulties with Overlap would also have problems with Constructional Conflict, since the latter also involves a mismatch between two (or more) parts of a sentence.[30]

Since 1981, considerable further research on memory processes has thrown a complicating light on Daiute's prediction. First, a distinction is now usually made between short-term memory and working memory, where the latter consists of an activated portion of memory subject to decay and size limitation and interacts with the attention-focusing component of the central executive (see, for example, Cowan 2006, 2009). Importantly, working memory is seen as not consisting of a simple, unitary storage device but as potentially several distinct modules that process in parallel. Thus, the limitation that Daiute proposed could logically have nothing to do with memory *capacity* but rather might be caused by deficits in the attention-focusing component or the serial processor during the writing exercise. That is, the distraction caused by the felt need to put together various bits of tenuously connected information may have the potential to disrupt the construction process as much as memory limitations might. This obviously raises many important questions for further research, among them whether and how cases of Constructional Conflict and Overlap might be remediable.

Lexical Confusion

In addition to Constructional Conflation and Constructional Conflict, there is a third general type of constructional problem that I find plagues young writers, and it is what I call *Lexical Confusion*. In a rules-based pedagogy, instances of Lexical Confusion are usually labeled "Wrong Word," but I assume the latter is not as helpful as further information about why the word is wrong and another might be a better choice. A good example of Lexical Confusion is in (3.36).

(3.36)   *Most of my professors have averted many of my exams and essays to next week whereby putting me under an enormous amount of pressure.

In this sentence the writer has used the two words "averted" and "whereby" in ways that are conventionally discordant in context. Notice that these are not cases of metaphor gone awry or of stretching the meaning of a word. The writer has simply picked words that make no sense where they are used, probably guessing that they mean something other than what is conventionally understood by them. You might speculate about what the writer really meant, but you would have no way of really knowing (unless you had a private understanding with him or her). Here follow a few more examples.

(3.37)   *He is known for emitting a sense of human decency in his works.

(3.38)   *I hope you can verify my question, as I do not want to miss out on studying the material.

(3.39)   *Do the essays in this course follow the writing format which absconds citation?

It is important to understand that Lexical Confusion does not necessarily involve a failure to cleave precisely to a dictionary definition. Dictionaries do not provide the final word on word meaning; communities do. Or, rather, the final judgment rests on whether the intended sense is well communicated to the intended audience. Dictionaries are extremely useful if you are unsure of the meaning a word has for a general audience or of the way a general audience spells that word. But they can be misleading in a number of ways. For one thing, they are only contemporaneous on the date of their publication and often miss trends in the evolution of the language. For example, the following sentences contain words used in ways that certain dictionaries deplore, but the writers may still be using them entirely in accord with their conventional meaning within the groups in which they circulate.

(3.40)   Because its hero was a boy my age, I found this book quite relatable.

(3.41)   The Smiths, the Maloneys, and the Martins comprised our little group.

(3.42) The steps any young adult needs to take to achieve independence are simplistic.

(3.43) She literally swept us off our feet with her performance.

That is, there are communities of people who use "relatable," "comprised," "simplistic," and "literally" in exactly these ways. The writers' errors, if any, lie in their insensitivity to or lack of awareness of the fact that there also exists a large community of people who share a significantly different convention. The only issue then is whether the writer has chosen the appropriate constructions for the particular audience he or she is writing for. Since I not only am not aware of any community of speakers that uses "emit," "verify," and "abscond" in the way they are used in (3.37) to (3.39) but also really can't imagine that such a community exists, I am fairly confident that those sentences contain instances of Lexical Confusion. But I certainly could be wrong. If a word like "mace" can have two very different meanings in English, why not "abscond"? There's no reason why "emit," "verify," and "abscond" couldn't be assigned meanings similar (but not quite identical) to those of "communicate," "answer," and "eschew." I will have much more to say about audience in chapter 4.

Lexical Underperformance

Another lexical problem that crops up in the work of aspiring writers is *Lexical Underperformance*, which sometimes goes under the rubric of "lazy writing" or "lack of concreteness." Here follows an example.

(3.44) *I liked Garrison Keillor's style, because it was easy to understand and his topics had a commonality that many people my age could relate to.

Although purists might complain that (3.44) contains an instance of Constructional Conflation (on the theory that the writer meant that it was Keillor's essay that was easy to understand, not his style), I want to focus on the use of "had a commonality that many people my age could relate to." It's possible that the writer has confused commonality here, understanding it to mean something like "an ordinary or common-place theme," but I will assume that it is appropriately deployed in the sense of "a shared feature." In that case, the question that immediately arises in the reader's mind is "What is that shared feature?" This might be discussed in the following text, but if it isn't, we'd want another construction in place of "commonality" that would shoulder more of the informational burden.

A useful way to think about Lexical Underperformance is in terms of taxonomical hierarchies. We put things into categories all the time: a Beagle puppy is a type of Beagle, and a Beagle is a kind of dog, and a dog is a type of mammal, and a mammal is a kind of animal, and an animal is a kind of living being. Following the work of Eleanor Rosch in the 1970s, cognitive scientists have concluded that concepts and the words we use for them are cognitively organized at a minimum of three levels. The *basic* level is cognitively the most salient level; Rosch describes it as the level in which commonalities in shape and overall look occur and at which the first categorizations are made by young children.[31]

Examples of words for basic level categories (for the average person) include dogs, cats, fish, chairs, sofas, desks, houses, clouds, trees, rocks, fences, cars, balls, snow, and wind. In psychological jargon, basic-level objects "maximize cue validity." Cue validity is the conditional probability that an object that has a particular feature falls in a particular category. For example, if the object is a member of homo sapiens, then the probability that that object has a cranium and a spine is 100% (by definition). Objects at the basic level maximize cue validity in that they have the greatest number of features that distinguish them from objects in other categories. Objects in superordinate categories (like the objects denoted by the words "mammals," "furniture," "dwellings," "machines," "forms of transportation," and "sports equipment") don't have as many distinctive features and therefore have lower cue validity than objects in basic categories. Because objects in subordinate categories ("Beagles," "Maine Coon Cats," "Northern Pikes," "rocking chairs," "bungalows," "cumulus clouds," "oak trees," "Hondas," and "footballs") share most of their features with other objects that belong to the same basic category, they too have lower cue validity than members of the basic level categories.

The important point is that basic-level categories are the ones that come to mind most readily when we seek to describe something. Driving to the country, we say to the children in the back seat something like (3.45).

(3.45) Hey look, there are horses in that field over there!

It would be most unlikely (unless we and our children were deeply into horse husbandry) that we would say something like (3.46).

(3.46) Hey look, there are two mottled Appaloosas and a gray Arabian mare in that unimproved sandy-soil pasture featuring mixed Kentucky blue and redtop grasses!

Most of the time, basic-level categories are the ones that are most useful, because in everyday conversation we usually don't need (and often are unable) to specify more detail. The problem is that the members of basic- and superordinate-level categories are mental abstractions.[32] There is no such thing in the physical world as a rock that is not a particular type of rock or a grass that is not a particular type of grass. You may not know the geological or botanical name, but any given piece of rock or blade of grass has features that distinguish it from other types of rock and grass. Thus, if the goal is to describe a concrete environment, one must reach below the abstract basic level to the more concrete subordinate level, where words carry more information.

For example, in paragraph (3.47) the noted writer Rachel Carson deploys words denoting objects in subordinate level categories in skillful combination with words denoting objects in basic level categories:

(3.47)   Near Samoa in the Pacific, the palolo worm lives out its life on the bottom of the shallow sea, in holes in the rocks and among the masses of corals. Twice each year, during the neap tides of the moon's last quarter in October and November, the worms forsake their burrows and rise to the surface in swarms that cover the water. For this purpose, each worm has literally broken its body in two, half to remain in its rocky tunnel, half to carry the reproductive products to the surface and there to liberate the cells. This happens at dawn on the day before the moon reaches its last quarter, and again on the following day; on the second day of the spawning the quantity of eggs liberated is so great that the sea is discolored.[33]

Notice that a subordinate-level category can be denoted by a phrase – "palolo worm," "bottom of the shallow sea," "holes in rocks," "neap tide," "rocky tunnel," etc. It's not necessary that the author pull out a single word to describe an object in a subordinate-level category.

And while I've been talking about objects, obviously the same sort of categorization can be applied to events, actions, and even abstractions. Think of the different words we have for explosive sounds—"burst," "pop," "crack," "bang," "smack," "splat," "snap," "knock," "tap," "blast," "boom," "peal," "roar." Jogging is a type of running, democracy is type of government, and so forth.

In the following passage, the great writer Zora Neale Hurston deploys a lovely mix of superordinate-level, basic-level, and subordinate-level diction:

(3.48)   Sometimes, I feel discriminated against, but it does not make me angry. It merely astonishes me. How can any deny themselves the pleasure of my company? It is beyond me. But in the main, I feel like a brown bag of miscellany propped against a wall. Against a wall in company with other bags, white, red, and yellow. Pour out the contents, and there is discovered a jumble of small things priceless and worthless. A first-water diamond, an empty spool, bits of broken glass, lengths of string, a key to a door long since crumbled away, a rusty knife-blade, old shoes saved for a road that never was and never will be, a nail bent under the weight of things too heavy for any nail, a dried flower or two still a little fragrant. In your hand is the brown bag. On the ground before you is the jumble it held—so much like the jumble in the bags, could they be emptied, that all might be dumped in a single heap and the bags refilled without altering the content of any greatly. A bit of colored glass more or less would not matter. Perhaps that is how the Great Stuffer of Bags filled them in the first place—who knows?[34]

It's not easy to write like Zora Neale Hurston or Rachel Carson, which is why "lazy writing" is a persistent problem among aspiring writers. However, as suggested with regard to (3.45) and (3.46), a subordinate-level word is not appropriate in every context. There are some circumstances where you really do want to talk about a horse rather than about a gelding. The trick is to give your audience exactly the right amount of information, the information they need to get the most out of what you are telling them – neither more nor less. This will be the subject of the next chapter.

The reason that rules-based approaches can do so little to improve the quality of writing of aspiring writers is that they are not especially designed to address fluency as defined earlier. Post-process approaches may free a writer from normal inhibitions and coax the diffident away from their fear of writing, but for the most part they do not address a writer's skills in using and understanding constructions. And although instruction with a rules-based approach may help a writer to avoid committing a handful of solecisms that a teacher finds particularly egregious, it leaves untouched most of the writer's fund of knowledge (or lack of knowledge) about his or her language. The result is that students can take and pass with high grades several writing or composition classes and still not be able to produce anything that comes close to good writing.

The Significance of the Input Problem

As indicated earlier, learning a language is a natural process, one fed by massive exposure to the language and strong motivation to communicate in that language (i.e., motivation to both understand others' messages and transmit messages of one's own). This would imply that if aspiring writers wish to improve their constructional fluency, they must significantly increase their exposure to the many constructions of their language and employ those constructions in an exchange that is meaningful to them.

We know, from an important study by Betty Hart and Todd R. Risley,[35] that variation in children's intellectual and language ability and their academic success at ages 9 and 10 is related to the amount of talk that they hear from birth to age 3. "With few exceptions," they say, "the more parents talked to their children, the faster the children's vocabularies were growing and the higher the children's IQ test scores at age three and later." So, then, does the advantage to children's language abilities of more speech input during infancy generalize to writing abilities later in life? That is, can it be shown that children and young people advance in writing skill according to the amount they read?

It is no secret that exceptionally fluent writers have read prodigiously throughout their lives, including, most notably, their formative years. For example, the writer Harold Brodkey, winner of the Prix de Rome, said that by the time he was 14, he was reading *Pride and Prejudice*, *The Three Musketeers*, and *Gone with the Wind* "over and over, partly to see how they worked, but also because I liked them. . . . These are the ones I adopted as setting the basic levels of narrative."[36]

More effusively, the great English poet Samuel Taylor Coleridge wrote of his child-hood as follows:

(3.49) My father's sister kept an every-thing shop at Crediton—and there I read through all the gilt-cover little books that could be had at that time, and likewise all the uncovered tales of Tom Hickathrift, Jack the Giant-killer, etc. and etc. etc. etc.—and I used to lie by the wall, and mope—and my spirits used to come upon me suddenly, and in a flood—and then I was accustomed to run up and down the church-yard, and act over all I had been reading on the docks, the nettles, and the rank-grass. At six years old I remember to have read Belisarius, Robinson Crusoe, and Philip Quarll—and then I found the Arabian Nights entertainments—one tale of which (the tale of a man who was compelled to seek for a pure virgin) made so deep an impression on me (I had read it in the evening while my mother was mending stockings) that I was haunted by spectres whenever I was in the dark—and I distinctly remember the anxious and fearful eagerness with which I used to watch the window in which the books lay—and whenever the sun lay upon them, I would seize it, carry it by the wall, and bask, and read. My father found out the effect which these books had produced—and burnt them.[37]

What I think is important to note here is not only the avidness with which Coleridge read and the variety of books he chose but also the profound effect they had on him. As Warwick Elley has shown,[38] children who are actively engaged in a story acquire new vocabulary in it at a faster rate than those who just passively listen. Moreover, children whose vocabularies are already large acquire additional new vocabulary at a faster rate than their peers with smaller vocabularies, and children with larger vocabularies are better at reading comprehension.[39] By age 16, the most significant predictors of text production are vocabulary and spelling.[40] In other words, the rich get richer, while the poor lag ever father behind.[41] In the psychological literature, this is known as the "Matthew Effect."

Good writers continue to press their advantage through their adult years. Jane Smiley, the novelist and biographer of Charles Dickens, said of the adult Dickens that he "sought out and delighted in all forms of writing and talk" and that "his relationship to the English language went beyond love to something more intimate, something more living, something like breathing."[42] The point, Smiley makes clear, is that the good writer takes in language in great gulps, thereby fixing in her or his mind "thousands of word usages and sentence structures, thousands of metaphors, similes, and circumlocutions." But it's not just the great who are raised in an environment copiously supplied with words. The researchers William E. Nagy and Richard C. Anderson estimate that the average seventh grade reader may be exposed to a million words of text in a school year and that avid readers may read up to fifty times that.[43] Of course, when discussing the number of words a person reads or knows, it is important to distinguish between total number of words including repetitions, graphically distinct words, and word families. For example, the word "play" belongs to the word family that includes the graphically distinct words "playing," "played," "player," "replay," etc. Assuming that the average high schooler knows between 25,000 and 50,000 graphically distinct words and that printed school English materials may expose students to approximately 600,000 graphically distinct words in 88,500 different word families (which works out to about seven distinct words for each word family), Nagy and Anderson conclude that in grades 6 through 9 students will normally encounter in a year 5,000 word families, of which 1,000 may be new to them. I. S. P. Nation, citing research by himself and others, indicates that well-educated native speakers know the words in around 20,000 word families, and he decides that secure knowledge of 7,000 to 9,000 word families is probably sufficient for a comfortable reading of novels like *Lady Chatterley's Lover*, *The Turn of the Screw*, and *The Great Gatsby*.[44]

Of course, unstructured reading in elementary and high school will provide only sporadic exposure to any particular word or pattern. The linguist Mark Liberman has calculated that 30 to 40 percent of the words in the bbc.co.uk website were from just the twenty most common word families found in that site.[45] Nagy and Anderson conclude that as many as half of the words of printed school English occur only once in a billion words of text or less. Thus, "any program of direct vocabulary instruction ought to be conceived in full recognition that it can cover only a small fraction of the words that children need to know. Trying to expand children's vocabularies by teaching them words one by one, ten by ten, or even hundred by hundred would appear to be an exercise in futility."[46]

Similarly, according to linguists Geoffrey Leech and Roger Garside, a large proportion of the phrasal and sentence patterns contained in the 45,000-word Lancaster-Leeds Treebank, which includes writing in various genres in English since 1960, were found only once in that corpus.[47] But as Adele E. Goldberg and others have shown, it is the already familiar words that most assist in the learning of pattern constructions. As Goldberg notes, "the high frequency of particular verbs in particular constructions facilitates children's unconsciously establishing a correlation between the meaning of a particular verb in a constructional pattern and the pattern itself."[48] Once the constructional pattern is learned, other words slotted in that pattern are acquired with comparative ease. To the extent that adults confront constructions in their native language that are new to them, the learning of these constructions presumably occurs in exactly the same way. The crucial factor, though, is frequency of exposure to the words and patterns themselves in a context where communication involving those words and patterns is highly valued.[49]

Is there, then, a substitute for avid reading of many books and conversation with many speakers, both of which consistently challenge the learner with a variety of new words and constructions to be learned? We know that a child must be exposed to an appropriate number of constructions of his or her language in an appropriate way for an appropriate number of times during the first dozen or so years of life because we know that, in the extreme case, the language capacity of a child deprived of that exposure will inevitably be permanently damaged.[50] We also know that there are differences among individuals in regard to how, and how fast, they learn. What counts as "appropriate" for each of the conditions in the next to the last sentence above in order to turn the learner into a good writer we can call the *Input Problem.*

The first condition of the Input Problem requires that we determine the appropriate number of constructions the learner must be exposed to, which is actually very simple to state: lots. We can't be more precise than this because we really don't know. What we do know is that, beginning in about the third grade, there is a strong correlation between the amount of time a student spends in reading outside of school and her or his success in reading skill, vocabulary development, fluency, comprehension, and general intellectual development.[51] Of course, there are many factors that could potentially lead a child to read outside of school. In a study of 149 fifth-graders in two schools in the American southwest, Sharon S. McKool found significant correlations between students' avid reading outside school (averaging over 45 minutes a day) and the following:

(3.50i)   parents read aloud to students before they began attending school
(3.50ii)   parents and siblings read for recreational purposes
(3.50iii) value placed on reading in the home
(3.50iv)   access to favored reading material at home
(3.50v)   ability to self-select reading material
(3.50vi)   positive self concept as a reader
(3.50vii) time available for reading both in and out of school
(3.50viii) preference for reading over watching TV[52]

A pertinent issue at this point is whether students who are impoverished according to the Matthew Effect can catch up to the richer members of their cohort. In an ingenious experiment, Nate Kornell, Alan D. Castel, Teal S. Eich, and Robert A. Bjork determined that, although adults' ability to learn declines with age, if learning opportunities are spaced at intervals rather than massed together, older adults (average age: 77) can learn almost as well as younger adults (average age: 21). This is true most strikingly when the learning is inductive (i.e., when it requires the learner to reach a general conclusion based upon exposure to a series of related but not identical items).[53] Not incidentally, this is just the kind of learning that Adele Goldberg and colleagues found was involved in establishing a particular pattern construction and then associating particular new words with that construction.

Of course, many of the world's great writers were prodigies. The Romantic poet John Keats died at age 25, having produced a body of work that stands as one of the greatest poetic achievements of any era. Then there are the teen-aged Jane Austen, Anne Frank,

Alexander Pope, John Stuart Mill, Arthur Rimbaud, T. S. Eliot, all of whom were prodigies. But what about late-bloomers? Is it possible to be a poor writer in your teens and
twenties and then later on to become a good writer? We do know of many writers who
did not come to the attention of the literary world until late in their lives—Cervantes
and Daniel Defoe come to mind. Perhaps the most sensational case is that of Harriet
Doerr, who published her first novel, the award-winning *Stones for Iberra*, at 74, though
we have no evidence that she was not a good writer already as a young student at Smith
College and Stanford in the 1930s. Students who have not done well in their English
classes may take heart from the fact that Carl Sandburg, the Pulitzer-Prize-winning poet
and biographer of Abraham Lincoln, failed his grammar entrance exam at West Point
when he was 21.[54] The writer David Sedaris has said that he didn't really begin to read
avidly until he was in his twenties and in fact didn't begin to write seriously until he was
in his thirties.[55] Note, however, that if you are a 21-year-old who has not been reading at
least 45 minutes a day outside of class for the last ten years, then you'd have to read eight
hours a day every day for almost a full year to catch up with those who have.

The question of what kinds of materials one needs to read to become a good writer is
somewhat more difficult to answer. On the Universal Grammar Hypothesis of Noam
Chomsky, much of the grammar comes already "hard-wired" in the brain: different languages end up with different grammars because this hard-wiring consists of a number of
parameters (switches) which start with a default setting and then get switched on or off
depending on the kinds of constructions of the language that the language learner is
exposed to.[56] On this hypothesis, it doesn't take much in the way of exposure to set a
parameter—perhaps even a single exposure will do (though, again, the ability to extract
the correct generalizations declines with age[57]). However, all vocabulary items, idioms,
frozen expressions ("so to say," "be that as it may"), and all exceptions to regular processes (*desire/desirous*, and *prosper/prosperous* but not *satire/*satirous* or *fire/*firous*) obviously must be learned by exposure. Exactly how much and exactly what kind of exposure
may vary with the constructions involved as well as with the age of the learner.[58]

Chomsky's hard-wiring hypothesis is not universally accepted by linguists and psychologists, a number of whom have proposed alternatives that do not require particular grammars to be so richly predetermined by the configuration of the brain at birth.
Constructionists, following the work of Michael Tomasello, Adele Goldberg, and
others, generally believe that there are more attractive models of language acquisition
available that posit that language is learned (like everything else) from the available
input by the operation of general learning mechanisms not specific to language. Such
models should be preferable because they are, all other things equal, simpler than
Chomsky's alternatives and thus obviously provide a simpler explanation for the
facts. The crucial phrase in the previous sentence clearly is "all other things equal,"
which presumes an equal accounting, something rarely achieved in a comparison of
scientific models. Nonetheless, there are empirical data that support the Constructionist view.

One important issue for both models concerns the role of correction, or negative feedback. Various studies have shown that children learning a language actually receive negative feedback infrequently and (at best) inconsistently. As a rule, parents respond to the content of their children's utterances, not to the form: they'll voice approval if the child utters a true but ungrammatical sentence (e.g., "Her curl my hair," with the meaning "She curled my hair"), but register dissent if the child says a false but grammatical sentence (e.g., "There's the animal farmhouse," where the building in question was a lighthouse).[59] In any case, children often prove resistant to explicit correction. The classic example is from a study by David McNeill:

(3.51) CHILD: Nobody don't like me.
MOTHER: No, say "Nobody likes me."
CHILD: Nobody don't like me.
[eight more repetitions of this]
MOTHER: No, now listen carefully; say "Nobody likes me."
CHILD: Oh! Nobody don't likes me.[60]

Thus, it does not appear at first glance that negative feedback can account for how children actually learn language. It certainly is not the case that they simply rely on the meaning of the words themselves. Tomasello gives these examples:

(3.52i)   He gave/sent/bequeathed/donated his books to the library.
(3.52ii) He gave/sent/bequeathed/*donated the library his books.
(3.53i)   She said/told something to her mother.
(3.53ii) She *said/told her mother something.[61]

The meanings of the verbs in (3.52i) and (3.52ii) are very close, as are the verbs in (3.53i) and (3.53ii). How does the child know that donated in (3.52ii) and said in (3.53ii) are excluded in the grammar of English? If the child is not explicitly told otherwise, why won't she just assume that "donated" and "said" can fill the same slot that "give" and "tell" respectively can fill? Thus, the appeal of the hard-wiring hypothesis: If the grammar is hard-wired in the brain, we can simply claim that whatever controls these facts is part of the human genetic endowment.[62]

Although the evidence for a "language organ" in the brain is not terribly strong,[63] this in itself doesn't falsify the "innateness" hypothesis—and it should be pointed out that the evidence so far that language is learned from general learning principles isn't conclusive either.[64] But it does provide an impetus for cognitive psycholinguists like Tomasello to look elsewhere to explain the phenomena. He points out that researchers have noticed that the more often children hear a particular word used in a particular construction, the less likely they will be to use that word in a novel construction that is similar but not identical. Moreover, if children hear adults using a somewhat more convoluted construction to express something that, if the rules were regular, should be expressible in a simpler form, the child will conclude that the simpler form is inappropriate.[65] Goldberg puts it this way:

(3.54) In a situation in which construction A might have been expected to be uttered, the learner can infer that construction A is not after all appropriate if, consistently, construction B is heard instead.[66]

If the learning strategy in (3.54) (or something like it[67]) is correct, neither explicit correction nor hard-wiring is needed to account for the learning of irregular constructions. What is needed is consistent exposure to the appropriate forms. Given the infrequency with which certain less familiar constructions appear in a random stretch of text, consistent exposure may therefore necessitate a sizable ingestion of linguistic material. This would nicely account for the fact that the amount of exposure to speech or text necessary for learning a particular construction (whatever your hypothesis and however you define consistent exposure) clearly varies from construction to construction and in some cases requires decades to accrue.[68]

During the past twenty years there has been a lively debate in second-language acquisition (L2) circles concerning whether correction is helpful or not in improving the grammaticality and fluency of a student's writing, with the results mostly inconclusive.[69] From my perspective, both sides are right to a limited extent. Correction is useless, as (3.52) demonstrates, when the learner has not acquired the appropriate cognitive apparatus to analyze the new construction and then generalize from it, and it can even be harmful if it confuses the student. And this is true for young and old and for both first- and second-language learners. If the correction is to have any effect at all, learners must be able to intuitively understand why the construction they used is not appropriate (i.e., the correction must provide data that is usable by their internal grammar). For example, Jean Chandler quotes one English-as-a-Second Language (ESL) student as saying "only Correction I feel I can't learn them," apparently meaning that if the teacher only provides the correct answer, the student isn't able to internalize the correction.[70] This is exactly as we would expect if the task of the learning mechanism is to subconsciously extract compatible construction patterns from large amounts of input data.

Fluent Speaking and Fluent Writing

If children are for the most part fluent speakers of their native language by the time they reach puberty, one may wonder why they have not become equally fluent writers by that age. The answer shouldn't be far to seek. Writing fluently requires a firm grasp of many more constructions than does speaking fluently, at least in everyday situations. In order to navigate safely though the communicative rapids that constitute the typical high school hallway, a teenager can get by with a vocabulary consisting of fewer word families than the 8,000 or so that he or she needs to read *The Great Gatsby*. The reason for this is that one reads mostly in order to expand one's knowledge of the factual or fictional world, and that means that the demands on vocabulary will typically be greater. The writers that teenagers read will generally be older and better read than they, with a better command of the language. Additionally, writers have the opportunity—if not the obligation—to search for the precise word, the precise construction, to convey precisely the information that they have to the reader, though that precision is rarely found in conversation. Consequently, as the psycholinguist Paul Bloom says, "The only way to explain how adults can acquire very large vocabularies—over 100,000 words in some cases—is through reading."[71]

But it's not just single words that one learns from reading; it's constructions of all types. We have seen earlier in this chapter that mistakes common to young writers often involve mismanagement of complex constructions that aren't typically encountered in their daily spoken intercourse with others. Mastery of these constructions depends on repeated exposure to them, and that generally occurs through wide reading.

The aspiring writer might wonder whether it would be possible to skip all that reading and just to focus on the constructions he or she must learn in order to become proficient. As pointed out earlier, a construction is not merely a linguistic form but a form paired with its meaning and conditions of use. Moreover, one can't learn these things if the construction is divorced from a context that makes the linguistic elements meaningful to the learner. Sure, one might read the dictionary and find there that a periplast is a "proteinaceous subcellular layer below the plasma membrane of a euglena," but for most of us this definition will never be anything other than gibberish. However, if one comes to study biology, and in particular the green scum that forms in stagnant ponds, and discovers that the euglena that make up that scum can be killed by a certain chemical that penetrates their membrane and periplast layer, then one has a reasonable context for understanding it. But the learner will surely forget this word along with its definition unless he or she is consistently exposed to it in meaningful contexts. Besides, as already pointed out, it would be a near impossibility to lay out all of the relevant constructions that a student would need to study in order to become fluent,[72] weighting each according to the amount of exposure required. The only reasonable recommendation for the aspiring writer is to follow the path that has proved most productive for generations of accomplished writers, which is to read widely and avidly. Any program meant to improve students' writing facility must be, first and foremost, a reading program.

If Colette Daiute's hypothesis that the errors I call Constructional Conflict are the result of short-term memory problems is correct, students who persistently have such problems may be helped by targeted lessons that train them to recognize the constructions involved, as Daiute proposes. However, if the cause is failure of the attention-focusing element of the executive function component, then such lessons may be fruitless. We know that writers like Gibbons, Dickens, Henry James, and Virginia Woolf composed elaborately long and highly complex sentences without apparent effort, though we can only speculate about the capacity of their short-term memory.

What Lies Ahead

Predicting the future is a fool's game, but isn't it possible, or even likely, that all of the fluency issues discussed in this and following chapters will soon be solved—at least from students' and teachers' points of view—by advances in computational linguistics? Several companies already are offering automated essay scoring (AES) software that purports to match the performance of human graders.[73] So, won't grammar checkers and automatic grading software become increasingly good at catching instances of Constructional Conflict, Constructional Conflation, and so on, so that all students or teachers will have to do is to click to correct or grade?

The only way I know to answer such questions is in terms of what seem to me to be the hard issues that will somehow have to be addressed to find such a solution. While Constructional Conflation might be addressed by grammar checkers that incorporate long lists of constructions acceptable to the writer's or grader's preferred audiences ("on a personal note," "in a personal vein") and at least some inferential mechanisms to rule out deviant ones (* "in a personal note," * "on a personal vein"), Constructional Conflict presents a problem of a different order. Think about how you might try to build a grammar checker to undertake the kind of analysis we offered for (3.14), (3.15), and (3.16), repeated here for convenience.

(3.14) *By this time I had known Ramona since I was young, throughout which we had talked of her wonderful success in sports.

(3.15) *We should not overly depend on prescription drugs for fear of becoming habituated.

(3.16) *Using the metaphor of disliking cilantro as a comparison to why some men do not like women bears truth and is also quite funny.

First, the checker would need to find phrases that don't go together—"by this time," "since I was young," and "throughout which" in the first instance—though this is not so simple as making a list. You can easily construct a sentence consisting of these elements that is perfectly acceptable:

(3.55) By this time, I had given my neighbor on the south side of my house that old hand lawnmower I'd had since I was young, so I could enjoy long stretches of the afternoon throughout which no bawling weed eater would disturb my peace.

In order to identify (3.14) as deviant, the automated grader or grammar checker would have to incorporate some very fancy semantics of tense and time reference, but even then, considerable challenges remain. As we'll see in the next chapter, knowledge of context is essential to assign a reading to a construction, and that means that the grader or checker must be able to access an entire, up-to-date encyclopedia of information about the world to render a human-like judgment. And whether or not it could deliver such a judgment, I'm not at all sure how it could help the author fix the problem, i.e., by pointing her toward what I decided she meant, which I said was something like (3.56):

(3.56)   I had known Ramona since I was young. Ever since we were first acquainted, she had talked of her wonderful success in sports.

From a computational perspective, the difficulty is that any deviant sentence can be mapped into an infinite number of acceptable sentences (or, if you prefer a philosophical approach, an inconsistent sentence implies every sentence). There's just no end to devising sentences that (3.14) could possibly be paired with. And even if we could agree on, say, (3.56), as an acceptable (to us) alternative, how can we be sure that this is what the author was directly aiming at—or should have been aiming at? Until we have software that somehow duplicates both the language capacity and the intelligence of the average professional writer (something that, if it's attainable at all, we're clearly still very far away from), we won't have a perfect "auto-correct" button for (3.14).

What AES can do is correlate strings of characters from writing samples with model features of text that programmers build into the program. The enduring issue is whether any plausible set of programmable model features can detect quality of writing in the samples in the way that human graders regularly feel they do. That is, AES (like Graham's meta-analysis or indeed any rubric-based scoring system) depends on proxies for good writing in order to mark deviations from it.[74] Researchers report high correlations with grading done by humans, but of course if the human graders have been trained and are grading to the instruction, then the validity of the construct is questionable.

4

Pragmatic Fluency

The Cooperative Principle

If constructional fluency provides the skeleton of good writing, pragmatic fluency provides the flesh and blood. A person who is pragmatically fluent knows exactly when to deploy a particular construction and for what purpose. It is all well and good to have command of the structural patterns of your language, but if you don't understand the principles governing their use you will bore and confuse and irritate your audience and your writing will end up like an unruly thicket in an uncultivated field.

All of us intuitively know these principles, though we may not realize precisely how or when to apply them. There is a logic to communicating information which the great philosopher H. P. Grice styled the Cooperative Principle, summarized in four maxims as follows:[1]

(4.1) Maxim of Quantity
    (i) Make your contribution as informative as is required (for the current purposes of the [communication]).
    (ii) Do not make your contribution more informative than is required.

(4.2) Maxim of Quality: Try to make your contribution one that is true
    (i) Do not say what you believe to be false.
    (ii) Do not say that for which you lack adequate evidence.

(4.3) Maxim of Manner: Be perspicuous.
  (i) Avoid obscurity of expression.
  (ii) Avoid ambiguity.
  (iii) Be brief (and avoid unnecessary prolixity).
  (iv) Be orderly.
(4.4) Maxim of Relation: Be relevant.

The point is not that you need to follow these maxims because otherwise your school-master might beat you with a stick,[2] but rather that there is a natural expectation on the part of any person you are communicating with that you are following them. If you spurn the maxims, unless it is obvious why you are doing so, you probably won't be understood.

In the next four sections I will summarize the content of these maxims, following which I will discuss a significant recent development from a cognitive perspective that unites them.

The Maxim of Quantity

Grice offers the following example. Let's say you are walking down a street in your neighborhood and you come across a car stopped at the side of the street. The owner says to you that he is out of gas. You respond, "There's a gas station around the corner." This will be quite helpful, unless you know that the gas station is in fact closed. If you don't mention that, you will have violated the Maxim of Quantity: although what you said may be entirely true, you haven't made your contribution as informative as required for the situation. The driver of the car is entitled to infer that you anticipate that the gas station is open, although no words to that effect were exchanged.

Getting the right amount of information into your communication requires that you know what your audience knows, doesn't know, and (most importantly) wants and needs to know. Although no person can ever see into another person's mind, much less have anything like a complete catalogue of that person's thoughts, beliefs, etc., we do the best we can—we are expected to do the best we can. Sometimes our past conversational or other social experiences can help us determine the state of the other person's mind when we're conversing. When reading or writing, it helps greatly to have a sense of the conventions of the literature. Much of the time an error in mind reading produces nothing more than confusion or irritation. But occasionally the result can be more consequential. There is an amusing scene in the movie *The Princess Bride* which nicely illustrates this. The characters in this movie include the Man in Black (the hero), Buttercup (the heroine), and the villain Vizzini the Sicilian. In this scene the Man in Black proposes a contest between himself and Vizzini for the freedom of Buttercup, whom Vizzini has captured. The Man in Black presents Vizzini with two wine goblets and bids him to choose one of them to drink from, further telling him that he has put the poison iocane in one of the two and that he, the Man in Black, will drink from the goblet that Vizzini doesn't choose. Vizzini then employs the following logic in an attempt to figure out which goblet contains the poison:[3]

(4.5i)   Vizzini figures that a clever man like the Man in Black might put the poison in his own goblet, believing that only a fool would reach for the goblet he was given.

(4.5ii) And since he, Vizzini, is not a fool, he cannot choose the wine in front of the Man in Black.

(4.5iii) But the Man in Black must have known that Vizzini wasn't a fool, so Vizzini decides he cannot select the goblet that is in front of himself.

(4.5iv) However, Vizzini also knows that iocane comes from Australia and that Australia was populated with criminals who felt they were trusted by no one, just as the Man in Black is not trusted by Vizzini, so Vizzini feels he cannot choose the goblet in front of the Man in Black.

(4.5v)   But since Vizzini thinks the Man in Black must have expected him to know where the powder came from, Vizzini concludes that he cannot choose the goblet in front of himself.

(4.5vi) Vizzini also knows that in a previous scene, the Man in Black beat a giant, which means the Man in Black must be very strong, possibly so strong as to convince himself that his strength will protect him from the poison.

(4.5vii) Furthermore, Vizzini knows that in another scene the Man in Black also defeated a very smart Spaniard, which suggests that the Man in Black has studied enough to know that humans are mortal. Therefore the Man in Black would probably have not put poison in front of himself.

Before making his final choice, Vizzini distracts the Man in Black long enough to switch the goblets. He then drinks from the goblet he has just placed in front of himself and, of course, promptly falls over dead. As the Man in Black later explains, both goblets had been poisoned but he had "spent the last years building up immunity to iocane powder."

At one point in their colloquy, the Man in Black tells Vizzini that his intellect is "truly dizzying." What makes Vizzini's reasoning dizzying is its potentially endless cycle of embedded assumptions: Vizzini assumes that the Man in Black assumes that Vizzini assumes that the Man in Black assumes that Vizzini assumes that the Man in Black assumes . . . well, it could obviously go on infinitely, with no resolution. In the end, though, what Vizzini does is to discard everything but the single assumption that the poisoned cup was put in front of him.

It is very important to understand the logical inferences that can and can't be made from what you say, since those inferences constitute part of the information you convey.

Good writers manipulate the inferences that their audience will naturally draw with considerable skill. For example, consider the following, which is the beginning of André Aciman's essay "In a Double Life":

> (4.6) There comes the time at every Passover Seder when someone opens a door to let in the prophet Elijah. At that moment, something like a spell invariably descends over the celebrants, and everyone stares into the doorway, trying to make out the quiet movements of the prophet as he glides his way in and takes the empty seat among us.[4]

Now, what I am interested in here is the third word of this excerpt, the definite article "the." You use the definite article when you assume your audience will understand which particular concept or individual is denoted by the following noun: when Aciman says "the time," he is making use of a convention that indicates he assumes his audience is familiar with that particular moment in the ceremony and will know what he is speaking of. If he didn't wish to make this assumption, the indefinite article "a" would be available to him instead: "There comes a time at every Passover Seder when . . ." However, this essay was published as an op-ed piece in the *New York Times*, which indicates that Aciman intended to speak to a broad audience, one consisting of both people familiar with the practice of opening a door at the Passover Seder and those unfamiliar with it. So, then, why did Aciman use the definite article, apparently excluding the latter group?

I believe he did so as an artful act of inclusion. The reader familiar with the practice is directly addressed (as she would not be if Aciman had used the indefinite article). Others, reading this sentence, accommodate to the assumption of familiarity: "All right," such a reader thinks, "Aciman is acting as if I can be counted on to follow what he's saying, to know, as he does, about this particular time in the ceremony. I'll play along, so long as it doesn't cause me difficulties in understanding what comes next."[5] For his part, Aciman does this because it allows him to figuratively put his arm around that reader, to make her or him feel comfortable as a sort of co-conspirator in the communicative transaction. He is saying, "I can talk to you because we share many things." Of course, his use of the definite article would cause confusion for the reader who knows nothing of the esoteric practice ("What time?") if it weren't followed immediately by the relative clause "when someone opens a door to let in the prophet Elijah," which specifically identifies it. And because with the addition of that clause the accommodation causes no difficulties, the author can breeze right by without further ado, having conveyed the subtle signal he intended.

All of us, I'm sure, have had at some point in our lives a conversation with a friend in which there's something about the way the friend phrased a sentence that assumes we know something we don't. For example, the friend might say

(4.7) Guess what? I've stopped eating muskrat meat.

You're puzzled, because you didn't know your friend was ever eating muskrat meat. Linguists say that (4.7) linguistically (or pragmatically) presupposes that its speaker had, in fact, been eating muskrat meat. What distinguishes a linguistic presupposition from just plain suppositions or guesses is that it must be true for the sentence to make sense. You can guess that your friend stopped eating muskrat meat because she's on a diet, or because she came to dislike its taste, or because it's too expensive, but (4.7) doesn't presuppose any particular reason for her decision—the sentence will still make sense no matter what reason she had, as long as it's true that she used to eat muskrat meat but no longer does. If you didn't know that fact, you can accommodate to her assertion by reasoning to yourself that it must be true because she wouldn't have said what she said otherwise, that is, by directly implying that it must be true. Possibly your friend forgot that she hadn't previously mentioned her consumption of this meat, or perhaps she did mention it and you simply forgot. No matter, because you can accommodate to it.

In narrative, and particularly in fiction, we, as readers, are used to accommodating in this way. Here follow the first sentences of three novels.[6]

(4.8) In the late summer of that year, we lived in a house in a village that looked across the river and the plain to the mountains.

(4.9) From the window, all that could be seen was a receding area of grey.

(4.10) Early in the morning, late in the century, Cricklewood Broadway.

In each of these cases, we don't mind that the author has not identified the year, the river, the plain, the mountains, the window, the century, because we are willing to follow along in the author's assumption that we either already know this information or can figure it out, even if we don't or can't at this point. That is part of the reader's contract with the author of a work of fiction: we won't demand more factual information than the author gives us, as long as it doesn't get in the way of our suspension of disbelief. And here, because the author is placing us in the midst of the action, we are prepared to take the facts as they come and accommodate where necessary. Saul Bellow's short story, "Leaving the Yellow House," begins:

(4.11) The neighbors—there were in all six white people who lived at Sego Desert Lake—told one another that old Hattie could no longer make it alone.[7]

Bellow might have just begun with an indefinite like "Neighbors," but notice how the use of the definite article makes it seem as if you had already had all the information you need to identify them. It serves again to put us *in media res*.

In the case of nonfiction, we are usually less willing to accommodate. If (4.11) had initiated a nonfiction article, we would probably sense that the author is engaging in literary or creative nonfiction, adopting a technique of fiction to provide atmosphere for the story. Here's another instance:

(4.12) It is a bright summer day in 1947. My father, a fat, funny man with beautiful eyes and a subversive wit, is trying to decide which of his eight children
he will take with him to the county fair. My mother, of course, will not go.[8]

This is the beginning of Alice Walker's lovely essay, "Beauty: When the Other Dancer
Is the Self." What is interesting here, of course, is the phrase "of course" in the third sentence. This implies that it should be obvious to the reader that the author's mother will
not go to the fair. But when we reach this phrase, we have been given precisely no information about the mother, other than the apparent fact that the author has (or has had)
one. Again, we must accommodate to this implication, and we do so by drawing the
conclusion that the author wants us to draw, which is that we all already know that her
mother will not go. It is inherent in the meaning of the phrase in its context. Now, we
can speculate about the reason for the mother's refusal (which may or may not be revealed in the following sentence), but that is not the point. The point is to intimate to us
a powerful clue about her mother's state of mind without directly describing it.

By manipulating the inferences that a reader can draw—through linguistic presupposition, accommodation, or just plain guess—an author can pack a great deal into a few
words. We might add to our list what is often called "literary compression," which is a
loose term suggesting terseness or laconicity, as in the writing of Raymond Carver as
edited by Gordon Lish. Here's the beginning of his story "Gazebo":

(4.13) That morning she pours Teacher's over my belly and licks it off. That afternoon she tries to jump out the window.
I go, "Holly, this can't continue. This has got to stop."[9]

Aside from having to infer the meaning of the two definite determiners ("That" in the
first sentence and "that" in the second), the reader doesn't need to accommodate here.
We are given information directly, in little compressed packets, but the information is
spare to the point of being telegraphic. The effect is almost that of a haiku, or even a
shopping list: there's this, then there's that, and then there are those other things. As in
a shopping list, there is little room for drawing linguistic inferences based upon the particular words used (though obviously one can speculate about both the narrator's and
Holly's personalities, as one might speculate about the motives of the writer of a shopping list that included rat poison, rope, knife, kerosene, matches). Contrast (4.13) with
the following opening of Toni Morrison's elegant essay, "Strangers":

(4.14) I am in this river place—newly mine—walking in the yard when I see a
woman sitting on the seawall at the edge of a neighbor's garden. A home-
made fishing pole arcs into the water some twenty feet from her hand. A
feeling of welcome washes over me. I walk toward her, right up to the fence
that separates my place from the neighbor's, and notice with pleasure the

clothes she wears: men's shoes, a man's hat, a well-worn, colorless sweater over a long black dress. The woman turns her head and greets me with an easy smile and a "How you doing?" She tells me her name (Mother Something) and we talk for some time—fifteen minutes or so—about fish recipes and weather and children. When I ask her if she lives there, she answers no. She lives in a nearby village, but the owner of the house lets her come to this spot any time she wants to fish, and she comes every week, sometimes several days in a row when the perch or catfish are running and even if they aren't because she likes eel, too, and they are always there. She is witty and full of the wisdom that older women always seem to have a lock on. When we part, it is with the understanding that she will be there the next day or very soon after and we will visit again.[10]

In order to interpret this, we must do some significant inferencing. Like Carver, Morrison uses a definite determiner in the first sentence ("this") that must be accommodated, but its head ("river place") is quite vague—a river place is a place associated with a river, which means it could be a place on, in, beside, near, above, or (for that matter) under a river. The place is "newly mine," which means the place is in addition associated very recently with the author in some unspecified way. It could be by means of ownership, temporary possession, affection, or interest—we're not told. When we get to "walking in the yard," we can conclude that the "place" must be a property with a yard near or beside a river, which is confirmed by the phrase "sitting on the seawall" and reinforced in the next sentence when water is positioned no more than twenty feet from the woman's hand at the seawall. The woman's relation to the author as neighbor or as just someone else who is occupying the neighbor's property is not made clear. It isn't until we come to the sixth sentence that we are given indirect evidence that the two of them have not met before. When the woman "tells me her name (Mother Something)" we can infer that she is a stranger to the author, for exchanging names is something one generally does only on first meeting. Finally, in the eighth sentence, we learn the woman's relationship to the property she is occupying, though we still haven't been told what the author's relationship is to the land on her side of the fence. We infer that the author must be occupying that land for several days at least when we come to the tenth sentence (the last in the excerpt).

Obviously, how much information the author needs to supply varies with the audience: different audiences require differential treatment. A book on advanced nuclear engineering requires (presumes) not only interest in that subject but also solid knowledge of the basics of the field. A common failing of aspiring writers is not writing a piece consistently for a particular group of readers, putting in more than they should here, less than they should there. That group of readers may be minuscule or enormous or anything in between, but the writer must have in mind a particular group with more or less common beliefs, experience, and enthusiasms in order to fashion a piece that is coherent and that is likely to appeal to that group. It's not that every person in the chosen audience must have exactly the same background,[11] but simply that the readers must, usually, be satisfied that the author is making an effort to speak to them.[12] But then, how does the writer know what the audience knows, since no one can see into another person's mind? As suggested earlier, close familiarity with the conventions of the genre helps enormously (and, in fact, is the only guide we usually have), which is why reading widely in that genre is so important to figuring out what your audience might like to know.

If providing too much information may bore your readers, providing too little may defeat your purposes. This is well illustrated by the following Jewish folk tale related by Judith N. Levi:

(4.15) Once upon a time in Moscow, there was a man who, due to grievous personal circumstances, was obliged to send a telegram to his brother in a distant town. So, writing out the message that he wanted to send, he took his money and himself down to the telegraph office. Here is the telegram that he wrote out:

Dear Moishe: Our grandfather Yosl is very ill. Come immediately. We fear the worst. Rest of the family is fine; don't worry. Love, Itzik

When he got to the telegraph office, he asked the clerk how much it would be to send such a telegram, but when he heard the answer, he winced and said, "Oy! So much money just for a little telegram? Don't I have enough trouble already?" So he decided to shorten it as much as he could.

So, beginning at the beginning, he read, "Dear Moishe." "'Dear Moishe'?" he said to himself. "Why should I write 'Dear Moishe'? When Moishe gets the telegram, he'll *know* it's for him; I certainly don't need to say so." So he crossed out the first two words.

Next he read, "Our grandfather Yosl is very ill." Raising his eyebrows, Itzik said to himself, "So who else in the family should be sick? Our grandfather Yosl is 97 years old already; naturally he's sick! And besides, would I be sending a telegram to say that he was well? Of course not!" So he crossed out the entire sentence.

The next words were "Come immediately." "'Come immediately'?" read Itzik, shaking his head at his own thoughtlessness. "If that nudnik doesn't even know that he should come immediately at a time like this, I don't even want to see his face—much less spend money on him." And he crossed those two words out with one emphatic stroke.

Next he read, "We fear the worst." "Really, Itzik; what could you have been thinking of?" he asked himself. "At 97 we should fear the best? Of course we fear the worst. But as my little Rochele always says, it's better not to talk of such things!" And so, crossing out those four words, he turned to the next sentence: "Rest of the family is fine; don't worry."

"Of course we're fine," said Itzik in disgust. "We're not 97 years old like our beloved Yosl! And besides, in a few days Moishe will be here and he'll see for himself how fine we are. No need to waste money on saying *that*!" And with a stroke of his pencil he crossed all that out.

So what was left? Not much—only the last two words, "Love, Itzik." "'Love, Itzik'?" cried Itzik, once again marveling at his own obtuseness. "I should send a telegram to my only brother—and at a time like this—just to tell him I love him? That's the most ridiculous thing I ever heard!" And with those words, he crossed out all that was left of the original message, picked up his money, and went home—to wait for Moishe to arrive.

Moral: In the eternal conflict between shortening the form and preserving the meaning, it's going to cost you at either end![13]

There is obviously a flaw in Itzik's reasoning, but who among us has always reasoned flawlessly?

The Maxim of Quality

Grice's Maxim of Quality seems, at first blush, to be merely a restatement of the biblical commandment against bearing false witness, but it's not quite that. And it's also more than that. We accept false witness quite readily in fiction. Moreover, Grice's subsidiary injunction not to say that for which we lack adequate evidence doesn't exactly amount to an injunction against lying, or vice-versa. If it did, that would put all of religious writing and a lot of political writing in jeopardy. (Of course, that would depend on what is to count as "adequate": to the clergy and the true believer, on the one hand, and to the agnostic and the skeptic, on the other, what is adequate won't be easily agreed upon.)

Grice gives the following example: "If I need sugar as an ingredient in the cake you are assisting me to make, I do not expect you to hand me salt; if I need a spoon, I do not expect a trick spoon made of rubber."[14] Grice obviously isn't talking about overt speech acts here; he is covering all acts of deception, and in speech, when we rightly expect an honest accounting from an interlocutor, we are entitled to be irritated if we don't receive it. It's the expectation that I think needs to be attended to. Grice does present a number of cases where we are quite content to let falsehoods—irony ("he's a fine friend"), metaphor ("you are the cream in my coffee"), meiosis ("he was a little intoxicated"), and speculation ("she is probably deceiving him")—pass, because we know that the speaker is flouting the Maxim of Quality intentionally, and we know the speaker knows that we know this. In other cases—"Not tonight, dear, I have a headache"; Q: "How are you?" A: "Oh, fine. Getting along"—we know how to interpret the meaning of the sentences in context. In fiction and in poetry we are not expecting veridicality, and so we are not irritated when we don't get it. But if we feel we are deceived, we are going to resent the transaction.

TABLE 4.1

Expectations Concerning Factuality, Truthfulness, and Bias in Different Genres

Type of writing	Factual	Truthful	Unbiased
Scientific article	Yes	NA	Yes
Journalism	Yes	Yes	Yes
History/Biography	Yes	Yes	No
Opinion essay	Mostly	Yes	No
Journal for publication	No	Yes	No
Autobiography	Yes	Yes	No
Humor	No	No	No
Fiction	No	No	NA

If there were simply three categories of writing—fiction, poetry, and everything else—and everybody were entirely clear about what the authors were up to, then there wouldn't be so much of a problem. We encounter difficulties when we come up against a multiplicity of genres the distinctions among which are occasionally blurred, and our expectations are dashed. The category of "literary" or "creative" nonfiction can be especially problematical, but autobiography, biography, journal writing, etc. can also lay traps for the unwary. In table 4.1, I've indicated my sense of reader expectations regarding whether an author's representations in different genres must be factual, truthful, or unbiased.

We expect the author of a scientific article to deliver facts; in ordinary understanding, there is no distinction to be made between what a scientist considers a fact and what she believes to be true—in a scientific article they are expected to be the same. The sentence, "It's a fact that hydrogen has one electron, but I don't believe it's true that hydrogen has one electron," is self-contradictory (whether or not accurate), on common understanding. We also expect scientists to be unbiased, even though there is a massive literature in science studies that demonstrates beyond doubt that they aren't. Nevertheless, our expectation is lack of bias and an honest accounting of the facts. We expect much the same of journalists, although sophisticated readers are aware that you can't believe everything you read in a print or online news source, nearly every one of which, if it's reputable, runs a column in which mistakes in earlier editions are corrected. Still, we rely on journalists to report the truth as they see it and attribute error to the pressure of deadlines. (Unlike journalists, scientists are not supposed to publish their results until those results have been thoroughly vetted for error.)

In the case of histories and biographies, we demand facts and we demand that their authors tell us what they believe to be true. In a book or an article, an author of history or biography is usually held to the strictest standards of fact and truth. Of course, what counts as a fact may change over time, for example, we may learn, on the basis of newly discovered evidence, that what was previously thought to be true is not. Still, we don't want to be fed anything the author doesn't earnestly believe to be the case. We would like an unbiased account but are prepared on occasion to accept one that isn't, especially if the history or biography has an ideological dimension and the author indicates this. Obviously, opinion essays will carry the biases of their authors and we expect that, though we don't want to be hoodwinked by false assertions or assertions their authors don't believe. Journals and autobiographies, like opinion essays, are not assumed to be unbiased, but because the journal is assumed to be more personal, more intimate than the autobiography, we anticipate with relish the possibly outrageous perspective. In autobiography, we do want and expect facts, although we know autobiographers will tend to portray themselves in the most advantageous light; we just don't want them to say that they served in the Vietnam War when in fact they never did.

A journal—even a journal that the author aspires to have published—will, we expect, be somewhat looser with facts than an autobiography. Not that there will be outright lies, but the purpose of the journal is to convey what it was like to be the author at that place and at that time, so the sun in the journal may shine more brightly than it actually did, or the rain fall more heavily. But if our author is not completely honest about what he or she believes she was feeling, doing, etc., then we become annoyed.

The error that James Frey made was in presenting his book, *A Million Little Pieces*, as autobiography rather than as creative nonfiction (or fiction). When readers discovered that not all of the incidents reported in the book were factual, and that Frey knew that they were not, Frey was subjected to a public humiliation broadcast internationally to millions on daytime television. Had Frey's book been explicitly labeled creative nonfiction, or fiction based on fact, he almost certainly wouldn't have been censured as he was (though perhaps his book would not have sold as well).

The Maxim of Manner

Grice's Maxim of Manner ("be perspicuous") seems similar to Strunk and White's injunction to "be clear," though he does provide a revealing example: "if I were to say X went into a house yesterday and found a tortoise inside the front door, my hearer would normally be surprised if some time later I revealed that the house was X's own." This is because the speaker has failed to be perspicuous when he could easily have been so by substituting "his house" for "a house." Failure to provide this detail in this situation implicates to the audience that the speaker is not in a position to be specific. That is, by saying "a house," the speaker can assume that the audience will pick up on the fact that the speaker has intentionally not resolved an ambiguity because that information isn't available or is irrelevant, which would hardly be the case if the speaker actually knew it were X's own house. You can see that, again, the point is to get the speaker/writer and audience on the same page as regards the facts that make the story worth telling to the audience in the speaker's mind. The multifarious resources of the language for obscuring, condensing, and circumventing detail can obviously produce confusion where and when the speaker/writer isn't careful. The speaker/writer must be aware—must anticipate—that the audience will constantly be making these sorts of inferences based on what is said/written.

As has been often noted, the Maxim of Manner and the Maxim of Quantity overlap. For example, in Grice's example just given, one might say that the speaker was violating the Maxim of Quantity as well as the Maxim of Manner, because the speaker was not supplying enough information. But there are clear cases where the two maxims diverge. If, as Grice suggests, the speaker did not know whether the house X went into was X's own, then the speaker is providing all the information she knows to be correct in accordance with the Maxim of Quality, even if the hearer might prefer to have the ambiguity resolved. The speaker is being perspicuous insofar as the information she has is concerned, though she must violate the Maxim of Quantity.

The Maxim of Relation

The kind of information an author supplies is certainly as important as the quantity and quality—hence Grice's fourth maxim, which is to be relevant. I grant that this maxim, on its own, seems also to be an instance of Strunk and White's "Be clear," though Grice does supply a nice example, which may help to clarify his meaning. A professor (Professor A) is writing a letter of reference for one of his students (Mr. X), who is applying for a job as a philosophy instructor. Professor A's letter reads as follows: "Mr. X's command of English is excellent, and his attendance at tutorials has been regular. Yours, etc." That's the extent of it. The writer here has brazenly flouted the Maxim of Relevance. Surely the recipient of the letter expects Professor A to be more forthcoming about Mr. X's qualifications for the position sought. And surely Professor A, as Mr. X's teacher, knows a good deal more about Mr. X than he is letting on. If the recipient believes that Professor A is being honest and not trying to be silly, she may infer that Professor A is trying in this oblique way to convey information that he would simply prefer not to write down, which is that Mr. X is not particularly qualified for the job.

What information is relevant obviously varies according to audience, just as how much information is sufficient does. Composition teachers, especially those whose theory of value favors a rhetorical approach, are quite used to emphasizing the importance of audience to their students. And among composition scholars, there has been much discussion of how audience should be identified (is it real? imaginary? "invoked"?) and, once identified, how it can be satisfied (by better argumentation? by attention to genre or discourse community?).[15] These issues, however, are largely intractable. The audience for a letter you're writing to your sister may be simply identified as your sister, but what about a poem addressed to no one in particular? In any case, how can you possibly know what is inside the heads of your audience so that you can satisfy at any particular moment their wants and/or needs?

Moreover, a focus on audience often means a lack of focus on the writer, which naturally puts rhetoricists and expressivists at odds. The expressivist believes that "the content of composition is the writer—as he reveals his self, thoughtfully and feelingly, in his own language, with his own voice."[16] Audience would more or less come along for the ride. Or perhaps not. Grice's Maxims do suggest various general strategies for attending to an audience (as well as what happens when you flout the maxims), but they don't go far enough to solve either the rhetorical or the expressive problem.

Relevance Theory

From the perspective of the cognitive scientist, an exclusionary expressivist or rhetoricist position on writers and their audiences is unhelpful, because it more and more appears to be a single communicative problem. This problem is directly addressed by Relevance Theory.

The primary proponents of Relevance Theory, Dan Sperber and Deirdre Wilson, have expanded on and extended the Gricean Maxims in their books *Relevance: Communication and Cognition* and *Meaning and Relevance*,[17] in an attempt to develop a general inferential model of communication. Sperber and Wilson offer two principles upon which they claim all human communication is based:

(4.16i) The Cognitive Principle of Relevance: Human cognition tends to be geared to the maximization of relevance.

(4.16ii) The Communicative Principle of Relevance: Every ostensive stimulus conveys a presumption of its own optimal relevance.

The Cognitive Principle is straightforward and, if you think about it, would make good sense for our species from a survival-of-the-fittest perspective. We want to pay attention to that which matters the most to the satisfaction of our needs. The Communicative Principle requires some elaboration. An ostensive stimulus is an attempt to communicate by pointing, speaking, writing, etc., and such a stimulus is optimally relevant if it's worth the audience's effort to process it and it's the most relevant one compatible with the communicator's abilities and preferences. Thus, communicators communicate with the presumption that what they are pointing at, speaking about, etc., is optimally relevant to their audience. Similarly, their audience assumes that the communicator thinks this will be optimally relevant to them. Sperber and Wilson's stance, like Grice's, is decidedly not prescriptive: "According to relevance theory, utterances raise expectations of relevance not because speakers are expected to obey a Co-operative Principle and maxims or some other specifically communicative convention, but because the search for relevance is a basic feature of human cognition, which communicators may exploit."[18]

On Sperber and Wilson's understanding, utterances automatically create expectations that direct the audience to what they infer is the communicator's intended meaning by the very fact that the communication is attempted. This means that all parties to a conversation are constantly trying to figure out everyone else's intentions, as exemplified in (4.5).

So, then, what is relevant? Sperber and Wilson say that something is relevant in a context if it has some contextual effect in that context (p. 122). They give (p. 120) the following example:

(4.17)   May 5, 1881, was a sunny day in Kabul.

The information conveyed by this sentence might have some relevance somewhere but not so far in this book. That information does not affect the context up to the point at which it was introduced—it doesn't alter my argument or add to or subtract from the information about my topic that I have given the reader so far. However, because I have introduced it, the reader will have the expectation that it must be in some way relevant to my exposition. And now the reader can see that I believe that its relevance is that the sentence itself is an example of irrelevance in its context, according to the definition of relevance just given. (Whether it was actually sunny or not in Kabul on that date, though, is irrelevant to this example.)

To have a contextual effect in a context is to change that context—that is, to change the common ground or the assumptions about shared information in that context. After I tell you straightforwardly that my friend Bill has gotten married, you now have information that you may not have had before (or at least I assume you haven't had it, and you assume that I assume that you didn't have it, otherwise why would I suggest, according to the Communicative Principle, that I think it's optimally relevant by telling you?). Of course, a statement can have indubitably large contextual effects ("My god, your house is on fire!") or minimal ones ("Apparently, you're reading *What is Good Writing?* right now"). Relevance Theory postulates that degree of relevance is determined by both cognitive effect and cognitive effort: "Everything else being equal, the greater the cognitive effects achieved by processing the input, the greater its relevance. The smaller the processing effort required to achieve these effects, the greater the relevance."[19] So a warning from the blue that one's house is on fire, because it requires more cognitive effort to process and reconcile with the standard assumption that one's house isn't on fire, may seem to be less relevant than the observation that one's house looks the same as it always did; however, everything else isn't equal here and because the cognitive effects are so much greater (making the input well worth the effort to process), being told one's house is on fire turns out to be on the whole a great deal more relevant. The speaker's intention, the audience's assumptions or inferences about the speaker's intentions, and the audience's knowledge at the time as well as other information the audience has available, all play a role.

Given all of this information that is available or being made available, the audience invariably attends to what's most (i.e., optimally) relevant at the time. As Sperber and Wilson point out, "Relevance theory claims that what makes an input worth picking out from the mass of competing stimuli is not just that it is relevant, but that it is more relevant than any alternative input available to us at that time."[20] Thus, when a reader reads a text, he or she gauges relevance "on the fly": as chunks of sentences are processed, their relevance is computed against, and their informational content integrated into, what has been processed up to that point. As new information is gained it becomes part of the common ground or shared knowledge of speaker (or writer) and audience. So relevance is never absolute or inherent in a particular utterance or sentence, but is relative to context, which is constantly shifting, being augmented by the new information available to it.

Relevance is also relative to the speaker or writer. That is, we communicate from an imperative of our own, not necessarily (or often even at all) from purely altruistic motives. We want to join a conversation to acquire food, sex, money, prestige, companionship, and other benefits of socializing, to proffer our opinions, to be appreciated, to seek useful information for ourselves, to impose our will on others. The poet, the writer of literary novels, the playwright, the author of books on good writing, all want to join a conversation as much as anyone else: I'll tell you what's relevant to me: revisiting the banks of the Wye River a few miles above Tintern Abbey. And isn't the way I've written about it grand!

The implications of this model for pragmatic fluency are profound. In fact, the Sperber and Wilson model entirely replaces (or subsumes) Grice's Maxims: we want just the right quantity of information because that's what's relevant to us, and we want it to be of the appropriate quality and to be delivered in an appropriate manner, because, again, we're constantly making instantaneous judgments of significance to us. In this sense, Quantity, Quality, and Manner all turn out to be aspects of Relevance. (Still, I will occasionally revert to Grice's terminology when it seems useful.)

But Relevance Theory not only replaces Grice's Maxims, it also pretty much covers all the old virtues of good writing as described by the prescriptivists—precision, concision, logic, clarity, cohesion, consistency. Ordinarily, all of these are virtues of relevance. One difficulty that attends conceiving of these virtues in prescriptivist terms is that there are times when you don't exactly want them. Concise versions of *War and Peace* and *In Search of Lost Time* simply will not satisfy some people in the way the complete versions do. Despite my occasional reservations about *Mrs. Dalloway*, I don't think I'd advocate for a rewritten edition. And as for precision, while I enjoy the extremely faithful Lattimore translation of *The Iliad*, I sometimes prefer the more discursive versions by Robert Fagles, Alexander Pope, and Samuel Butler. The advantage of Relevance Theory is that instead of simply decreeing the value of concision, precision, etc., it permits the reader to decide for himself or herself what is relevant at one time or another.

Experimental Pragmatics

Another advantage of the Sperber and Wilson Relevance Theory is that it, like Construction Grammar, has explanatory force.[21] This means that the principles of Relevance Theory should be empirically motivated. And, indeed, Sperber himself, in a 1995 paper with F. Cara and V. Girotto,[22] has provided some persuasive empirical support for the Communicative Principle. This paper describes an experiment in which participants were shown four cards lying on a table, one displaying a 6, a second displaying a 4, a third displaying an E, and a fourth displaying an A. Each participant was then given one instruction from the following set:

1. A machine manufactures cards. It is programmed to print at random, on the front of each card, a number. On the back of each card, it prints a letter at random. The person in charge, Mr. Bianchi, examines the cards and has the strong impression that the machine does not really print letters and numbers at random. "I think," he says, "if a card has a 6 on the front, it has an E on the back."

2. A machine manufactures cards. It is programmed to print at random, on the front of each card, a 4 or a 6. On the back of each card, it prints either an E or an A at random. The person in charge, Mr. Bianchi, examines the cards and has the strong impression that the machine does not really print letters and numbers at random. "I think," he says, "if a card has a 6 on the front, it has an E on the back."

3. A machine manufactures cards. It is programmed to print at random, on the front of each card, a number. On the back of each card, it prints a letter. When there is a 6, it prints an E. When there is not a 6, it prints a letter at random. One day, Mr. Bianchi, the person in charge, realizes that the machine has produced some cards it should not have printed. On the back of the cards with a 6, the machines has not always printed an E: sometimes it has printed any letter at random. Mr. Bianchi fixes the machine, examines the new printed cards and says, "Don't worry, the machine works fine. If a card has a 6 on the front, it has an E on the back."

4. A machine manufactures cards. It is programmed to print at random, on the front of each card, a 4 or a 6. On the back of each card, it prints a letter. When there is a 6, it prints an E. When there is a 4, it prints an E or an A at random. One day, Mr. Bianchi, the person in charge, realizes that the machine has produced some cards it should not have printed. On the back of the cards with a 6, the machine has not always printed an E: sometimes it has printed an A instead of an E. Mr. Bianchi fixes the machine, examines the new printed cards and says, "Don't worry, the machine works fine. If a card has a 6 on the front, it has an E on the back."

Each participant was then told, "Your task is to indicate which cards need to be turned over in order to establish whether what Mr. Bianchi said is true or false, at least as far as these four cards are concerned. Indicate only the cards that it is absolutely necessary to turn over."

Note that in each of the four cases the correct answer is the same: turn over the card with a 6 and the one with an A. However, Mr. Bianchi's statement "if a card has a 6 on the front, it has an E on the back" may imply to the participant that (a) any card with a 6 on it has an E on the other side, or (b) there are cards with a 6 and an E, or (c) there are no cards with a 6 and without an E on the other side, or (d) some combination of these. Just looking at Mr. Bianchi's statement outside the context of the instructions, you should be able to see that implication (c) is harder to process than (b), even though at first blush it doesn't seem to deliver more information. At the same time, it is easier to conclude (wrongly) from (b) that the correct answer is either 6 or 6 and E than it is to derive the correct answer (6 and A) by processing (c). Thus, Sperber and his colleagues predict from the Communicative Principle that unless the instructions somehow suggest to the participants that the implication in (c) is worth processing (as instruction 4 does), the participants will be less likely to make the effort to process it. What they found in their experiment was that where the instructions were as in 1, 38 percent more participants chose the incorrect answer of 6 or 6 and E. But when the instructions were as in 4, 52 percent more participants chose the correct answer (6 and A). When instructions 2 and 3 were given, more participants made the correct choice, but by a smaller (14 percent) margin. This finding is consistent with the premise that effort and effect work as the Communicative Principle indicates.

In another experiment that is worth our notice, Aiden Feeney, John D. Coley, and Aimée Crisp, investigating category-based inductive reasoning, demonstrated that participants require significantly greater cognitive effort to process premises in an inductive argument that are inconsistent with the inferences they are making on the fly about the significance or salience of the properties of the objects in those premises. For example, when participants are given the two premises "White doves have a certain property, which is that they are _____" and "Polar bears have this same property, which is that they are _____" (where the blanks are not filled in), they form an expectation, based on the Communicative Principle, about the nature of the property in the two premises—and usually, in this case, the expectation after they see the two premises is that the property would have something to do with whiteness, as that would be the most salient or relevant property shared by white doves and polar bears. The cognitive process of pattern and category recognition relies on induction from instances of this sort: we observe that goldfish, perch, salmon, and trout have gills and live in water, and we conclude that fish in general have gills and live in water. If a possible conclusion that might be drawn from the two premises is now presented to us, such as "All animals have this same property, which is that they are _____," then we may judge the argument to be pretty weak.

In Feeney, Coley, and Crisp's experiment, the first premise about white doves was displayed on a computer screen in front of a participant, and after the participant had read it, he or she pressed a key to continue. Then the first premise disappeared and the second premise about polar bears appeared on the screen, and again the participant pressed a key after reading it. At this point a third premise appeared on the screen, which was

"Snow tigers have this same property, which is that they are _____." Again, after reading it, the participant pressed a key and the third premise disappeared and was replaced by the conclusion "All animals have this same property, which is that they are _____. After the participant finished reading it, he or she pressed a key to indicate the strength of the argument from the three premises to the conclusion. In some versions of the test, the initial premise was varied, and instead of snow doves, the participant was shown a sentence about grizzly bears or donkeys.

The experimenters measured how long it took participants to press a key after the third premise was displayed. This premise was the same in all cases, but the interesting result was that the time varied depending on the animal named in the first premise. When the third premise (snow tigers) was consistent with the first two premises (white doves, polar bears), participants took less time to process it than when it contradicted an assumption they might have formed after reading the first two premises (grizzly bears, polar bears). When it did contradict the first two premises, those participants who took longer to read it also indicated that they found the conclusion from the premises weaker. This confirms that cognitive effects like belief change are related to cognitive effort, which is predicted by Relevance Theory, but not by prominent competing theories of categorization.

The implications of these experiments extend well beyond the test situations. For example, consider some facts of first language acquisition, as explored in an interesting paper by Ewa Wałaszewska.[23] In this paper Wałaszewska considers how children arrive at an adult's understanding of the meaning of words, especially basic-level terms like dog, fish, stone, coat. As is well known, children both overextend and underextend these terms when learning them—they might use dog as a generic term for animal, or they might use it as the name only for the type of dog their family has (say, a collie). Wałaszewska argues that both overextension and underextension are strategies children use to pinpoint relevant meaning in the absence of an extensive vocabulary: "overextensions make it possible for a child to bypass limitations in production vocabulary and to produce verbal stimuli relevant enough to be worth the audience's processing effort" (p. 324). But adults use this process as well when they can't bring up an appropriate word from their own vocabulary (think of the many computer terms that derive from overextensions from previous usage—"file," "mouse," "button," "menu," "window," "mail," "cut," "paste," "cloud," etc.). Underextensions, by contrast, represent underestimations of scope, which adults are less frequently given to. For example, Wałaszewska repeats the following anecdote from Timothy Jay: "I once observed two toddlers who were arguing over the word 'daddy' when their fathers arrived to pick them up at day care. When one child called his father 'Daddy,' the other said, 'That's not daddy. Daddy's my daddy!'"[24]

Still, there are adults who would not categorize the sun as a star or a whale as a mammal. In either case, the child or adult is grasping at the most relevant word he or she has at hand. Minimizing overextensions and underextensions may constitute only one aspect of the transition from child language to adult language, but they are central to an understanding of metonymy and metaphor in literature as in everyday language, as we will see in chapter 7.[25] As we've noted, the psycholinguist Michael Tomasello maintains that Sperber and Wilson's Relevance Theory explains a central feature in the origins and development of human communication.[26] The recognition of others' intentions in their acts of pointing or uttering or writing and the calculation of the relevance of those acts in context are foundational: you simply cannot have communication without them.

The experimental evidence in support of Relevance Theory at this point is obviously far from conclusive. But the arguments in the papers just summarized make a strong case that an empirical theory of pragmatic fluency is not only possible but already well grounded. Moreover, the experimental results in these papers demonstrate Relevance Theory's potential for explaining how the inferential system actually works in human communication.

Audience and Relevance

Much of what I've been discussing so far under the rubric of relevance may seem to compositionists and rhetoricians to be merely a restatement of what they've always understood as the importance of audience, about which there has been much discussion in the literature. A particularly popular model involves the distinction that Lisa Ede and Andrea Lunsford make between "audience addressed" and "audience invoked," and the many roles that these two audiences consist of: "the term audience refers not just to the intended, actual, or eventual readers of a discourse, but to all whose image, ideas, or actions influence a writer during the process of composition."[27] Ede and Lunsford suggest that, in this particular sense, the term may be overdetermined. However, from the perspective of Relevance Theory, it is both overdetermined and underdetermined. For one thing, it is very difficult to imagine that a writer runs through all the potential invoked audience roles (self, friend, colleague, critic, mass audience, future audience, past audience, and anomalous audience) and potential addressed audience roles (future audience, mass audience, critic, colleague, friend, and self) in formulating a sentence or even a plan for her or his communication. For another thing, this leaves out the difficulty of mind reading mentioned earlier.

Relevance Theory, being an inferential model, does not assume that communication is simply a process of encoding and decoding. Rather, it assumes that it is a complex of intention and inference. The difference is that in a coding model, the hearer or reader responds to conventional representations because, well, because they are conventional representations. Relevance theory recognizes that the linguistic content of any sentence always radically underdetermines its interpretation, even if it contains within it certain conventions. Speakers and writers do the best they can on their own understanding, while hearers and readers must choose the most salient meaning from a range of contextually available meanings of multiply ambiguous stimuli – because this is not only the best way but sometimes the only way of inferring the speaker's or writer's intentions.[28]

So I don't think the failure of much school writing is the students' for having not understood the nature of their audience and what that audience might infer. We, their teachers, are their audience and they knew that quite well, although they couldn't know what we were thinking. The problem, I am fairly certain, is that they rarely have any idea what literary conversation they are supposed to be joining or why they might want to join it. And if we were to give them a sample of a literary discourse as a target, I'm fairly sure that most of them wouldn't know what to do with it. As suggested in chapter 2, it's only after developing a compelling motivation to join a discourse that a person learns (intuitively) how to participate in it. Without that motivation, no instruction will suffice to bring that person into the conversation.

Pragmatic Conventions

Of course, learning the pragmatic conventions tied to specific constructions is an important part of learning a language. Gabriele Kasper lists a few examples under the broad category of apologies:

> (4.18) *Apologetic formula*: "I'm sorry," "I apologize," "I'm afraid"
> *Assuming Responsibility*: "I haven't read your paper yet."
> *Account*: "I had to prepare my TESOL plenary."
> *Offer of Repair*: "But I'll get it done by Wednesday."
> *Appeaser*: "Believe me, you're not the only one."
> *Promise of forbearance*: "I'll do better after TESOL."
> *Intensifier*: "I'm terribly sorry, I really tried to squeeze it in."[29]

It should be unsurprising that most empirical work on the acquisition of pragmatic conventions has been done in the context of studies of second-language learning, since L2 learners have a doubly difficult task: the particular conventions they have learned in their first language for associating form with pragmatic effect are not always in a one-to-one correspondence with the conventions of the second language, which means in many cases they must calculate the inferences on the basis of the information content rather than the form itself. Consider, for example, calculating the relevance of a response like "Whatever" upon hearing it the first time. This leads to some of the most obvious, and most serious, problems that second-language learners have in communicating in their second language.

Moreover, as Kathleen Bardovi-Harlig and Rebecca Mahan-Taylor point out, L2 learners who demonstrate high proficiency in the grammar of the second language will not necessarily show equivalent skill in its pragmatics, nor will they usually develop this skill on their own.[30] So instruction that might lead to competence in pragmatics has become an important desideratum of second-language instruction.[31]

Consciousness-Raising

There is one strategy used extensively in second-language learning for achieving prag-matic competence that may be seen to have application to writing skills, and that is "consciousness-raising" or "awareness-raising," (i.e., directing students' conscious atten-tion to particular features of language). While the positive effects of consciousness-raising have been demonstrated primarily in the L2 learning arena,[32] the same principles necessarily apply to teaching pragmatic skills to those who have similar difficulties in writing in their first language.

The premise of consciousness-raising is that learners don't know the appropriate verbal and/or written routines for particular social situations and require specific in-struction in these routines. Consciousness-raising activities usually focus on common types of social exchange, such as greetings, valedictions, requests, or apologies. Learners are exposed, via video or role-playing, to conversations of native speakers, and relevant aspects of those conversations are identified.

Consciousness-raising is far from a panacea, however. There are so many different kinds of social situations calling for so many different linguistic conventions that in-struction in the necessarily limited number that can be covered in a class will hardly confer native speaker (or professional writer) skills on the pragmatically challenged. Moreover, at least in the first-language context, it's not as if students don't know most of these conventions. They are quite adept in the hallway and in the pub with their friends. But when it comes to writing, they seem overwhelmed by the performative pos-sibilities. Should one try to write like Dickens? Or Hemingway? Or J. K. Rowling? It's not just the academic context: when these students write messages asking for permis-sion to hand in a paper late, they can be quite eloquent and rarely make the wrong prag-matic assumptions.

It is interesting in this context that similar consciousness-raising activities are em-ployed as a therapeutic strategy with patients who have suffered Traumatic Brain Injury (TBI) of the frontal lobe and especially the prefrontal cortex, where so-called executive function, involving self-regulation, allocation of attention, planning, and task manage-ment, is located. Jacinta Douglas[33] identifies several kinds of deficits involving executive function experienced by people with frontal lobe TBI, including impaired attention, poor response inhibition, distractibility, initiation difficulties, and reduced flexibility. In an interesting study, she tracked the perceived frequency of different kinds of language deficits experienced by executive function patients and categorized them according to Grice's Maxims. Among these were the following:

(4.19i) Thinking of the particular word (Manner)
(4.19ii) Get sidetracked by irrelevant parts of conversation (Relation)
(4.19iii) Hesitate, pause, or repeat (Manner)
(4.19iv) Go over and over the same ground (Quantity)

(4.19v)   Thinking of things to say to keep conversation going (Relation)

(4.19vi)   Change speech style according to the situation (Relation)

(4.19vii)   Use a lot of vague/empty words (Quantity)

(4.19viii)   Leave out important details (Quantity)

In her study, Douglas found that TBI patients reported experiencing pragmatic difficulties of the sort in (4.19) significantly more frequently than a control group with normal brain function. Since the patients' pragmatic difficulties represented violations of three Gricean Maxims (Quantity, Relation, and Manner), she concluded that there is a significant association between executive impairment and the pragmatic communication difficulties experienced.[34]

Two of the more popular training therapies for TBI patients involve social skills intervention, such as consciousness-raising and self-coaching. For example, Shari L. Wade and her colleagues in Ohio had teenaged TBI patients use an online problem-solving exercise to improve their executive function skills.[35] This exercise, which Wade et al. call the "ABCDE" exercise, involved (1) stopping and thinking, (2) identifying the problem (Aim), (3) brainstorming possible solutions (Brainstorm), (4) analyzing the potential consequences of various courses of action (Choose), (5) implementing the plan (Do it), and (6) evaluating the outcome (Evaluate). They found that teens with severe executive function deficits benefited significantly from the exercise, though those with moderate deficits performed not much differently from a control group. A possible explanation for this difference between patients with severe TBI and those with moderate TBI may lie in the degree of executive function retained after injury: where the function remained mostly intact, consciousness-raising would have less dramatic effects, producing detectable results perhaps only under a more sensitive analysis than that used in the study.[36] But if so, consciousness-raising activities in the writing classroom are unlikely to be the solution for writing problems that some instructors assume them to be.

Agrammatic and Anomic Aphasias

Executive function deficits differ from the effects of agrammatic and anomic aphasias typically observed in patients with TBI or atrophy of the left cerebral hemisphere, where constructional functions are generally understood to reside.[37] A person suffering from severe agrammatic aphasia produces sentences so bizarre that it appears they are speaking no recognizable human language at all. By contrast, in the case of anomic aphasia, the patient seems to be speaking the target language because the structure and function words are normally deployed, but the nouns are often used strangely or are unrecognizable. An example of an agrammatic aphasiac's writing follows in (4.20),[38] while (4.21) is an example of the speech of an anomic aphasiac.[39]

(4.20) Mary + Penny apoligies
re: mail forg ton
for nex forgahr
forget womet
and collect
com ne lt
upduirl, world
connetc frodn
correlt. Accas
cheo urcol ibris

(4.21) The toys are stirring to keep their tethote [/tə'ðot/] the keeping of teedrive
[/'tidraiv/]. Him pushing his bike [pointing to a man carrying a suitcase].
He's got his books to take to the car [pointing to a boy carrying a bucket
and spade]. A stedly [/'stɛdli/] pin, crystal, two pelidemens [/pə'lidmənz/]
and a dustman [pointing to a bunch of safety pins, a nailbrush, a mug, and
a spoon].

Clearly the language deficiencies in (4.20) and (4.21) are of a different order than the
executive function problems described in (4.19), and the ABCDE exercise would be in-
applicable. The point here is not that anyone who hesitates or gets sidetracked or uses the
wrong word is displaying evidence of TBI. We all are guilty of the lapses in (4.19)—we
all forget words and leave out important details and use vague, empty, or inappropriate
words now and again. It's a matter of degree; TBI patients display this kind of behavior
much more frequently than people without TBI. What is important is that pragmatic
function seems to be governed by brain structures separate from those that govern construction function, and this offers some hope that the sort of remediation Wade et al.
advocate for TBI patients may also be useful for non-TBI students who are not pragmatically fluent in their writing.

5

Narrative Fluency

NARRATIVE FLUENCY IS accomplished skill in storytelling. It is one kind of pragmatic fluency, and as such is covered by Relevance Theory, but I am giving it its own chapter here because it ramifies in its own way and bears so significantly on the success of any particular written piece.

While narrative has been variously treated in both writing texts and literary criticism as the process of selling an argument, of creating tension, suspense, or emotion, of knitting a tapestry, or of finding unity in diversity, within Relevance Theory it receives a simple and uniform account. A narrative is a story, and stories command our attention exactly insofar as we deem their elements as presented relevant to us. The information stories convey, and the way they convey that information, must continue to be compelling or we will lose interest. That is all there is to it.

However, for many aspiring writers, it's one thing for an instructor to say that they must compose a relevant sentence here or there but entirely another to ask them to compose a 12,000-word essay or 120,000-word book every single one of whose sentences must be relevant. How are they to do that?

In large measure, of course, they already know. As suggested in the previous chapter, they string sentences together comfortably in conversation with friends. They know what follows and what doesn't. They have a sense of what the people they're talking to are interested in and how those people want to receive the information given them. And they know, and have used in conversation, the several different strategies for ordering information, for creating context, and so on that make stories work. When it comes to extended creative writing, however, they often freeze in the face of the many options available to them along with the sheer amount of information that they think they should be conveying.

This narrative problem for writers, once they have a topic, is threefold. First, they must populate a storehouse or database of information concerning their topic that they guess will be relevant to the audience they are writing for. Second, they must create and execute a plan for presenting the information that's in the database in an interesting and logical way. And third, they must sustain their focus throughout the presentation.

The first problem is a research problem, and I won't pursue it here.[1] The third requires a sort of mental discipline that is also beyond the scope of this book. It's the second that I'd like to concentrate on.[2]

Discourse Analysis

To explore the dimensions of the planning/execution problem, I will first introduce some preliminary concepts from Discourse Analysis, which for convenience we might say is a branch of linguistics that studies pragmatics as evidenced in actual instances of language use beyond the sentence and employs a particular methodology in that study.[3]

Wallace Chafe, in his book *Discourse, Consciousness, and Time*, includes a useful discussion of the mental processes involved in the communication of ideas from speaker (or writer) to hearer (or reader). He distinguishes between extroverted consciousness, which is our consciousness of the external world as a result of our perceiving, acting, and evaluating what we experience, and introverted consciousness, which is what we experience purely through the operation of our minds on our extroverted consciousness. When we remember or imagine experiences triggered by our senses, they are represented in our introverted consciousness. The original stimulus is "distal," that is, it is distant from our minds at the point of remembering or imagining. By remembering or imagining the stimulus, we make it "proximal," or near to us. Using language, we can encode the information represented in our introverted consciousness for conveying to others. "The speaker's represented consciousness receives its input from a distal consciousness that is remembered from some time in the past or imagined for some hypothetical time," Chafe says. "The intent of the speaker is to influence the listener's consciousness in such a way that the listener imagines a distal experience resembling the speaker's own distal experience. . . . The speaker's intent is realized by means of language designed to produce in the listener a vicarious introverted consciousness which, like the speaker's, is actively focused, not on the immediate environment of the conversation, but on the distal experience the speaker is imagining or remembering."[4]

But, of course, the challenge for the speaker or writer is to arrange the contents of introverted consciousness in such a way that when converted into language, the result "influence[s] the listener's [or reader's] consciousness" so that the listener or reader can vicariously experience the distal stimuli that the speaker or writer originally experienced or imagined. This arrangement is what we call a story or argument or narrative.

Standard treatments of narrative focus on logical structure in terms of arrangements such as the five-paragraph essay with beginning-middle-end, or issue-discussion, or topic-argument-summary. While attempting to teach students such logical patterns may help them with their expository writing in class, my concern is that this approach can have the unfortunate effect of pulling aspiring authors away from what they need to cleave to most firmly, which is a commitment to relevance for their audience, to influencing the reader's consciousness. In conversation, we (and they) don't often adhere to a logical 1-2-3 structure, and when we deviate from it, we don't necessarily lose our audience. This is because relevance isn't solely or even mainly a matter of logical structure. True, a narrative must be coherent and make sequential sense, but it also must be interesting to the audience, and that depends on factors other than (or in addition to) logic.

In chapters 8 and 9, I will look in some detail at repetition and surprise, which I think are also important to relevance, but in this chapter I want in particular to discuss topical structure, which precedes logical structure and which provides the structural foundation for relevance. Discourse Analysis is just the tool we need for this.

Michael Stubbs, in his book *Discourse Analysis: The Sociolinguistic Analysis of Natural Language*,[5] offers an interesting study of Ernest Hemingway's short story, "Cat in the Rain." Hemingway's story concerns an American couple who are staying at a hotel in Italy or another country where Italian is spoken. It is raining. The wife looks out the window of their room on the second floor and sees a cat huddling under a table in front of the hotel. She tells her husband that she is going to go down and get the kitty. As she is leaving the hotel, the manager sees her and has a maid bring her an umbrella. The wife appreciates this gesture on the part of the manager and conceives a liking for him. But when she gets outside, the cat has gone. She returns inside, manifestly disappointed. In their room upstairs, the husband, who is called George, is lying on the bed reading. The wife expresses her longing for a cat and for a new hair style. George tells her to shut up and resumes reading his book. The story ends as follows:

(5.1) Someone knocked at the door.
"Avanti," George said. He looked up from his book.
In the doorway stood the maid. She held a big tortoise-shell cat pressed tight against her and swung down against her body.
"Excuse me," she said, "the padrone asked me to bring this for the Signora."

Stubbs is concerned with the question whether the cat that the maid brings in is the same cat that the wife had seen from her window. Hemingway is coy about this, not explicitly saying one way or the other, but Stubbs concludes that it is not the same cat, cannot be the same cat. His reasoning proceeds as follows: Hemingway does not describe the cat that the wife initially sees huddling under the table. It is simply "a cat." But the wife refers to it as a "kitty." This appears at least superficially inconsistent with the description of the cat that the maid brings in in the next to last sentence as being "a big tortoise-shell cat." At any rate, one wonders why Hemingway would not have used this description earlier in the story when the cat seen from the window was first introduced, if it were indeed the same cat. But even if Stubbs is correct that Hemingway meant the reader to conclude that it was a different cat, it is clear that he did not intend to give the reader any information about whether the wife believed it to be a different cat. Her reaction is unrecorded.

Stubbs's conclusion is an inference from the ordering of information in Hemingway's story as much as from what information Hemingway chose to present. Both determine what the reader takes away from the narrative. Unless the writer has a fair idea of how the arrangement of the information in a narrative will affect what the reader will understand, he or she will be unlikely to produce good writing.

It should be said that nothing in Hemingway's story actually hinges on whether the cat was the same or not; the principal point is that there is tension in the marriage and that the padrone is filling a void in the wife's life that the husband can't or won't fill. If it were to be made explicit that the cat is the same cat, it might tie the knot a little too neatly, so Hemingway settles for an ambiguity. Or perhaps Hemingway didn't care one way or the other, or didn't even think about the issue.

So much is uncontroversial from a literary standpoint, but if you wished to codify rules for this in a writing class, or to teach these concepts in some other way, how would you go about it? Aside from simply rehearsing the analysis already given, there isn't a great deal of leeway for you. The inferential process is crucial, but determining what the reader will infer isn't something the aspiring writer can be explicitly taught how to do (though, of course, she can be urged to use her native intelligence to do it).

Common Ground, Scenes, and Frames

Earlier, I introduced the concept of the common ground, which is information that the writer can assume is shared with the reader. The common ground includes what an ordinary adult knows about how things work in the world, and this is usually information that the writer doesn't need to expressly convey in his narrative. As the author tells the story, the information in it is added to the common ground as it is encountered, and what's in the common ground at any one point determines what can follow. I've already pointed out that a definite article (such as "the") will usually not be used with a noun unless whatever is denoted by the noun is included in the common ground. So one might start a story with (5.2) but not (5.3).

(5.2)   A minister, a priest, and a rabbi walked into a bar.

(5.3)   The minister, the priest, and the rabbi walked into the bar.

Once the minister, priest, rabbi, and bar have been introduced by a sentence like (5.2), the author can follow with a sentence like (5.4).

(5.4)   The minister said to the priest and the rabbi, "I only drink ginger ale, but you can have whatever you want."

Chafe looks at definite articles used in another of Hemingway's stories, "Big Two-Hearted River." In this story, Nick, the protagonist, is on a camping and fishing trip by himself. After Nick strikes camp, he engages in some activities, which Hemingway describes as follows:

(5.5) He took the ax out of the pack and chopped out two projecting roots. . . . He started a fire with some chunks of pine he got with the ax from a stump. Over the fire he stuck a wire grill, pushing the four legs down into the ground with his boot. Nick put the frying pan on the grill over the flames.

What Chafe finds interesting is that to this point, the ax and the frying pan haven't been mentioned in the story. Chafe suggests that because Nick is on a camping trip, we can expect him to have brought with him an ax and a frying pan. Hemingway doesn't need to introduce these items with an indefinite article because they are already part of the common ground, part of our understanding of what camping consists of. However, a wire grill, as an optional piece of equipment, probably benefits from an indefinite article.

Every time we evoke a common scene or "frame," as it is often called, such as a camping or fishing trip, the elements of the frame will all be part of the common ground. On a fishing trip, the rod and reel, net, and creel will be there, for a baseball game, the bats and balls and gloves and bases and foul lines will be there, and for a criminal trial, the judge and jury and defendant and prosecutor and witnesses will all be there too.

In the common ground, items can be active or inactive. An active item has been recently mentioned in such a way that you might expect it to be mentioned again. An inactive item may be simply evoked by the frame but not explicitly mentioned or may have not been taken up for a period after introduction. For example, Talmy Givón has pointed out that by using the demonstrative article "this" in conjunction with a noun that is being introduced for the first time, the speaker/writer indicates that the item should be kept active in common ground.[6] Having been presented with (5.6), we know that the lawyer is going to play a prominent role in the narrative.

(5.6) This lawyer walks into a bar.

Of course, in a 200,000 word novel, it is not going to be easy for the reader to activate in chapter 49 some inactive item that was last mentioned in chapter 2. Thus, what is in common ground is not only a function of what an author may assume others know but also what the reader can readily pull up from memory.

Activating an inactive item in common ground is similar but not identical to adding a new item to common ground. Thus, the reader of the 200,000 word novel will undoubtedly appreciate, in a hypothetical chapter 49, a reintroduction of sorts:

(5.7) John Bracegirdle, the farmer whom we last met in chapter 2, appeared one afternoon at Celia's door with a basket of tomatoes.

But in a hypothetical chapter 3, the unrestrictive relative clause in (5.7) probably wouldn't be necessary, under the assumption that the character is still fresh in memory (active in common ground).

I've already pointed out how authors can sometimes force a reader to accommodate to something that isn't in the common ground by acting as if it is. Thus, there are narratives (especially fictional or literary nonfictional narratives) that begin with a definite article, as we saw in (4.9).

(4.9) From the window, all that could be seen was a receding area of grey.

Here, we are placed in the scene as if we were in the room looking out the window. The definite article supplies a sense of immediacy, of familiarity. Contrast (4.9) with (5.8), where the definite article has been replaced by an indefinite. In (5.8), the indefinite article has the effect of placing the reader at a distance from the scene, outside it.

(5.8) From a window, all that could be seen was a receding area of grey.

We immediately want to know: Which window? Who could see a receding area of gray?

Chafe discusses the general tendency of speaker and writers to reserve the subject position of a sentence for trivial information or information in the common ground and to introduce only one new piece of information (usually in the predicate) at a time. This makes good sense from an information processing perspective, as it minimizes the processing burden on addressees/readers, as illustrated in (5.9), where OI = trivial or old information in common ground and NI = new information. New information introduced in the predicate of one sentence may subsequently become old information in the subject of the next

(5.9) $\text{OI} + \text{NI}_i \quad \rightarrow \quad \text{OI}_i + \text{NI}_j \quad \rightarrow \quad \text{OI}_j + \text{NI}_k \cdots$
      Subj + Pred   Subj + Pred   Subj + Pred
      Sentence 1   Sentence 2   Sentence 3

A sequence of sentences like (5.10), modeled on the pattern of (5.9), is easy to process relative to a sequence like (5.11), which bounces from new subject to new subject.

(5.10) There was an old man who was sitting in a bar. He wore a clean suit and a dapper cap. The cap was of the alpine sort, with a yellow feather. But the feather had been dislodged and was hanging precariously at the brim.

(5.11)   An old man was sitting in a bar. His suit was clean. A feather in his cap was yellow. The brim of the cap barely kept the feather, which had been dislodged from its more secure position in the band, from falling off.

But can we say that (5.11) is not fluent writing? Might there not be a perfectly valid pragmatic reason for producing (5.11) in a narrative in preference to (5.10)? If the writer wants to demonstrate the old man's psychological detachment from the physicality of the situation, this might be turn out to do just the trick. We've already come across several examples where new information is treated syntactically like old (see (4.6), (4.8), (4.9), (4.10)) or where new information comes in an unlinked series or where old information follows new (e.g., (1.2), (3.4viii), (3.5ii)). Indeed, the content of all opening sentences is necessarily new.

Moreover, as Sara W. Smith and her colleagues demonstrate,[7] different writers/speakers can approach the task of producing a given narrative differently, making different assumptions about what can be considered to be in common ground. Smith and her colleagues also show that writers/speakers avail themselves of a diverse store of grammatical constructions to introduce important new information, often signaling in advance the arrival of a new person or object on the scene. These strategies include presentational structures (5.12), discourse markers (5.13), and metalinguistic expressions (5.14).

(5.12)   There was a woman who lived in a shoe.

(5.13)   He met, you see, a woman to whom he gave all his money.

(5.14)   So, the people I'm going to tell you about were on a trip to America.

Because in colloquial discourse students are used to informal methods of presentation in which a variety of such cues can help to establish reference, they sometimes are at a loss when they feel constrained to not use such cues in formal writing. In an experiment, Smith et al. looked at how student volunteers activated inactive content from common ground in colloquial discourse. In the experiment, Smith et al. asked pairs of subjects to watch the Charlie Chaplin silent movie *The Immigrant* (1917). The first member of the pair ("A") watched the entire movie, but the second member ("B") watched only the first half. After the movie ended, Smith et al. asked A to summarize for B the part of the movie that B didn't get to see. Smith et al. provide their own summary of the movie as follows:

(5.15)   The movie has two main settings, the boat on which the immigrants cross the ocean and a restaurant with an intimidating waiter. A young woman on the boat attracts Chaplin's interest, but they part when the boat lands. He re-encounters her in the restaurant and invites her to join him, despite having just discovered that he has lost his money through a hole in his pocket. Several events make it clear that the waiter will have no mercy if Chaplin cannot pay the bill.

It is important in what follows that B stopped watching when the boat lands. Here is an excerpt from A's summary of the part where Chaplin reencounters the young woman in the restaurant; in this excerpt A mentions the young woman to B for the first time.

(5.16) A: and then he was turning around,
and it's you know there's that lady remember that lady that he saw on the ship?
B: uh huh
A: that he kind of fell in love with or whatever?
B: yeah.
A: so and he saw her

Smith et al.'s analysis of this dialogue is as follows:

(5.17) [A's] first mention of the young woman uses the definite expression "that lady," implying that the listener would know which one is intended. But before she proceeds with the story, she uses a variety of devices to ensure that relevant common ground has been activated and that the listener can connect the young woman introduced at this point with the young woman from the earlier part of the story. She uses discourse markers "you know" and "so." She also uses a metacognitive device "remember." She reminds the listener of both the context "that he saw on the ship" and the role "that he kind of fell in love with." And she twice uses a 'try marker' intonation (i.e., a rising intonation, typically designed to seek confirmation) to solicit acknowledgements that the appropriate memories have been activated.

Simply transferring A's part of the dialogue to a simple narrative, we would have the following (with some additional punctuation added for clarity):

(5.18) . . . and then he was turning around, and it's, you know, there's that lady, remember, that lady that he saw on the ship? That he kind of fell in love with or whatever? So, and he saw her . . .

A Bearing of Grass

The text in (5.18) would be fine in written narrative if presented either as speech or as an imitation of speech, but as straight explication, it would seem odd. Sorting out what works in speech from what works in narrative explication is an essential part of learning narrative fluency. Moreover, when students begin to be exposed to writers of narrative who use poetic language, they may conceive the mistaken idea that anything goes.

Here's a paragraph from near the beginning of Michael Ondaatje's highly regarded novel, *The English Patient*:

> (5.19) They unwrapped the mask of herbs from his face. The day of the eclipse. They were waiting for it. Where was he? What civilization was this that understood the predictions of weather and light? El Ahmar or El Abyadd, for they must be one of the northwest desert tribes. Those who could catch a man out of the sky, who covered his face with a mask of oasis reeds knitted together. He had now a bearing of grass. His favourite garden in the world had been the grass garden at Kew, the colours so delicate and various, like levels of ash on a hill.[8]

The first thing to notice about Ondaatje's paragraph is the lack of relevant sequence, the lack of connection from one sentence to the next, at least in the first four sentences. Prior to this paragraph it has been established that a nurse and a "silent" male attendant have been taking care of an unnamed male soldier who was injured and burned in a plane crash in the desert. However, there has been no mention of a mask of herbs or reeds or of grass, or of El Ahmar or El Abyadd or the northwest desert tribes. There had been one earlier mention of the moon in the following context: "I have spent weeks in the desert, forgetting to look at the moon, he says, as a married man may spend days never looking into the face of his wife." The "he" in this sentence presumably refers to the patient.

The paragraph as written does convey the disjointed thoughts of the patient—perhaps all too well. I have never been able to figure out exactly what Ondaatje means by the sentence, "He had now a bearing of grass." No semantic construal of that sentence that makes sense to me fits the syntax and the meanings I attach to "bearing." Granted, the word "bearing" used as a noun is polysemous: on my understanding (now fortified and enlarged by looking it up in several dictionaries, including the *Oxford English Dictionary* and the *Canadian Oxford Dictionary*), it can refer to the activity of carrying, supporting, enduring, conveying, or giving birth, or to a person's behavior, comportment, or carriage, or to a direction, tendency, course, or result, or to a position relative to surroundings, or to a part of a machine which takes or reduces friction, or (in heraldry) to a device or ornament on a shield. None of these seems to fit. Perhaps Ondaatje meant "He now carried himself like grass," suggesting that the patient was supple, as bendable as a blade of grass in the wind, but then I would have expected "He had now the bearing of grass." Or he might have meant, "He was now lying on a stretcher made of reeds on which he had been borne," or "He had now a piece of machinery made of grass"; but neither of those really works in context. At first blush, especially given the sentence following about the grass at Kew, one might think that Ondaatje had in mind a compass bearing where, for example, "a bearing of 60°" is the angle between north (0°) and a line drawn through a point to the center (vertex) of the compass measured clockwise. This would make sense only if the word "grass" stood in for a certain number of compass degrees from 0°, which it clearly does not; to reach his desired meaning in this case Ondaatje would have had to say, "He had a bearing toward grass" or "He had a bearing in the direction of grass." I suppose it's remotely possible that Ondaatje had the heraldic sense of "bearing" in mind (so that the patient had an ornament of grass on the mask that covered his face), and that would indeed fit the syntax, but the problem is that the mask has been removed at the beginning of the paragraph, which would be contradicted by the word "now." Is this an instance of Constructional Conflation or Lexical Confusion? Well, you might say, maybe we're just dealing with poetic license. If so, it's a license I myself wouldn't issue, since the constructions used in the sentence don't actually make any sense to me in the context in which they're used. I don't receive an impression or a feeling from the way the words are put together. I'm just confused.

What the aspiring writer wants here, really, is some way to operationalize the Strunk and White maxim, "Be clear." As Strunk and White (and countless other writing masters including Joseph M. Williams in his *Style: Toward Clarity and Grace*) well understood, clarity does not come easily in writing: 'tis paid in sighs aplenty—and is marked by, if nothing else, extensive revision. The writer's obligation to the reader to be clear is part of the Cooperative Principle, an essential component of Relevance Theory. Has the writer thought everything through to the point where the piece entirely coheres, where each point logically follows from a previous point, and no further sharpening of ideas is possible? That's a very tall order. As I've suggested, Ondaatje's language in (5.19) is not effective for me, perhaps because I'm not part of the target audience or because he hasn't tried hard enough to clarify his language for me. But surely we must say that Ondaatje is a fluent writer of English. Surely we would not want to say that he has abused the conventions of his language. Thus, I have to assume an attitude of indulgence with respect Ondaatje's choice of phrase. Moreover, if most everything else in the larger passage works well for me, then, even if I attribute the problem I have with "a bearing of grass" to a certain slovenliness of thought or composition on Ondaatje's part, I might forgive this slip, even if I don't think it's justified. How much leeway I'm willing to give him will narrow with every succeeding difficulty I have in subsequent passages.[9]

Accommodation

Note that the poetic license that Ondaatje is apparently invoking is not the more general kind of permit that authorizes a pragmatically complex sentence (i.e., makes it meaningful in context), where pragmatic complexity is a measure of the minimum number of logical steps required to authorize sentence B from an arbitrary starting point A in the inactive common ground. This is what we called accommodation in the previous chapter. For example, in (5.20), the opening of Virginia Woolf's *To the Lighthouse*, it takes a minimum of seven steps (5.21) to accommodate the first sentence and twelve steps (5.22) to accommodate the fourth sentence from an arbitrary sentence in the inactive common ground.[10]

(5.20) "Yes, of course, if it's fine tomorrow," said Mrs. Ramsay. "But you'll have to be up with the lark," she added.

To her son these words conveyed an extraordinary joy, as if it were settled, the expedition were bound to take place, and the wonder to which he had looked forward, for years and years it seemed, was, after a night's darkness and a day's sail, within touch. Since he belonged, even at the age of six, to that great clan which cannot keep this feeling separate from that, but must let future prospects, with their joys and sorrows, cloud what is actually at hand, since to such people even in earliest childhood any turn in the wheel of sensation has the power to crystallize and transfix the moment upon which its gloom or radiance rests, James Ramsey, sitting on the floor cutting out pictures from the illustrated catalogue of the army and Navy Stores, endowed the picture of a refrigerator, as his mother spoke, with heavenly bliss.

(5.21i) The first sentence constitutes an answer to a question that has been asked by some unidentified person of Mrs. Ramsay.

(5.21ii) The question must have to do with an activity that depends on the state of the weather tomorrow.

(5.21iii) Mrs. Ramsay would have warrant for answering the question definitively.

(5.21iv) Mrs. Ramsay would have warrant for allowing or commanding the activity if the weather is fine tomorrow.

(5.21v) Mrs. Ramsey's answer is relevant to the person who asked the question.

(5.21vi) Mrs. Ramsey's answer is relevant to the reader.

(5.21vii) Mrs. Ramsey's character is relevant to story.

(5.22i) There is a clan that cannot keep feelings separate.

(5.22ii) James Ramsey belongs to that clan.

(5.22iii) James Ramsey is the person who asked the question to which Mrs. Ramsey responded in the first sentence.

(5.22iv) James Ramsey's character is relevant to the story.

(5.22v) Separating future prospects from what is at hand is a case of keeping feelings separate.

(5.22vi) In early childhood, people of this clan may have their moods fixed for a considerable period by a turn of events.

(5.22vii) James Ramsey is in early childhood.

(5.22viii) Mrs. Ramsey's answer constitutes one such turn of events.

(5.22ix) What is at hand is a picture of a refrigerator.

(5.22x) James Ramsey has received Mrs. Ramsey's offer positively.

(5.22xi) This has fixed his mood positively.

(5.22xii) Thus, James Ramsey looks at the picture positively.

A complex sentence that is interpretable—such as any of those of (4.20)—because it conforms to the usual constructional and pragmatic conventions, needs no excuse, though it may be difficult to unpack. Virginia Woolf, like the later Henry James, is difficult, but for the most part requires no extraordinary license. All one needs with *Mrs. Dalloway* and *To the Lighthouse* is patience (in quantities that I confess I sometimes don't possess).

Compare (5.20) with (4.12), which we've already said requires, in the first four sentences, only a single instance of accommodation related to the phrase "of course."

(4.12)   It is a bright summer day in 1947. My father, a fat, funny man with beautiful eyes and a subversive wit, is trying to decide which of his eight children he will take with him to the county fair. My mother, of course, will not go. She is knocked out from getting most of us ready.

It would perhaps not be surprising if, inspired by the poetic language of writers like Ondaatje, a student were to produce something like the following in a homework assignment designed to elicit a similar kind of feeling:

(5.23)   The moon has started to rise and the owl hoops in tandem to the inhalations and exhalations of every breath. A waggle to the fingers breathes life into the cold limbs. Craving warmth the limbs stretch to the ends of the earth, ever so careful as to not be exposed to the frigid air awaiting its embrace. Slowly one leg moves in preparation for releasing from the sitting.

This is not entirely uninterpretable, though the reader will probably note instances of Constructional Conflict, Constructional Conflation, Lexical Confusion, and Lexical Underperformance, along with a lack of relevance. The author is evidently writing about a person who has been sitting outside on a cold night and begins to get up, perhaps to return inside. To achieve a poetic effect, presumably, the author has not identified the person. In the terminology of Discourse Analysis, the identity of the person is neither old nor new information, nor, consequently, is the idea of that person either active or inactive in discourse. We are introduced to, one by one, the person's breathing, his or her fingers, and leg. "Fingers" does activate the idea of a person (or at least a primate), so at that point we readers are likely put on the right track. But we wonder why there is this coyness about identifying the person. Does it achieve anything positive here? I'm not able to see that it does, though I'm open to argument; and perhaps others will see in this passage what I do not. Unfortunately, what students often learn in literature classes is that obscurity is not altogether a bad thing. They learn this because they themselves have had difficulty understanding the work of "difficult" poets and novelists who have been held up as paragons. They will naturally try to imitate these poets and novelists in order to share in their success. Since they don't understand what they are imitating, they may try to write poetry and prose that seems (to them) equally opaque, with predictably unsatisfying results for those who must read their work.

Narrative Strategies

When I am going to write an essay about a topic, where should I start? At the beginning, of course, but what is the beginning? Let's say the subject is dogs, and let's just assume that I am already motivated to write about them (perhaps, as a dog-lover, I have been asked by my community newspaper to write an article). All right, then, what do I want to say about dogs? What they look like? Whether I like them or not? Do I want to concentrate on one dog I had named Moe that I think was crazy? Or on dog physiology? Or on dog mating behavior? This is the part of essay arrangement that many aspiring writers find problematical. But by now the reader should be able to sniff out what I'm going to say about it. First and foremost, it's an audience problem: It's figuring out who the audience consists of and what they might find relevant, interesting. Using the ABCDE exercise introduced in the previous chapter, I might try to answer this question. Well, the editor wants me to write an article about dogs and he and his newspaper's subscribers constitute the audience (Aim). So if I were in a conversation with him or one of his subscribers about dogs, what sort of story could I tell him that they might find relevant (Brainstorm)? Perhaps they'd be interested in a story about our family dog Moe's tendency to bark at clouds (Choose). That seems to me to be unusual enough as a topic for an essay that anyone would be interested in it. OK, so that's what I'll write about (Do it), and when I'm finished with my draft I'll see how it came out (Evaluate).

At the Do-it stage, however, I'm still unclear about where I should begin in my narrative about Moe. Our family had Moe for fourteen years, and as far as I can remember he barked at clouds during all fourteen of them. He found a single cumulus cloud moving along in an otherwise blue sky particularly threatening, and he would bark and leap and snap his jaws at it as if in an effort to pull it down. Should I start there, with a behavior that probably even a squirrel would find perplexing, or should I start at a particular event of cloud-barking? There was one time when Moe was so distraught about a flock of altocumulus clouds that he worked himself into a barking frenzy at the end of which he fainted. We thought he had apoplexy. When he revived himself, he looked unsteadily up and then began barking furiously again until he fainted a second time. We took him to the vet and he was examined, but the vet said there was nothing physically wrong with him. The vet said it was just his personality. Then the vet corrected herself. "His dogality, I mean."

That's one possibility. Or I could perhaps start with Moe's appearance (perpetually unkempt) or how we came by him (our local humane society). Alternatively, I suppose I could research craziness in dogs and begin with a summary of findings. Or I could talk about Moe's faithfulness and his ability to tolerate, with quiet dignity, just about any physical assault we children would launch at him and then introduce his cloud paranoia.

There is, of course, no "correct" way to begin an essay. But by rooting around you can easily find numerous different forms of topical arrangement that good writers have used with impressive results. Here follow three simple ones.

LINEAR FORM: ABC

The ABC Linear Form (not to be confused, of course, with Wade et al.'s ABCDE exercise) is the simplest and the most logical. We've already met with it in the excerpt from Toni Morrison's "Strangers" (4.14). Here the narrative line merely follows an established sequence either of events in time or places in geographic space or steps in a logical argument. In (5.24), which is the beginning of a retrospective review by Anthony Lane of the movie the *Sound of Music*, the linear form is temporal.[11]

(5.24) Let's start at the very beginning. (It's a very good place to start.) Maria Augusta Kutschera was born in 1905. As a young woman, she became a postulant at the Nonnberg Abbey, in Salzburg, Austria, but suffered from ill health. It was deemed beneficial that she should venture outside and adopt the post of governess in the home of a naval captain. She married him in 1927, which put an end to any postulating. The captain already had seven children; Maria bore him three more and formed a family musical group, whose success was cut short when Hitler invaded his native land. Even now, no historian has been able to ascertain if this was a genuine bid for power or the only possible means whereby the Fuhrer could eradicate the threat of close-harmony singing. Maria and her family fled to Italy, England, and, finally, the United States. The captain died in 1947; two years later, Maria published "The Story of the Trapp Family Singers." In 1956, the book was turned into a hit German movie; theatrical producers began to sniff around, and in November, 1959. "The Sound of Music," with original songs by Rogers and Hammerstein, opened on Broadway.

Lane is a witty writer and throws in some wonderful surprises which we'll discuss later, but the historical assertions are sequentially ordered by year of event: 1905, 1927, 1947, 1956, 1959. We can follow the narrative easily.

It is true that writers sometimes play with sequence for effect. Lane might have said, "'The Sound of Music' opened on Broadway in 1959, after the book had been turned into a hit German movie in 1956." While this arrangement might work if Lane had been focusing on Broadway musical from the beginning and had not already set up his paragraph in the ABC Form. But as it is, placing the 1956 date after the 1959 date might disrupt the flow of the narrative.

In his novel *The Naked and the Dead*, Norman Mailer often employs the ABC Linear Form not to provide a historical summary but to drive the plot forward:

(5.25)   It was beginning to rain, and Red covered his head with the blanket. His body was slowly sinking into a weary slumber in which different parts of him fell asleep at separate intervals, so that long after he had stopped thinking, a portion of his mind could feel the quivering of an exhausted limb or a cramp in one of his limbs. The shelling was becoming steady, and a half mile away from him a machine gun kept firing. Almost asleep, he watched Croft return and spread out a blanket. The rain continued. After a time, he no longer heard the artillery. But even when he was completely asleep, one last area of his mind noticed what was happening. Although he didn't remember it when he awoke, he heard a platoon of men march by, and was conscious of some other men beginning to push the antitank guns to the other side of the bivouac. There's a Jap road leads into the bivouac, he said in his sleep. They're going to protect it now. Probably he was feverish.[12]

This is probably the most common narrative form: this happened, then this happened, then this happened. The reader follows the action along, almost in "real time." It doesn't matter what tense the author uses; for example, in the following excerpt from Ann Beattie's short story, "Weekend," the first four sentences are in linear form, in active present tense. But then, with the fifth sentence, the action shifts to the habitual present, though again the form is linear:

(5.26)   On Saturday morning Lenore is up before the others. She carries her baby into the living room and puts him in George's favorite chair, which tilts because its back legs are missing, and covers him with a blanket. Then she lights a fire in the fireplace, putting fresh logs on a few embers that are still glowing from the night before. She sits down on the floor beside the chair and checks the baby, who has already gone back to sleep—a good thing because there are guests in the house. George, the man she lives with, is very hospitable and impetuous; he extends invitations whenever old friends call, urging them to come spend the weekend. Most of the callers are his former students—he used to be an English professor—and when they come it seems to make things much worse. It makes him much worse, because he falls into smoking too much and drinking and not eating, and then his ulcer bothers him. When the guests leave, when the weekend is over, she has to cook bland food: applesauce, oatmeal, puddings. And his drinking does not taper off easily anymore; in the past he would stop cold when the guests left, but lately he only tapers down from Scotch to wine, and drinks wine well into the week—a lot of wine, perhaps a whole bottle with his meal—until his stomach is much worse. He is hard to live with.[13]

Here, Beattie is developing her story as one would discuss the action in a movie: this is the "I Am a Camera" method of storytelling. But an author can also tell a story by painting a picture, by directing the reader's attention to various locations in a scene. In the following excerpt from near the beginning of F. Scott Fitzgerald's *The Great Gatsby*, for example, the reader is given (literally) a bird's-eye view of the geography where the action of the novel will take place.

(5.27) It was a matter of chance that I should have rented a house in one of the strangest communities in North America. It was on that slender riotous island which extends itself due east of New York—and where there are, among other natural curiosities, two unusual formations of land. Twenty miles from the city a pair of enormous eggs, identical in contour and separated only by a courtesy bay, jut out into the most domesticated body of salt water in the Western hemisphere, the great wet barnyard of Long Island Sound. They are not perfect ovals—like the egg in the Columbus story, they are both crushed flat at the contact end—but their physical resemblance must be a source of perpetual confusion to the gulls that fly overhead. To the wingless a more arresting phenomenon is their dissimilarity in every particular except shape and size.[14]

The ABC Linear Form also typically appears in logical arguments. Consider the following paragraph from an article by the distinguished scientist Stephen Jay Gould (I've numbered the clauses for convenience):

(5.28) (1) Our species has not won its independence from nature, and (2) we cannot do all that we can dream. Or (3) at least we cannot do it at the rate required to avoid tragedy, for (4) we are not unbounded in time. (5) Viral diseases are preventable in principle, and (6) I suspect that an AIDS vaccine will one day be produced. But (7) how will this discovery avail us if (8) it takes until the millennium, and (9) by then AIDS has fully run its exponential course and saturated our population, killing a substantial percentage of the human race? (10) A fight against an exponential enemy is primarily a race against time.[15]

This paragraph has the following sentence structure, where the Ss are the numbered sentences:

(5.29) NOT S1, and NOT S2.
Or NOT S3, for NOT S4.
S5, and S6.
But how S7, if S8, and S9?
(Therefore) S10.

Or, to put it in logical terms that might be slightly more easily understood:

>(5.30)   We cannot do A & B or C, because D.
>
>We can do E & F.
>
>But if G and H and I, what good are E & F?
>
>Therefore J.

Logic depends on laying out plausible premises leading to a rational conclusion, but it is not only a question of arranging sentences in a rational order. It's important that all the elements of a sentence cohere logically as well. This is our old friend Relevance again. For example, the second and third sentences of (5.23) seem a little strange because waggling fingers doesn't literally breathe life, and if limbs stretch to the ends of the earth, why wouldn't they be exposed to the frigid air? (And shouldn't "its embrace" be "their embrace"?)

>(5.23)   The moon has started to rise and the owl hoops in tandem to the inhalations and exhalations of every breath. A waggle to the fingers breathes life into the cold limbs. Craving warmth the limbs stretch to the ends of the earth, ever so careful as to not be exposed to the frigid air awaiting its embrace. Slowly one leg moves in preparation for releasing from the sitting.

The writer was almost certainly employing metaphor here, but one needs to be careful not to use a metaphor that contradicts other elements of the sentence. For example, one would be well-advised to avoid composing sentences like (5.31) and (5.32), although, strictly speaking, they are perfectly grammatical and meaningful.

>(5.31)   Foxes live in a dog-eat-dog world.
>
>(5.32)   After his neighbor Mary scolded him, Larry henceforth bent over backwards to pick up every leaf from his tree that dropped on her lawn.

Linguists have identified many sentences containing internal contradictions that are strange to the point of being uninterpretable because of their structure. A good example is (5.33), which makes no sense, in contrast to (5.34), which does:

>(5.33)   *Todd, who was transformed by magic into a swarm of bees, dispersed.
>
>(5.34)   The swarm of bees that Todd had become dispersed.

Other sentences, like "*All bachelors are married," are uninterpretable because of a conflict between the meanings of their lexical components. But to exactly the extent that such sentences are uninterpretable they are, of course, irrelevant. Note that they are irrelevant because they are uninterpretable, not vice-versa.

SONATA FORM: ABA

The ABA Sonata Form is familiar from the toastmaster's formula: "tell 'em what you're going to tell 'em, then tell 'em what you have to say, then tell 'em what you've told 'em." In this form, a theme is stated at the beginning, then there is a development of the particulars of the theme, and all is tied up at the end with a recapitulation of the theme, now buttressed by the particulars in the middle. John Updike's magisterial short piece, "Beer Can," nicely illustrates this technique.

(5.35) This seems to be an era of gratuitous inventions and negative improvements. Consider the beer can. It was beautiful—as beautiful as the clothespin, as inevitable as the wine bottle, as dignified and reassuring as the fire hydrant. A tranquil cylinder of delightfully resonant metal, it could be opened in an instant, requiring only the application of a handy gadget freely dispensed by every grocer. Who can forget the small, symmetrical thrill of those two triangular punctures, the dainty pfff, the little crest of suds that foamed eagerly in the exultation of release? Now we are given, instead, a top beetling with an ugly, shmoo-shaped tab, which, after fiercely resisting the tugging, bleeding fingers of the thirsty man, threatens his lips with a dangerous and hideous hole. However, we have discovered a way to thwart Progress, usually so unthwartable. Turn the beer can upside down and open the bottom. The bottom is still the way the top used to be. True, this operation gives the beer an unsettling jolt, and the sight of a consistently inverted beer can might make people edgy, not to say queasy. But the latter difficulty could be eliminated if manufacturers would design cans that looked the same whichever end was up, like playing cards. What we need is Progress with an escape hatch.[16]

This astonishing bit of virtuoso writing is simply structured—the A parts of the form comprise the first and last sentences, and everything else in the middle is the B part—but manages to comment simultaneously on a problem with "pop-top" drink cans of the 1960s (when this was first published in *The New Yorker*) and a larger issue about the nature of progress itself. This two-tier commentary is integral to the success of the piece.

There is a sense in which Updike's essay contains a simple argument: his premise is B and his conclusion is A. But B is merely one instance or illustration of A—instead of B we might label the middle part with the lowercase letter a (hence AaA), to show the relationship between the parts. Moreover, it's the last sentence, with its neat twist, that gives the paragraph its punch. It's not merely a restatement; it adds to the original statement with a trenchant metaphor. So we might call the last part A', giving us AaA'.

There is much about (5.35) that makes me rate it very highly and admire and appreciate it every time I read it. The symmetry of the combinations "gratuitous inventions" and "negative improvements"—where the adjective has a negative connotation and the noun a positive one—is especially pleasing. This adjective-noun pattern is repeated throughout—"tranquil cylinder," "resonant metal," "handy gadget," "symmetrical thrill," "dainty pfff," "shmoo-shaped tab," and so on—and each time we are bid to consider the unusual relation between the two elements of it. The way that Updike plays with "thwart" in the sixth sentence, is arresting. I will have more to say about this piece in Part III.

SPIRAL FORM: ABCABC

A more complex but often very effective thematic strategy involves creating a widening spiral of description, where the writer returns again and again to a few important themes, continually building on each. Each return to a theme expands the domain of that theme, so the reader has an expanded understanding of it. A brilliant use of this technique can be found in E. B. White's classic essay, "Once More to the Lake":

(5.36) One summer, along about 1904, my father rented a camp on a lake in Maine and took us all there for the month of August. We all got ringworm from some kittens and had to rub Pond's Extract on our arms and legs night and morning, and my father rolled over in a canoe with all his clothes on; but outside of that the vacation was a success and from then on none of us ever thought there was any place in the world like that lake in Maine. We returned summer after summer—always on August 1st for one month. I have since become a salt-water man, but sometimes in summer there are days when the restlessness of the tides and the fearful cold of the sea water and the incessant wind which blows across the afternoon and into the evening make me wish for the placidity of a lake in the woods. A few weeks ago this feeling got so strong I bought myself a couple of bass hooks and a spinner and returned to the lake where we used to go, for a week's fishing and to revisit old haunts.[17]

In this extract, which constitutes the first paragraph of the essay, there are three principal themes: the members of White's family (F), the place where they took their vacations (P), and time (T). You can chart how White goes from one theme to another by listing the nouns in order and then placing them in an array. (See figure 5.1. I have ignored the nouns that don't reference either of the three major themes; these are in italics.)

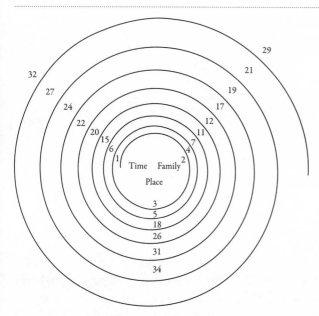

FIGURE 5.1 A diagram of the themes in the first paragraph of "Once More to the Lake"

1. F father
2. P camp lake Maine
3. F us
4. P there
5. T August
6. F we
7. *(ringworm)*
8. *(kittens)*
9. *(ponds)*
10. F our (arms & legs)
11. F father
12. *(Canoe)*
13. *(Clothes)*
14. T vacation
15. *(Success)*
16. F us
17. P place lake Maine
18. F we
19. T summer August one month
20. F I (salt-water man)
21. T summer days

22. *(Tides cold water wind)*
23. T afternoon evening
24. *(Placidity)*
25. P lake woods
26. T weeks ago
27. *(Feeling)*
28. F I myself
29. *Bass hooks spinner*
30. P lake
31. T week's
32. *Fishing*
33. P old haunts

Notice how White develops his three themes by alternating his topics, skipping from one theme to the next and back around again. The effect is to intertwine the three, creating a dynamic in which they are all implicated—family, time, and place. The form of the narrative beautifully mirrors its content, because White's concern is the very relationships that exist between his themes. Meanwhile, the reader's understanding of each theme expands as the spiral expands, so that he or she gains a wider appreciation of what White is up to with each turn.

But, and this is an enormous but, none of these three strategies is a necessary component of fluent writing. Yes, these writers did use them to dramatic effect, but there are many ways to skin this cat—so many, actually, that discussing only these three might mislead the aspiring writer into thinking that there is something special and privileged about them. Well, you might ask, wouldn't there be at least some value to teaching students these three forms to get them going?

Perhaps, but the important point is that each form is not independent of the content of the piece being written. The beauty of White's use of the spiral form is inseparable from the fact that it is integral to the story itself, the relationship between time, place, and self (as son and father). Teaching the spiral form independently of the very special circumstances in which it works well would be nugatory. Teaching it together with those circumstances may well help advanced students to appreciate the potential of this and other narrative strategies, but as a technique for teaching average students how to write well, I await convincing that it will contribute in any measurable way to doing the job. What we'd like students of writing to appreciate is the multiplicity of such strategies. And, of course, we'd like them, through their avid reading, to build up their own storehouse to use in their writing.

Choices

The problem of choice in narrative strategy is there wherever you look, down to the word itself. For example, as Todd Oakley points out,[18] if you want to discuss your trip to the Frick Collection in New York City, you might describe it in any of the following three ways, depending on whether you consider it relevant to your audience to include information about your starting point, your path to your destination, or the destination itself:

(5.37i)   We went to the Frick Collection.
(5.37ii)   We left our hotel and came to the Frick Collection.
(5.37iii) We came upon the Frick Collection while walking from our hotel through Central Park and onto 70th Street.

Or, you might wish to compress (5.37iii) into a single event:

(5.38)   We came upon the Frick Collection.

Or, you might wish to add a metaphor:

(5.39i)   We stumbled upon the Frick Collection.
(5.39ii)   Our stroll in the park turned into a trip to the Frick Collection.

Or, you might wish to integrate or blend two thoughts:[19]

(5.40)   When we got there, we couldn't digest the Frick Collection as we'd hoped to because the crowds were nauseating.

Or substitute more precise words for "went," "left," and "came upon":

(5.41i)   We strolled to the Frick Collection.
(5.41ii)   We ran from our hotel to the Frick Collection so as to arrive there before closing.
(5.41iii) We were pulled up short at the Frick Collection.

Or add description:

(5.42i)   After lunch, we left our cozy hotel for a lovely afternoon stroll to the Frick Collection on 70th Street.

And so on. The English language offers various alternatives for different points of view ("John kissed Mary"; "Mary was kissed by John"), different moods ("John must have kissed Mary"; "John should have kissed Mary"), different aspects ("John was kissing Mary"; "John began to kiss Mary"), different conceptual spaces ("John would have kissed Mary if he'd had the chance"; "John regretted not kissing Mary"). The options are daunting, but are in fact controlled by relevance. Which of the examples in (5.37) to (5.42) would be the best choice for someone who wishes to write well? Obviously, it depends on context: what information is in common ground, what information your audience would consider most relevant at that point in the narrative, what information you have to offer that you think might satisfy your audience, etc. Knowing these distinctions is part of what it means to be fluent in the language, but being able to teach them is a challenge of a much different order.

6

Graphemic Fluency

PRESCRIPTIVE WRITING TEXTBOOKS much concern themselves with rules of spelling and punctuation, and with good reason. While it is possible to be a constructionally and pragmatically fluent writer and at the same time a poor speller, it is rarely the case that a reader will forgive a writer of a confusingly spelled and punctuated piece, no matter how good the writing otherwise.[1] This is because consistency in spelling, punctuation, and other graphemic conventions, including headings and display typography, tables, and figures, directly aids the reader in processing the material read. Unlike the principles that determine constructional and pragmatic fluency, the rules of spelling are codified (if not entirely consistently) in dictionaries, and so deviations from the norm are reasonably easy to identify. Punctuation, although not convincingly codified in any universally authoritative source, is still standardized to a much greater degree than, say, narrative practice—and is to a significant degree easier to learn.

From a pedagogical perspective, teaching rules of spelling and punctuation also has its benefits, in that reliable and valid test scores can be derived from objective tests regarding those rules. A teacher who tires of frequent battles with students over the grades they received on their essays can avoid such hassles by focusing on spelling and punctuation, where there isn't much to argue about.

Admittedly, fluency in spelling and punctuation is not nearly so highly prized in the world at large as fluency in the constructional and pragmatic aspects of language. Yet spelling and punctuation do significantly influence how people rate the quality of a piece of writing. We, as readers, are not terribly good at isolating different kinds of fluency and simply assume (sometimes wrongly) that if something as obvious as spelling or punctuation is off-kilter, then everything else probably is too.

In this chapter, I will not have much more to say about spelling. But I think it worthwhile to look closely at the conventions English textbooks promote for punctuation, because more is at stake than these textbooks often let on.

In 2003, the sportswriter Lynn Truss published a surprisingly popular book entitled *Eats, Shoots and Leaves*,[2] which entertainingly denounced what she perceived as society's unforgivable tendency toward licentiousness in matters of punctuation. Ms. Truss was upset with, among a number of other solecisms, the ubiquity of the so-called grocer's apostrophe ("apple's for sale"), and she encouraged her readers not to countenance such things anymore. Apparently stimulated by her book, some youths were arrested for defacing signs they considered to be in contravention of Ms. Truss's teachings.[3] It may be all very well and good to take, in theory, an absolutist stance with regard to punctuation, but in practice, as these youths found out, it could lead to jail time.

Actually, I'll argue that it isn't even good theory to take the sort of absolutist position that Ms. Truss took. As the linguist Geoffrey Nunberg has pointed out, the conventions we use for punctuation supply an important argument for considering writing to be not simply a means of transcribing spoken language but rather an autonomous language system in its own right, one that, while it bears significant similarities to spoken language, is in important ways independent of it. Nunberg offers the following examples:

(6.1) He reported the decision: we were forbidden to speak with the chairman directly.

(6.2) He reported the decision; we were forbidden to speak with the chairman directly.

In (6.1), the decision reported is that we were forbidden to speak with the chairman directly. In (6.2), the nature of the decision is not stated; the fact that we were forbidden to speak with the chairman directly is supplied as the reason that "he" reported the decision to us rather than the chairman. Both sentences would normally be pronounced identically; only the written version would disambiguate them. Other examples of language that appear exclusive to writing include footnotes, so-called deictic elements like "herein" (meaning "in this book or article"), "above" (meaning "previously in this book or article"), "op. cit." (meaning "previously cited in this book or article), graphs, tables, and charts, headings and subheadings, chapter and section numbers, page numbers and running heads, tables of contents, copyright notices, bibliographies, colophons, and so on.

If punctuation is a part of an independent writing system, however, then that commits us to a position that is somewhat problematic. Will we argue that the writing system as a whole and ordinary speech are independently formed? Or do we wish to maintain that the former is derived from the latter, with perhaps a few added (and largely unimportant) quirks? There are arguments on both sides.

Perhaps the strongest case that literary language differs significantly from ordinary speech is that poetry (a form of literary language) can impose meter and rhyme schemes on the words and phrases that are external to the syntax and meaning of the words and phrases themselves and that wouldn't be found in ordinary speech. Against this argument, Nigel Fabb, in an interesting article from 2010,[4] investigates, and ultimately defends, what he calls the Development Hypothesis, which argues that "literary language is formed and regulated by developing only the elements, rules and constraints of ordinary language." His point is that if a feature is added to literary language that is developed from the constraints of ordinary speech, then that feature adds cognitive complexity (and, hence, interest) to the literary piece. However, if the feature is entirely independent of normal language (he gives the example of a novel composed without the letter "e"), it adds no cognitive complexity to the piece at all. Cognitive complexity being prized, it is just those elements of literary language that provide cognitive complexity that we should be most ready to identify with it.

This argument is suggestive and not conclusive, but it behooves a language teacher to be clear about which parts of any of its systems and subsystems are systematic and which are arbitrary. For example, the grocer's apostrophe during the Early Modern English period was systematically motivated, because at the time, apostrophes indicated a missing element, often an "e" after a consonant and before a plural or genitive "s": Middle English *croppes* ("crops") → Early Modern English *crop's* → Modern English *crops*. This is not to say that those grocers (and others) who today write "Apple's for sale" are merely caught up in nostalgia for Early Modern English; but it does suggest that scorn for them, based on the mistaken assumption that an apostrophe so-placed is illogical, is undeserved.

Nevertheless, Contemporary Standard Publisher's English (if I may be permitted to coin a term) today does not use the apostrophe to indicate an ancient dropped "e" before "s" in plurals, and English teachers should, of course, want their students to know this. Most students at the university level, in fact, already do. Think about Strunk and White's very first rule: "Form the possessive singular of nouns by adding 's." This is straightforward enough (although there is no hint how to handle a plural—for that you'll have to turn to another style manual). But when one begins to apply the rule to various constructions in the real world, complications inevitably arise. Consider the examples in (6.3) to (6.9):

> (6.3) I told its author, Penelope Fitzgerald, that I found *At Freddie's*'s title inappropriate for that book and therefore suggested that she change it to something else.
>
> (6.4) I found "Who's Afraid of Virginia Woolf?"'s plot confusing
>
> (6.5) Mary (who formerly was married to Henry)'s daughter, lives in Rome.
>
> (6.6) Was it Mary Smith—and here I'm assuming that that was her original name (before her adoptive parents changed it)—'s daughter who married a sword-swallower?

(6.7) "Las Vegas (What?) Las Vegas (Can't hear you! Too noisy) Las Vegas!!!!"'s author, Tom Wolfe, was critical of those who were critical of him.

(6.8) "Las Vegas (What?) Las Vegas (Can't hear you! Too noisy) Las Vegas!!!!"— yes, that's the correct title (or at least the one that's in the database)—'s author, Tom Wolfe, was critical of those who were critical of him.

(6.9) "Las Vegas (What?) Las Vegas (Can't hear you! Too noisy) Las Vegas!!!!"— yes, that's the correct title (or at least the one that's in the library's digital database; in the printed catalog, which I believe was published in 1992; and in the bibliography in the department)—'s author, Tom Wolfe, was critical of those who were critical of him.

I expect the English teacher who marginally tolerates (6.3) and (6.4) will ask the writer of any of (6.5) to (6.9) to rephrase. But on what principled grounds? What rule of punctuation has been violated? Strunk and White say nothing about situations like these.

Nunberg explores some additional complications involved in combining commas, parentheses, dashes, and question marks that are generally untreated in the manuals:

(6.10) The bombings were announced by (then Secretary of State) Henry Kissinger.

(6.11) *The bombings, (then Secretary of State) Henry Kissinger announced, were an important step toward peace.

(6.12) *(Not surprisingly), she left.

(6.13) And (not surprisingly), she left.

(6.14) What we want to know is when?, but he has told us only why.

(6.15) *What we want to know is when?—up to now you've told us only why—, and until you answer that question, we cannot come to a decision.

(6.16) *Who could get away with it—not John, surely—? and why would anyone want to?[5]

Nunberg's theory of such cases makes the following predictions: (1) parentheticals won't occur phrase initially; (2) an end dash will be absorbed by a following question mark; (3) a comma or a beginning dash following a question mark won't be absorbed. As before, Strunk and White don't cover such complexities, and, so far as I'm aware, neither do any of the other style books. How are aspiring writers to learn these rules?

I suppose one must first ask whether it is important that they do so. My sense is that once one has become familiar with the function of parentheticals and dashes, results like those in (6.10) to (6.16) shouldn't be difficult to infer.

Nunberg's point—and it's one that makes a good deal of sense to me—is that the punctuation subsystem operates in service to the writing system as a whole. It's impossible to grasp the rules of that subsystem without having a firm grip already on the system. What a writer should want punctuation to do is to contribute to the reader's understanding and appreciation of the text, not merely to assist the writer in stringing ideas together.

Problems of inconsistency in punctuation practice—and of other lapses of judgment in deploying punctuation—should be kept separate from what I'll call homonymic and finger errors, which are largely unconscious. Homonymic errors include the substitution of "it's" for "its" or "they're" for "there" or "their," or vice versa, which many (most?) professional writers continue to commit no matter how many years they've been working with language. Finger errors, such as typing "teh" instead of "the" and leaving out the period at the end of a sentence, are also not usually associated with lack of expertise, but should be caught by a writer (or the writer's word-processing software) at some stage.

Punctuation and spelling are, of course, only two of the several graphical elements integral to written language, and fluency in these others (headings, etc.) is similarly important for a professional writer. Nevertheless, I don't think much of an argument can be mounted that these fluencies are anywhere near as important in professional writing as the constructional and pragmatic fluencies we have so far discussed.

As Nigel Hall has demonstrated,[6] children in the lower grades learning punctuation often treat it as entirely extrinsic to writing, as something that has no function in writing but that is to be added after the fact to please the teacher. These young students adopt a graphical strategy, for example, placing a period after every line in a page of text rather than at the end of a sentence. At some point, these students must be weaned from the graphical strategy and transition to a linguistic strategy. For some, that transition can occur as late as entry into secondary school.

If there is a problem with Contemporary Standard Publisher's English, it's that there are too many versions of it, including (among many others) the various systems advocated in the *New York Times Style Manual*, the *Chicago Manual of Style*, the *Associated Press Stylebook*, the *Modern Language Association Style Manual*, the *Oxford Guide to Style*, and the *Yahoo! Style Guide*, not to mention the many different elementary and secondary school textbooks. Any one of these style guides would be largely adequate for most circumstances, but their multiplicity promotes confusion on the part of students. Newspapers and magazines have in the past eschewed the Oxford or serial comma (the use of two commas instead of one in a conjunction of three elements, as in "blood, sweat, and tears"); but this is reputedly a consequence of the cost of space in traditional print serial publications, a consideration that does not obtain to the same degree in print books or digital publications. British practice with respect to the order of period or comma punctuation and quotation marks also differs from American practice: Americans prefer a comma or period inside quotation marks, the British, outside or inside, according to sense. Academic and technical publications often have their own style manuals, which specify punctuation policies idiosyncratic to them. Add to this the propensity of creative writers to play with punctuation, and the result is that there appears to be no single "correct" way to punctuate anything. This should not be seen as the student's problem, but as the publisher's problem. The lack of consistency in the English spelling system, so often the subject of fruitless attempts at revision, is another publisher's problem. Perhaps if students were allowed to adopt one particular punctuation system early on in their schooling and to stick closely to it through university, the world would be a better, or at least more relaxed, place.

However, as long as spelling and punctuation are taken by many people (especially people who can determine their future) as proxies for overall literacy and fluency in language, students would be well-advised to develop their graphemic fluency to the extent they can.

Form and Content

7

Figurative Language

AS THE FIRST-CENTURY writer known as Longinus said, "the natural power of figurative language is great, and metaphors conduce to sublimity." At least since that time, it has been common to identify figurative language with highly accomplished writing. Samuel Johnson put it well: "metaphorical expression . . . is a great excellence in style, when it is used with propriety, for it gives you two ideas for one; conveys the meaning more luminously, and generally with a perception of delight."[1] Certainly modern writers and critics have embraced figurative language as a signal mark of literary art.

The question about figurative language most relevant to us in this book is what place it plays in the conception of writing fluency we have been developing. Some educators see the use of figurative language as an indication of literary complexity, others of confusion. But what counts as figurative language is not always obvious, nor is its role in indicating complexity of thought.

First, a little background. On the Classical view, figurative language (metaphor, meiosis, puns, irony, etc.) has always constituted an added decoration to literal language, a poetic fillip included for the delight of the reader. Metaphor and other tropes may then be studied as embodying a particular and special use of language, different in kind from literal language. By contrast, the Romantics turned the tables by viewing metaphoric language as elemental and literal language as derivative and inferior. In either case, the literal and the figurative were assumed to be separate modes of linguistic communication, each with its own use, value, and interpretation. Under the influence of Nietzsche, postmodernist thought has denied that figurative language can be separated from literal language—or, rather, that literal language exists at all. Thus, belief in the impossibility of an objective stance has become the hallmark of postmodernism: since no language is literal, it cannot get at truth.

The brief summary in the preceding paragraph suggests the possibility of a confusion to which discussions of figurative language are sometimes heir—namely, the identification of a stance on meaning with a stance on ontology. We very well may mean precisely (and believe) that old age is the autumn of life when we say "Old age is the autumn of life" without committing ourselves to belief in the truth of the equation of autumn and old age. The Nietzschean view that no language is adequate to describe what actually exists does not preclude our meaning what we say and saying what we mean.

Even postmodern compositionists like James Seitz, who decry the attempt to rid student essays of metaphor in order to encourage clarity, still see metaphor, while pervasive, as distinct from literal language: he speaks of "the need to 'disinter' dead metaphors in the interest of enlivening and complicating both the rhetoric and the aesthetics of discourse about reading and writing. . . . It is tempting to say that metaphor 'creeps into' language when we are not looking; but in fact it is metaphor that allows us to look—and to speak our looking—in the first place."[2]

Among cognitive linguists and psychologists there are those, such as George Lakoff and Mark Johnson,[3] who would probably see Seitz as agreeing with them that metaphor is integral to thought: "metaphor is pervasive in everyday life," they say, "not just in language but in thought and action. . . . [M]ost of our ordinary conceptual system is metaphorical in nature."

Relevance Theory, which we discussed in chapter 4, rejects the idea that figurative language is cognitively different from literal (or nonfigurative) language, at least as regards the inferential mechanisms we employ in interpreting them. These inferential mechanisms use relevance as an aid to interpretation, whether the language is vague, loose, equivocal, or ambiguous or contains obvious original metaphors, "dead" metaphors, metonymy, irony, sarcasm, hyperbole, idioms, clichés, misspellings or mispronunciations, colloquialisms, omissions, repetitions, and so on. According to Sperber and Wilson, metaphor is not a theoretically significant notion: "we see metaphors as simply a range of cases at one end of a continuum that includes literal, loose, and hyperbolic interpretations. . . . There is no mechanism specific to metaphors, no interesting generalization that applies only to them. In other terms, metaphor is not a natural kind."[4] Seitz might agree with Sperber and Wilson as well, since he says (drawing on work by Paul Ricoeur) that "it is the reader who constructs 'sense' out of the metaphor."[5]

As was pointed out earlier, Sperber and Wilson stress that spoken or written language greatly underdetermines meaning. We need the information provided by context and our cognitive inferential system to make sense of the simplest sentence. For example, they mention sentences like "That surgeon is a butcher" and "That butcher is a surgeon." We need contextual cues to tell us which butcher or surgeon is indicated. But to get the apparently intended meanings ("That surgeon is incompetent, careless, dangerous, etc.";

"That butcher is an accomplished artist with the knife") we have to infer that the speaker or writer intends the sentence to be optimally relevant and not nonsensical. Because incompetence, carelessness, etc. are not necessarily properties of butchers, we can't derive the intended meaning from the meaning of the words themselves. But we do know that surgeons perform intricate operations, usually taking exquisite care to avoid damaging internal tissues, while butchers use their knives roughly to separate particular cuts of meat from a carcass. It is this inferential meaning which we derive from the basic semantic meaning of the constructions by picking out what is optimally relevant from our encyclopedic knowledge that allows us to make sense of them.

Concupiscent Curds

Sperber and Wilson distinguish between the range of inferences that can be derived from a particular statement and the strength of those inferences as intended by the writer or speaker of the statement. In their terminology, to strongly implicate a weak implication is to intend a specific interpretation which, however, doesn't provide strong grounds for the inference. This sort of mixing of broad or narrow range and strong or weak inference is most apparent in instances of hedging. Sperber and Wilson give the following example: You are at the airport and see that your flight has been delayed. You say to the airline employee at the desk, "I need to be in Dallas by 3 p.m. to catch my connecting flight to Mexico City. Am I going to make it?" Now, the employee might answer with a simple "yes" or "no," but probably she doesn't really know. Instead, she might say something like, "Your flight is going to be delayed by at least an hour," leaving you to draw the appropriate inference. In this case, the employee may have weakly implied the specific proposition that you won't make your connecting flight. The really interesting cases, however, are weak implications that are weakly implied, because these are what paradoxically attend the most effective and powerful metaphors. Consider the first lines of Wallace Stevens's "The Emperor of Ice Cream":

> (7.1)   Call the roller of big cigars,
>   The muscular one, and bid him whip
>   In kitchen cups concupiscent curds.[6]

I will ignore the alliteration for the moment and concern myself just with the phrase "concupiscent curds" and how we construe it. Since concupiscence is an occasional property of humans (or animals) and curds are inanimate (at least, they are to a naked eye unable to detect any living microorganisms that may be inhabiting them), we are confronted with a logical impossibility. But if we believe (under the Communicative Principle of Relevance) that Stevens had something in mind that he felt it might be optimally relevant to us to convey, then we will engage our normal inferential mechanisms to discover what that might be. The implication that the curds are concupiscent is weak—certainly Stevens did not want to be taken as providing strong grounds for the reader to infer the particular proposition that curds have desire, which wouldn't make much sense. Moreover, he no doubt intended that the range of inferences the reader might draw from the word "concupiscent" in its context be broad—"concupiscent curds" brings together a lustful sense of desire with the appetizing appeal of rounded spoonfuls of the whipped ice cream of the title. The curds could be themselves voluptuous, or their appearance could be appealing to a voluptuary, or the muscular roller of big cigars who will be bidden to whip the ice cream could be so concupiscent in his activity that that concupiscence will be evident in the curds.

Hypallage

If the last, then the phenomenon in question—the transference of the meaning of the modifier concupiscent—to the subject (the cigar roller) is what is called *hypallage*. P. G. Wodehouse was an eminent practitioner of hypallage, and his novels and stories contain many amusing examples of it.

> (7.2) In every dance, however greatly he may be enjoying it, there comes a time when a man needs a meditative cigarette apart from the throng. (*The Intrusion of Jimmy*)
> I balanced a thoughtful lump of sugar on the teaspoon. (*Joy in the Morning*)
> He uncovered the fragrant eggs and I pronged a moody forkful. (*Jeeves and the Impending Doom*)
> As I sat in the bath-tub, soaping a meditative foot . . . (*Jeeves and the Feudal Spirit*)

In "The Transferred Epithet in P. G. Wodehouse,"[7] Robert A. Hall Jr. entertained two possible analyses of such constructions. In the first, the seemingly misplaced adjective is interpreted as modifying the subject's action: "There comes a time when a man needs to meditatively smoke a cigarette apart from the throng." "I balanced a lump of sugar thoughtfully on the teaspoon." "I moodily pronged a forkful." "As I sat meditatively in the bath-tub, soaping a foot." Hall ultimately found this analysis unsatisfactory, however, and opted for one much closer to Sperber and Wilson's, in which the constructions semantically "are simply a slightly incongruous extension of the type of reference involved in those with nontransferred epithets," such as "He uttered a surprised snort"; "She gave a sardonic laugh"; "I could not suppress a contemptuous sneer." Think about "happy day," "cheerful weather," "sad moment," "careful design." Note that the constructions in all the cases remain the same: Modifier + Noun. In such constructions, the modifier is interpreted as being in some unspecified semantic relation to the noun, which the Communicative Principle is required to sort out. In hypallage, the relation is typically loose—sometimes so loose that the meaning of the modifier seems to be floating freely, entirely unattached to that of the noun. But it is hard to draw a line. We might decide that an "inhaled circumference" crosses it, but perhaps not without assessing all plausible contexts. What we think of as hypallage are just cases on a continuum that begins with ordinary modification.

Applying the Hall/Sperber and Wilson analysis to Stevens's poem, we might let the Communicative Principle suggest for us that the poet's meaning is that passion and desire commingle with the curds and the roller of cigars. This is a stretch, and that's both the virtue and the problem with weak implications weakly implicated. It is possible that this is what Seitz had in mind when he says, "the most compelling metaphors are precisely those that suggest numerous imaginative possibilities (rather than 'quick and easy' access), possibilities that may move us to synthesis or analysis, a putting together or a taking apart. Metaphor—itself a metaphor of movement—sets in motion the motions of thought."[8]

Let's look at the extract in the context of the whole poem:

(7.3) Call the roller of big cigars,
       The muscular one, and bid him whip
       In kitchen cups concupiscent curds.
       Let the wenches dawdle in such dress
       As they are used to wear, and let the boys
       Bring flowers in last month's newspapers.
       Let be be finale of seem.
       The only emperor is the emperor of ice-cream.

       Take from the dresser of deal.
       Lacking the three glass knobs, that sheet
       On which she embroidered fantails once
       And spread it so as to cover her face.
       If her horny feet protrude, they come
       To show how cold she is, and dumb.
       Let the lamp affix its beam.
       The only emperor is the emperor of ice-cream.

On Stevens's own account, he had no particular meaning in mind when he came up with the phrase "concupiscent curds" in line 3: he said in a letter to a Leonard C. van Geyzel dated May 16, 1945, that "the words 'concupiscent curds' have no genealogy. They are merely expressive: at least, I hope they are expressive. They express the concupiscence of life, but, by contrast with the things in relation to them in the poem, they express or accentuate life's destitution, and it is this that gives them something more than cheap luster."[9] So from the very start we actually haven't been in a position to extract the poet's precise intention, since he seems not to have had one. (Or, at least, twenty-three years after publishing the poem he didn't remember having one.) In the same letter, Stevens also said that "the point of a poem is not its meaning . . . a poem must have a peculiarity, as if it was the momentarily complete idiom of that which prompts it, even if that which prompts it is the vaguest emotion. This character seems to be one of the consequences of concentration." In "The Emperor of Ice Cream" the "vaguest emotion" that prompted the poem is expressed peculiarly—that is, with weak implications weakly implicated. Presumably, Stevens felt intuitively that the construction "concupiscent curds" worked well in its context. He must have liked the alliteration of "whip / In kitchen cups concupiscent curds." But why kitchen cups necessarily (except for the fitting phonology)? And does anyone ever whip (as opposed to dispense) ice cream in kitchen cups, rather than kitchen bowls? I don't know, and my inferential mechanisms don't help me. Perhaps it doesn't matter, since Stevens was aiming at expression of the "vaguest emotion." The general idea of the poem, which appears to be that, in the end, one dies and the most powerful force only is able to whip concupiscent ice-cream in the face of that, doesn't help me either, though I like the coda of the first stanza, "Let be be finale of seem / The only emperor is the emperor of ice cream"—which I interpret as something like when "what seems to be true" is finally realized as "what is true," all we ultimately have to appeal to as a higher power is a carnival-type king, a muscular guy who rolls big cigars. Does this idea come across? Yes. Is the word "concupiscent" successful in its context to furthering this idea, to "accentuat[ing] life's destitution"? No—or so I would vote—and not only because Stevens himself seemed to rule out hypallage as a possible interpretation of the modifier + noun construction ("the words express the concupiscence of life," rather than the concupiscence of the roller of big cigars), but more importantly because it calls attention to itself by its constructional peculiarity without that peculiarity contributing anything to the meaning of the poem.

Fog

Sperber and Wilson discuss Carl Sandberg's poem "Fog" as another example of weak implications weakly implicated:

(7.4) Fog
       The fog comes
       on little cat feet.
       It sits looking
       over harbor and city
       on silent haunches
       and then moves on.

They point out that the phrase "on little cat feet" "evokes an array of implications having to do with silence, smoothness, stealth. Taken together with the following four lines, the phrase evokes a movement which appears both arbitrary and yet composed. . . . [The] metaphor weakly implicates an ever-widening array of implications which combine to depict a place, an atmosphere, a mood, achieving a powerful overall effect that varies from reader to reader and reading to reading."[10] In contrast with Stevens's ice cream poem, Sandberg's fog poem doesn't leave one scratching his head about the "peculiar" meaning of a construction. The relation between cat and fog is straightforward and isn't compromised by a syntactic oddity. We'll return to the meaning of this poem in chapter 9.

It is important to recognize that the Relevance Theoretic approach is not merely a restatement of Seitz's "metaphor of movement," since the former is an instantiation of an empirical theory of cognition and the latter is an interpretation that doesn't take us any further than the interpretation itself. From a literary point of view, the critic must decide whether the weak implications weakly implicated actually do the job. But without a sense of how the constructions work linguistically, a justifiable conclusion may be difficult to reach—in the case of Stevens's ice-cream poem, I would say, impossible. Indeed, it would be a rare class in composition or creative writing or English that taught how weak implications weakly implicated actually work. Such constructions occur to us as writers—and we are able to understand them as readers—because of certain properties of our brains that the Communicative Principle captures. An advanced course in creative writing might offer instruction that distinguishes "the most compelling metaphors" from not-so-compelling metaphors, but the mental processes involved in creating and processing the metaphors are necessarily unconscious.

If good writing is a display of fluency, as discussed, and the manipulation of metaphor is a feature of fluent writing, where fluency requires sensitivity to relevance in context, then we must be prepared to find that what is relevant in one context will not inevitably be relevant in the next. A weak implication weakly implicated may be merely confusing, as, for example, would be my saying on a foggy day, "Boy, this fog arrived on foot," or at the bedside of a deceased woman, "I wonder if the ice cream in her fridge is concupiscent."

However, judgment of Constructional Conflict, as in the selection from Stevens (7.1)—and earlier in the selection from Ondaatje (5.19)—is not a mere subjectivity, in the way that, say, preference for Woolf over Hemingway (or vice-versa) is. Nor is it the same as preferring the relative pronoun "that" instead of "which" in restrictive relative clauses or condoning or disparaging the word "irregardless." With cases of Constructional Conflict, which we have in the Stevens and Ondaatje examples, we have a violation of the implicit constructional conventions that make up our language and need an easy pragmatic way out (via the principles of relevance) if we are to make sense of it, or else we remain hooked on it in an unproductive way (i.e., a way that does not lead to greater insight or understanding). Thus, in my view, (5.19) and (7.1) are examples of writing badly, though, of course, both Ondaatje and Stevens are unquestionably good writers in the sense developed in this book. I don't doubt that if a vote were taken, some voters would see nothing wrong with either (5.19) or (7.1) and be happy to accept them as consistent with the poet's special license.

The general inferential principles we've been discussing in relation to metaphor are equally at work with other figures, though occasionally requiring additional machinery to get us where we want to be. An expression, such as "This is a fine day," said in the middle of a cold downpour, could be ironic (assuming one doesn't like cold downpours) or not (if one does). Sperber and Wilson argue that for an ironic reading the expression must echo or mimic an actual or generally understood statement or comment, where the information available from contextual cues suggests the speaker's sarcastic attitude toward that statement or comment. This may not work for constructions like "I could care less" (meaning "I couldn't care less") or "to coin a phrase" (meaning, unironically, "to repeat a phrase coined by someone else"), where we accept the phrases as imperfect substitutes or mistakes for the implicated meaning. Indeed, these two constructions have become so embedded in popular speech these days that one might not even need to go through the inferential process to access their intended meaning, which attaches naturally to the constructions themselves. Now, if you actually did mean to say "I could care less" (meaning, literally, "I could care less"), then you would have to distinguish the construction by, for example, emphasizing the word "could," showing your commitment to the non-negated form. "To coin a phrase" might be meant ironically if the phrase wasn't actually coined by the speaker, but it would be confusing given its established interpretation, even if accompanied by distinctive intonation or an eye wink.

8

Surprise, Repetition, and Complexity

THERE ARE SEVERAL other aspects of good writing frequently mentioned in composition texts that are susceptible to a Relevance Theoretic account, among them surprise, repetition, and complexity. As emphasized earlier, the virtue of Relevance Theory is that it is explanatory and not merely descriptive or taxonomic. You might say, for example, that a writer shouldn't repeat herself, but sometimes excellent writers use repetition to make a point. When is it all right to repeat and when is it not? And, most importantly, why? To answer questions such as these, a taxonomy of errors is insufficient. We need an explanatory theory.

Surprise

We've seen that figurative language is prized because it presents us with new information or a new way of conceptualizing the world around us. But language need not be blatantly figurative to surprise.

According to Relevance Theory, as readers we expect authors to consistently give us information optimally relevant to our interests. Intercalated with those interests is a strong attraction to salient information that we haven't previously had. We want to be able to adjust the common ground so that we stand shoulder to shoulder with the author. But if an author provides information we perceive to be simply irrelevant to us, that information will not surprise us. In Hamlet, for example, the audience and the title character learn simultaneously that the person he has impaled on his sword behind the curtain is Polonius rather than his uncle, the usurper. In the context of the play, this is a significant, unexpected, and consequential piece of new information, and hence a surprise. But if you have no interest whatever in the play, haven't been paying attention, and have been counting the minutes until the play ends, then receiving this bit of news would be useless to you. Thus, when we talk about surprise, we really mean "surprise in context," where the context will inevitably be different from person to person depending upon what interests and information each has.

We've looked at several examples of surprise already. Recall the concluding sentence of John Updike's "Beer Can":

(8.1)   What we need is Progress with an escape hatch.

Updike has in his essay been putting words together in unusual ways that for a reader like me are interesting: I've remarked on the pleasurable surprise of the negative-positive combinations "gratuitous inventions" and "negative improvements," the striking figurative phrase "a top beetling with an ugly, schmoo-shaped tab," the play on "thwart." All of these have the potential, in the appropriate context, to delight with their inventiveness. He concludes his argument in his final sentence with an arresting metaphor, "Progress with an escape hatch." Had anyone to that point conceived of progress as, say, a vessel hurtling through an ocean of inventions that requires an escape hatch when things go awry? Perhaps, but it's not terribly likely. Yet the image sticks because it is so apt in the context of what has preceded it.

Often, writers try to stick a surprise at the very beginning of a story, to inveigle the reader into wanting to read further. Here is the opening of Michael Chabon's *The Mysteries of Pittsburgh*:

(8.2)   At the beginning of the summer I had lunch with my father, the gangster, who was in town for the weekend to transact some of his vague business.[1]

The reference to the narrator's father with the appositive, "the gangster," makes us sit up and pay attention. If Chabon had used "extortionist" or "money-launderer," it would have perhaps supplied a surprise, but wouldn't have packed quite the punch of "gangster." We want, naturally, to know more. The author seems—at least on the basis of this introductory sentence—to be intelligent, careful, and perceptive, as well as, perhaps, a little impish. The situation seems unusual, and our natural interest in unusual stories, especially those told by a charming narrator, is aroused.

I've heard the writer Bruce Jay Friedman say that writing the first sentence of a short story is "the diamond-cutter's art," and that seems quite right to me, for that's where the reader forms his first impression, positive or negative, of the writer and her story. The linguist Geoffrey Pullum gives a trenchant analysis of the first sentences (8.3) of Dan Brown's *The DaVinci Code*:

(8.3)   Renowned curator Jacques Saunière staggered through the vaulted arch-
way of the museum's Grand Gallery. He lunged for the nearest painting he
could see, a Caravaggio. Grabbing the gilded frame, the seventy-six-year-
old man heaved the masterpiece toward himself until it tore from the wall
and Saunière collapsed backward in a heap beneath the canvas.[2]

Pullum says that it was the "very first sentence, indeed the very first word, that told me
instantly that I was in for a very bad time stylistically."[3] The problem, as he points out, is
that there's no justification for beginning with the adjective "renowned": "Putting curriculum vitae details into complex modifiers on proper names or definite descriptions is
what you do in journalistic stories about deaths; you just don't do it in describing an
event in a narrative." This is, of course, a complaint about relevance in the sense discussed. Pullum doesn't like other things about this paragraph, including the term "masterpiece" (which he feels is unnecessary: "it's a Caravaggio hanging in the Louvre, that
should be enough in the way of credentials, for heaven's sake") and the phrase "in a heap"
("Surely a single man can't fall into a heap (there's only him, that's not a heap)"). Pullum
concludes (after reading the entire book) that Brown is "one of the worst prose stylists in
the history of literature . . . Brown's writing is not just bad; it is staggeringly, clumsily,
thoughtlessly, almost ingeniously bad."

I've said earlier that I could agree that Dan Brown is a fluent writer of English, though
not that every sentence he writes accords with my sense of what a fluent writer would
produce. So, is he a good writer or not? The problems with Brown's writing that Pullum
identifies strike me as mostly problems of relevance in the Sperber and Wilson sense, and
there is certainly room for debate about them. James Joyce opens his book *Ulysses* with a
construction similar to the one Brown chooses to open *The DaVinci Code*: "Stately,
plump Buck Mulligan came from the stairhead, bearing a bowl of lather on which a
mirror and a razor lay crossed." Is there reason to prefer "Stately, plump Buck Mulligan"
to "Renowned curator Jacques Saunière"? Clearly Joyce's physical descriptors help to
give us a visual image of Buck Mulligan and therefore to advance the narrative. Pullum's
point, in contrast, is that the curricular detail that Saunière was a renowned curator is
entirely incidental to setting the scene of the action. Yes, the reader needs eventually to
learn that Saunière was a renowned curator, but is this the right place to put that information? Consider how different the opening of Joyce's book would be had he cast his
sentence as follows: "Medical student Buck Mulligan came from the stairhead, bearing
a bowl of lather on which a mirror and a razor lay crossed." Well, we'd know that Buck
was a medical student, but how would that help us to understand the scene that con-
fronts us? Is that where we'd want Joyce to present the information about Buck's
occupation? Similarly, does the fact that Saunière was a renowned curator help us to understand his physical distress and his seizing of the Caravaggio? I think we can agree
with Pullum that it doesn't. However, I wouldn't say that this bit of infelicity on
Brown's part by itself makes his writing "staggeringly . . . bad," but an accumulation of

sub-optimal pragmatic decisions like this can surely affect the reader's enjoyment and appreciation of the novel.[4]

Surprise can, of course, be achieved in many different ways, since surprise is merely the expression of the unexpected. J. D. Salinger begins his famous novel *The Catcher in the Rye* in a kind of colloquial, confessional mode:

> (8.4) If you really want to hear about it, the first thing you'll probably want to know is where I was born and what my lousy childhood was like, and how my parents were occupied and all before they had me, and all that David Copperfield kind of crap, but I don't feel like going into it, if you want to know the truth. In the first place, that stuff bores me, and in the second place, my parents would have about two hemorrhages apiece if I told anything pretty personal about them.[5]

Here, the narrator, Holden Caulfield, tells us explicitly what he considers irrelevant to his story, but the way he tells us this is highly relevant to our understanding of his character. The first sentence—"If you really want to hear about it"—is surprising because of what it presumes. To accommodate it, we have to assume that whomever Holden is speaking to or writing for has already expressed an interest in his story. The "really" in this sentence signals a resistance on Holden's part—the "it" is not something he is anxious to tell. This, combined with the colloquialisms ("lousy," "and all," "kind of crap") and exaggerations ("my parents would have about two hemorrhages apiece"), as well as his determination to tell the story on his own definite terms, forcefully implies a charismatic adolescent persona. When Holden says at the end of the first paragraph that "I'll just tell you about this madman stuff that happened to me around last Christmas before I got pretty run-down and had to come out here and take it easy," we get another surprise. The meaning of the challenge in the first sentence now becomes clearer: the addressee is not a family member but someone for whom the information about "this madman stuff" would be most relevant—as most assume, a therapist.

Holden's narrative bears some resemblance to the beginning of Twain's *Adventures of Huckleberry Finn*.

> (8.5) You don't know about me without you have read a book by the name of *The Adventures of Tom Sawyer*; but that ain't no matter. That book was made by Mr. Mark Twain, and he told the truth, mainly. There was things which he stretched, but mainly he told the truth. That is nothing. I never seen anybody but lied one time or another, without it was Aunt Polly, or the widow, or maybe Mary. Aunt Polly—Tom's Aunt Polly, she is—and Mary, and the Widow Douglas is all told about in that book, which is mostly a true book, with some stretchers, as I said before.

As in *The Catcher in the Rye,* Twain's narrator introduces himself by establishing a context for his confession that concedes nothing. What is striking in both books, however, is the dialect chosen for the narration—in Holden Caulfield's case a sort of urban preppy condescension, in Huckleberry Finn's case an uneducated country hick who is wise far beyond his years and circumstances. Both use language that stands out not only for its particularity and peculiarity but also for its directness and incisiveness. The language is the surprise, the hook, that makes us want more.

Both Salinger and Twain deploy a natural narrative voice that achieves a sort of verisimilitude—it seems real enough to us that we don't question its authenticity, despite the fact that it is wholly constructed. And what is constructed is narrative in which the unexpected appears in a context that makes perfect sense. Is it not what makes Shakespeare so consistently exciting?

(8.6) Not poppy, not mandragora,
      Nor all the drowsy syrups of the world,
      Shall ever medicine thee to that sweet sleep
      Which thou ow'dst yesterday.[6]

That stunning language—the "drowsy syrups," the use of "medicine" as a verb—it's no wonder that we look to virtually every sentence Shakespeare ever wrote for a linguistic thrill.

E. B. White's "Once More to the Lake" is perhaps as un-Shakespearian as they come; no fancy language in that piece. But White's language, plain as it is, is so perfectly expressive and evocative as to almost take our breath away. We can feel with White the "restlessness of the tides" and the "fearful cold of the sea water" which make him wish for "the placidity of a lake in the woods."

(5.36) One summer, along about 1904, my father rented a camp on a lake in
      Maine and took us all there for the month of August. We all got ringworm
      from some kittens and had to rub Pond's Extract on our arms and legs
      night and morning, and my father rolled over in a canoe with all his clothes
      on; but outside of that the vacation was a success and from then on none of
      us ever thought there was any place in the world like that lake in Maine.
      We returned summer after summer—always on August 1st for one month.
      I have since become a salt-water man, but sometimes in summer there are
      days when the restlessness of the tides and the fearful cold of the sea water
      and the incessant wind which blows across the afternoon and into the eve-
      ning make me wish for the placidity of a lake in the woods. A few weeks
      ago this feeling got so strong I bought myself a couple of bass hooks and a
      spinner and returned to the lake where we used to go, for a week's fishing
      and to revisit old haunts.

The real surprise in this piece, however, comes at its very end, where White talks about the children, including his son, returning to the water after a thunder shower:

> (8.7) When the others went swimming my son said he was going in too. He pulled his dripping trunks from the line where they had hung all through the shower, and wring them out. Languidly, and with no thought of going in, I watched him, his hard little body, skinny and bare, saw him wince slightly as he pulled up around his vitals the small, soggy, icy garment. As he buckled the swollen belt suddenly my groin felt the chill of death.

White has very subtly foreshadowed this last sentence earlier in the essay, but it still is enormously powerful. There has previously been only one mention of the word "death," and this in the complex construction "deathless." (The boys, swimming in the rain, perpetuate "the deathless joke about how they were getting simply drenched.") That contrast itself serves to emphasize that final word all the more. We've already discussed how White used the Sonata Structure to organize his essay around three themes: time, place, and family. Time runs quickly in this place, and sons become fathers who will inevitably fade away in a cycle from which there is no escape.

In terms of Relevance Theory, something is relevant in context if it has a contextual effect. As indicated earlier, to have a contextual effect in a context is to change that context, that is, to change the common ground or the assumptions about shared information of what is relevant. "So, you see, John has to be the one who murdered Sam and George," appearing at the end of a murder mystery and intoned by the hero-detective, has a very significant contextual effect. A relevant contribution has an especially potent effect when it simultaneously answers many questions or entirely reframes an important idea or theme. Joycean epiphanies, dramatic revelations (Jocasta is Oedipus's mother! Your house is on fire!), and inductive conclusions generally fall into this category.

This doesn't mean that surprise can't in some sense be predictable or foreshadowed. "Chekhov's gun"—the dramatic formula that says that if a gun is shown in the first act, then it must fire in the final act—can still supply surprising effects. It's even quite possible for repeated information to be surprising.

Repetition

The consequential repetition of elements in a written piece attracts our attention—it can be startling when it is unexpected in the normal course of things. Repetition presents us with a kind of pattern. According to the Cognitive Principle of Relevance, we are geared to the maximization of relevance, which means that we are especially sensitive to patterns. It's the recognition of patterns, after all, that keep us alive. When we locate a pattern in a written piece, according to the Communicative Principle of Relevance, we will attribute relevance to that pattern. Thus, when beginning writers repeat words or phrases unintentionally, it usually leads to unhappy results.

But in a master's hands, repetition can contribute importantly to the impact and meaning of a piece. Consider the famous opening of Ernest Hemingway's *A Farewell to Arms:*[7]

> (8.8) In the late summer of that year we lived in a house in a village that looked across the river and the plain to the mountains. In the bed of the river there were pebbles and boulders, dry and white in the sun, and the water was clear and swiftly moving and blue in the channels. Troops went by the house and down the road and the dust they raised powdered the leaves of the trees. The trunks of the trees too were dusty and the leaves fell early that year and we saw the troops marching along the road and the dust rising and leaves, stirred by the breeze, falling and the soldiers marching and afterwards the road bare and white except for the leaves.

The repetitions here—of words ("house," "river," "white," "road," "troops," "dust," "leaves," "trees", "marching"), and of constructions (noun-phrase, verb-phrase, and sentential conjunction involving "and," the noun phrase with the definite article "the")—lend a seductive rhythm to the paragraph. That rhythm almost obscures the startling fact that the paragraph is about troop movements prior to a military engagement. The piece begins languorously, and the troops, who cause the dust to rise, appear almost as part of the natural environment of the pebbles and boulders and trees around the house. This backgrounding of the war—at the same time as the foreground is populated with leaves and breezes and dust—surprises, but with a beguiling subtlety.

All consequential repetitions attract attention, but not all consequential repetitions surprise. Here is the beginning of Tom Wolfe's "Las Vegas (What?) Las Vegas (Can't hear you! Too noisy) Las Vegas!!!!" again:

> (1.1) Hernia, hernia, hernia, hernia, hernia, hernia, hernia, hernia, hernia, hernia, hernia, hernia, hernia, HERNia; hernia, HERNia, hernia, hernia, hernia, hernia, HERNia, HERNia, HERNia; hernia, hernia, hernia, hernia, hernia, hernia, hernia, eight is the point, the point is eight; hernia, hernia, HERNia; hernia, hernia, hernia, hernia, all right, hernia, hernia, hernia, hernia, hard eight, hernia, hernia, hernia, HERNia, hernia, hernia, hernia, HERNia, hernia, hernia, hernia, HERNia, hernia, hernia, hernia, hernia.

What impresses us is the fact of the repetition of "hernia" rather than any meaning attached to the word itself. The precise number of repetitions is also irrelevant, as is the variation in emphasis indicated in capitals and the insertion of references to "eight." When we learn in the following paragraphs that the person uttering this improbable sentence is playing craps at a Las Vegas gambling house and his vocalizations apparently constitute an irritating nervous tic as he tries to will the dice in his favor, we begin to get a vivid picture of him. That is the precise point—and, in fact, an effective one—of the repetition.

Wolfe plays with repetition in a slightly different way in "The Last American Hero":

(8.9)   Ten o'clock Sunday morning in the hills of North Carolina. Cars, miles of cars in every direction, millions of cars, pastel cars, aqua green, aqua blue, aqua beige, aqua buff, aqua dawn, aqua Malacca, Malacca lacquer, Cloud lavender, Assassin pink, Rake-a-Cheek raspberry, Nude Strand coral, Honest Thrill orange, and Baby Fawn Lust cream-colored cars are all going to the stock car races, and that old mothering North Carolina sun keeps exploding off the windshields.[8]

The different colors are part of a list here, with each color perhaps irrelevant in itself. But what is relevant is the subtle distinctions between the various pastel colors, as indicated by their names. That's what we're meant to pay attention to. We don't have to know what colors "aqua buff" and "Rake-a-Cheek" raspberry actually refer to. What we need to know, and what the sentence nicely conveys, is that we are at a place where some people take these distinctions very seriously.

The mere fact of repetition can sometimes be swallowed in convention:

(8.10)   "Hello, Tom" said Sam.
         "Hello, Sam," said Tom.

We don't draw any conclusions beyond the idea that this is exactly what happened. But consider a paragraph like (8.11):

(8.11)   I am particularly fond of cherries. You might wonder why, particularly. I'd say that it is particularly because when I was a child, we had a particular cherry tree in our garden that we used to gather cherries from in the late spring. They were a particular favorite in our family.

Is there any point to the repetition of the stem "particular" here? As readers, we search for relevance. Finding none, we move on.

In George Orwell's great essay, "Shooting an Elephant," the narrator tells of the instant of the shooting:

(8.12)   When I pulled the trigger I did not hear the bang or feel the kick—one never does when a shot goes home—but I heard the devilish roar of glee that went up from the crowd. In that instant, in too short a time, one would have thought, even for the bullet to get there, a mysterious, terrible change had come over the elephant. He neither stirred nor fell, but every line of his body had altered. He looked suddenly stricken, shrunken, immensely old, as though the frightful impact of the bullet had paralysed him without knocking him down. At last, after what seemed a long time— it might have been five seconds, I dare say—he sagged flabbily to his knees. His mouth slobbered. An enormous senility seemed to have settled upon him. One could have imagined him thousands of years old. I fired again into the same spot. At the second shot he did not collapse but climbed with desperate slowness to his feet and stood weakly upright, with legs sagging and head drooping. I fired a third time. That was the shot that did for him. You could see the agony of it jolt his whole body and knock the last remnant of strength from his legs. But in falling he seemed for a moment to rise, for as his hind legs collapsed beneath him he seemed to tower upward like a huge rock toppling, his trunk reaching skyward like a tree. He trumpeted, for the first and only time. And then down he came, his belly towards me, with a crash that seemed to shake the ground even where I lay.[9]

Here I'm interested in the lines: "He looked suddenly stricken, shrunken, immensely old . . . he sagged flabbily to his knees. His mouth slobbered. An enormous senility seemed to have settled upon him." All those sibilants! The onomatopoetic alliteration evokes the *sssss!* sound of air being let from a balloon. When the narrator fires for the third time, the sounds become percussive, plosive, and finally velar, the death cough: "the shot that did for him. You could see the agony of it jolt his whole body and knock the last remnant from his legs." The elephant "collapse[s]," "like a huge rock toppling . . . with a crash."

This kind of alliteration is, of course, unremarkable—even expected—in poetry, but it obviously has a significant role to play in literary prose as well.

E. B. White, in "Potter's Field," uses repetition to much different effect:

(8.13) New York's pauper dead are buried in a sandy hill on the north end of Hart's Island in Long Island Sound, a mile from Execution Light. They lie in big graves, tier on tier, unclaimed. It was blowy the day we went out there to see the field, and the low storm-swept island looked particularly weather-beaten. Michael Breen, warden of the island prison, met us, smiling broadly, glad of a visitor.

Twice a week the boat comes up from Bellevue. The prisoners bury the dead, solemnly and without ceremony, one hundred and fifty to a grave, one white headstone for the lot. It is a beautiful spot—the seep of the Sound, the restless clang of the bell buoy at the point. An incongruous spot, too, for directly across the water are the homes of the millionaires. Hearst's place on Sands Point, the broad lawns and grandeur of Great Neck.[10]

White does something quite extraordinary here with an ordinary construction—he takes a sentence and then extends it by pasting a modifier or an appositive onto the end. And does it time and again. The last two sentences are not sentences at all but fragments that mimic this process. There are two sentences that are not extended, the third sentence of the first paragraph and the first sentence of the second paragraph. Two extended sentences precede the first unextended sentence, and one separates it from the second unextended sentence, which is in turn followed by two extended sentences (assuming the fragments to be extensions of the sentence that precedes them). It's a nice symmetry. The effect is of a fully descriptive conciseness—we are getting all the description we need, though White is parsimonious with his words. Each extension gives us a bit more—not too much, just what we need.

Sometimes authors combine both repetition and surprise. You might think this contradictory, since repetition by definition is a presentation of information that has been presented before, but because the recognition of pattern brings with it its own surprise, the effect is doubled. We all know the "Song of Hiawatha," by Longfellow:

(8.14) By the shores of Gitche Gumee,
       By the shining Big-Sea-Water,
       Stood the wigwam of Nokomis,
       Daughter of the Moon, Nokomis.
       Dark behind it rose the forest,
       Rose the black and gloomy pine-trees,
       Rose the firs with cones upon them;
       Bright before it beat the water,
       Beat the clear and sunny water,
       Beat the shining Big-Sea-Water.

The prosodic meter here (trochaic tetrameter) has been associated with many things, including drumbeats, Finnish poetry, the rhythm of a rant, pidgin English; but because it defies the standard iambic flow of English, it is surprising. (To achieve this affect, note how Longfellow begins each line with a verb, bare noun, predicate adjective, or preposition, each able to bear primary stress.) The point is that the pattern draws attention to itself, and what we make of that pattern is not necessarily explicit in the text.

The long, single sentence that opens Jane Austen's *Persuasion* is also instructive for its combination of surprise and repetition:

(8.15) Sir Walter Elliot, of Kellynch-hall, in Somersetshire, was a man who, for his own amusement, never took up any book but the Baronetage; there he found occupation for an idle hour, and consolation in a distressed one; there his faculties were roused into admiration and respect, by contemplating the limited remnant of the earliest patents; there any unwelcome sensations, arising from domestic affairs, changed naturally into pity and contempt, as he turned over the almost endless creations of the last century—and there, if every other leaf were powerless, he could read his own history with an interest which never failed—this was the page at which the favourite volume always opened: "ELLIOT OF KELLYNCH-HALL."

So easy are the repetitions of the preposed adverbial there-construction that we almost overlook the repetitions inside them—the "occupation"/"consolation" and "sensations"/"creations" pairs, the sound of "limited remnant of the earliest patents," and of course the whole, beginning and ending with "Elliott of Kellynch-hall." The first main surprise is not that he read the Baronetage, but that he never read any other book but that. And the second is that, in that book, what he most liked to read was the passage about himself. Both are ironic and begin to sketch a recognizable caricature of the man. Yet I think what to me presents itself as the greatest surprise is simply the language, phrase after phrase of unexpected combinations of words—faculties being "roused into admiration and respect," "unwelcome sensations arising from domestic affairs changed naturally into pity and contempt," an interest in his own history "which never failed." In this respect I find in Austen what I enjoy so much in a number of the authors we've surveyed in this chapter: there is an especially high proportion of unexpected ways of looking at common things, of uncommon insights into human behavior, in most of what they wrote. And, what is so maddening about it, they seemed able to create this kind of work almost effortlessly. In the domain of speech, we are familiar with people (sportscasters, preachers, politicians) who are naturally glib, articulate, perhaps even eloquent, people who seem to be able to find their words and string them together rapidly and with surprising ease. They contrast with the rest of us who hesitate, pepper our speech with "um"s and "uh"s, and rarely think of the right thing to say before the occasion has passed. Are such individual differences, in speech as well as in writing, the result of nature or nurture? I don't know, but I don't think it matters to our question about what good writing is. It does matter, of course, to those who have to struggle to produce good writing. Still, there have been some great writers, such as E. B. White, for whom writing was apparently an extremely arduous adventure but who nonetheless consistently produced a highly engaging and polished product.

Complexity Yet Again

As mentioned earlier, readers—especially novice readers—are often tempted to associate the difficulty of a text with quality. Since Shakespeare, Milton, Johnson, Melville, James, Woolf, Joyce, and so on are considered both difficult and good writers, one might think that perhaps writing material that is difficult to interpret is the key to being good. We saw in chapter 4 that this is not and cannot be the case.

In her book, *Why We Read Fiction*, Lisa Zunshine usefully brings some concepts from cognitive science to bear on literary analysis, locating aspects of literary complexity in what we think about what others think—in other words, "mind reading," as discussed in chapter 4. She is especially interested in what philosophers call intentionality, which is roughly the forming of a mental attitude toward a proposition. For example, the sentence "John believes that Mary is pregnant" indicates that John has formed a certain mental attitude (belief) toward the proposition that Mary is pregnant. Things do get complicated when the proposition in question itself encodes an intention, as in the sentence "John thinks that Alice believes that Mary is pregnant." Such cases include what some have called "recursive mind reading," which occurs when two or more people try to figure out each other's intentions. We saw an example of this in the scene from the movie *The Princess Bride* involving the Man in Black and Vizzini, where the latter tried to figure out what the former thought that he (Vizzini) thought that the other thought, and so on. The more embedded and recursive the mind reading is, the more complex it becomes. Zunshine sees six levels of intentional embedding in the following paragraph from Virginia Woolf's *Mrs. Dalloway*:

> (8.16) And Miss Brush went out, came back; laid papers on the table; and Hugh produced his fountain pen; his silver fountain pen, which had done twenty years service, he said, unscrewing the cap. It was still in perfect order; he had shown it to the makers; there was no reason, they said, why it should ever wear out; which was somehow to Hugh's credit, and to the credit of the sentiments which his pen expressed (so Richard Dalloway felt) as Hugh began carefully writing capital letters with rings round them in the margin, and thus marvelously reduced Lady Brunton's tangles to sense, to grammar such as the editor of the *Times*, Lady Brunton felt, watching the marvelous transformation, must respect.

In this scene, four named characters have gathered in a room in an elegant home in London: Lady Millicent Brunton (whose home it is), Miss Brush (who is Lady Brunton's secretary), and Lady Brunton's good friends Richard Dalloway and Hugh Whitbread. Lady Brunton had drafted a letter to the editor of the *Times* and had asked Richard and Hugh to help her with it. The passage in (8.16) describes what ensues.

Zunshine ascribes the difficulty of this paragraph to the multiple levels of intentional embedding she sees in it. On the first level, Zunshine suggests, is the proposition that the makers of the pen think it will never wear out. The second level, she says, constitutes Hugh's saying that the makers of the pen say that it will never wear out.[11] Skipping up to the fourth level, Zunshine posits that Hugh desires that Lady Brunton and Richard believe that, because the makers of the pen think that it will never wear out, the editor of the *Times* will publish the sentiments expressed by the pen. At the fifth level, she says, Richard is aware that Hugh wants Lady Brunton and Richard to believe that, because the makers of the pen say that it will never wear out, the editor of the *Times* will publish the sentiments expressed by the pen. Then, finally at the sixth level, Zunshine proposes that the author Virginia Woolf intends that we recognize that Richard is aware that Hugh wants Lady Brunton and Richard to believe that because the makers of the pen believe that it well never wear out, the *Times* editor will publish the sentiments expressed by the pen.

This is indeed dizzying, in the words of the Man in Black in *The Princess Bride*. Or it would be, if correct. But I believe that Zunshine has overinterpreted the passage from *Mrs. Dalloway*. Consider what is public knowledge (part of the common ground) for the four characters in this scene, simply because they are there and can observe what each other is doing:

(8.17i)   Miss Brush went out, came back, laid papers on the table

(8.17ii)   Hugh produced his silver fountain pen

(8.17iii)   Hugh unscrewed the cap

(8.17iv)   (Hugh) said: "[his silver fountain pen] had done twenty years service"

(8.17v)   "it was still in perfect order"

(8.17vi)   "he had shown it to the makers"

(8.17vii)   "they [the makers] said: 'there was no reason why it should ever wear out'"

At this point, everyone in the room is aware of all the facts in (8.17). The reader is aware of them, too, being privileged to view the scene from Woolf's omniscient viewpoint. No mind reading is necessary to derive any of these facts.

Now Woolf adds the relative clause in (8.18) to Hugh's reporting that the makers of the pen said there was no reason why it should ever wear out:

(8.18)   which was somehow to Hugh's credit, and to the credit of the sentiments which his pen expressed (so Richard Dalloway felt)

Woolf doesn't explicitly indicate whether only Richard Dalloway had formed a mental attitude (feeling) toward the proposition that this was to Hugh's credit or whether all in the room had: either reading is possible. However, she does make clear, at least, that Richard Dalloway had formed a mental attitude (feeling) toward the proposition that this was to the credit of the sentiments the pen expressed. It is also possible (and I think the "somehow" in the first conjunct and the comma after "Hugh's credit" recommend this) that Woolf is indicating that the three other people in the room understood that Hugh felt that his pen's longevity was to his own credit. But this would require only a single level of mind reading on their part.

Woolf next offers another piece of information that would be in the common ground, since, presumably, everyone in the room could see what Hugh was doing:

(8.19)   Hugh began writing capital letters with rings around them in the margin

Following this, Woolf adds an unattributed proposition:

(8.20) [the way that Hugh] reduced Lady Brunton's tangles to sense [was marvelous]

Woolf doesn't indicate who marveled at Hugh's writing. Perhaps everyone in the room did, or perhaps only Richard or Lady Brunton did, depending on how widely the scope of the phrase in "Lady Brunton felt" in (8.21) is interpreted.

(8.21) to grammar such as the editor of the *Times*, Lady Brunton felt, watching the marvelous transformation, must respect

Or, it could simply be Woolf's own description of Hugh's act, not necessarily shared by anyone in the room. Naturally, the fact that Lady Brunton was watching the transformation was in the common ground, but evidently only she felt that the editor of the *Times* must necessarily respect what Hugh has done. Again, only one level of mind reading would be involved if all in the room deduced that Lady Brunton felt this way.

Zunshine's suggestion that Woolf's intention that we readers recognize Richard's intentions also causes me problems. When Woolf, as an omniscient and reliable narrator, describes the thoughts of her characters, she isn't mind reading. Consider the following dialogue:

(8.22) Virginia Woolf: "Elizabeth knew that her mother was resting."
You: *No, Elizabeth didn't know that.

It would be distinctly odd for you to say that, because here we actually do know that Elizabeth knew her mother was resting simply because Woolf tells us so. That's the convention that's operative when we read the novel. That is, the omniscient, reliable narrator doesn't need to deduce from a character's overt behavior what he or she is thinking: the omniscient, reliable narrator knows it as if the thoughts were on a par with observed behavior. Woolf doesn't explicitly say what other mental attitudes Elizabeth had toward the fact that her mother was resting. We may conjecture that it pleased her or irritated her or that she was indifferent to it based upon what Woolf has told us (i.e., based upon what is in our common ground with Woolf). When the author isn't entirely clear, we make our own judgment. But that isn't mind reading, strictly speaking. By the time the reader of *Mrs. Dalloway* reaches the passage in (8.16), Woolf has said already that "Richard was nearly driven mad by [Hugh]" and later in the novel she will have Richard call Hugh "an intolerable ass." But Woolf leaves us to interpret what additional mental attitudes Richard may have formed at that specific point after he "felt" that Hugh's remark redounded to the credit of the sentiments expressed by the pen. We can infer, as Zunshine does, that Woolf intends her readers to recognize that Richard is unimpressed by

Hugh's comments about his pen. However, this is not part of the linguistic meaning of the sentences that Woolf wrote, and the reader does not have to deal with many levels of embedded intentionality to understand that meaning.

But if it's not depth of intentional embedding that is the cause of the difficulty in Woolf, what is? I would argue that what makes Woolf's writing difficult is the burden placed on the reader by three different rhetorical strategies she employs. The first, which is evident in (8.16), consists of providing considerable detail while withholding explicit information that would precisely clarify the context in which the detail appears. I noted earlier that (8.16) doesn't say who marveled at Hugh's writing and is ambiguous as to whether only Richard felt that the longevity of the pen somehow redounded to Hugh's credit. She leaves us to guess what the nature of Richard's feelings was about Hugh's actions in this scene. This is a situation where mind reading is incapable of informing us as readers what a particular fictional character is thinking, or even what the author intends us to infer about that character's thoughts.

The second rhetorical strategy is to require the reader to actively accommodate in order to understand the linguistic meaning of the sentences. We met with accommodation in chapters 4 and 5 (in the latter case, in relation to another of Woolf's novels, *To the Lighthouse*):

(5.20) "Yes, of course, if it's fine tomorrow," said Mrs. Ramsay. "But you'll have to be up with the lark," she added.

To her son these words conveyed an extraordinary joy, as if it were settled, the expedition were bound to take place, and the wonder to which he had looked forward, for years and years it seemed, was, after a night's darkness and a day's sail, within touch. Since he belonged, even at the age of six, to that great clan which cannot keep this feeling separate from that, but must let future prospects, with their joys and sorrows, cloud what is actually at hand, since to such people even in earliest childhood any turn in the wheel of sensation has the power to crystallize and transfix the moment upon which its gloom or radiance rests, James Ramsey, sitting on the floor cutting out pictures from the illustrated catalogue of the Army and Navy Stores, endowed the picture of a refrigerator, as his mother spoke, with heavenly bliss.

I pointed out in chapter 5 that it takes a minimum of seven logical steps to accommodate the first sentence and twelve logical steps to accommodate the fourth sentence from an arbitrary sentence in the inactive common ground. This is pragmatic complexity of a high order.

The third strategy involves constructional complexity. In (5.20), subordinate clauses, adverbial phrases, and multiple conjunctions abound. The burden placed on the reader's syntactic interpreter by sentences of these sorts is well known to be considerable.[12] The more facility a reader has with the constructions at play, the less the burden, although some of the elaborately constructed sentences in Henry James's late novels, for example, can tax even the most experienced and sophisticated reader.

What is interesting from my perspective is the tension between the writing instructor's call for simplicity and clarity, on the one hand, and the literary critic's admiration for the kind of multidimensional complexity evidenced in the work of Virginia Woolf and Henry James (among many others). The obvious point is that in the case of Woolf and James the effort one has to expend to understand the difficult passages should in the end be rewarded, because the logic is solid. But if accommodation fails, if vagueness and ambiguity prevent the inference of the logical steps required to make sense of the passages, then we begin to find them irrelevant. This is, of course, where the composition studies scholar will want to invoke audience: If the writer is not writing for fans of Woolf and James, then the admonition to keep it simple applies. But I think this is too sweeping, because complexity is, well, complex. A child can handle and delight in multiply embedded subordinate constructions (as in the nursery rhyme "The House that Jack Built"). Complexity and clarity aren't mutually exclusive, and simplicity doesn't necessarily mean clarity (think of the sentences "All men are created equal" and "In the beginning, God created the heaven and the earth"). Moreover, in dealing with information that we don't understand, a natural inclination is to ignore it and focus on what we more easily comprehend.[13]

A focus on audience rather than relevance is also not ideal because it may be understood by the writer to shift the communicative burden qua conversation entirely onto his or her shoulders. The important question is: In consequence of your reading this far, what written conversations are you, the writer, inspired to want to participate in? Not inspired to join any conversations? Don't have anything to say? Then surely the prescription is to read more widely.

Relevance Theory as applied in this book does not directly account for all of the constructional, pragmatic, narrative, and conventional rules found in writing handbooks, but what it does cover is sufficient to explain the quality of writing found in fluent writers. The human capacity for language in all its beautiful and intricate complexity derives phylogenetically from the development of neural machinery to accommodate the drive to communicate, to participate in discourse. To become fluent, one only has to exploit that natural capacity.

9

Verbal Art and Craft

"YES, BUT IS it art?"

In the prologue, I briefly introduced the distinction between art and craft, and it's now time to take up that topic again. Everyone is entitled to an opinion, but in the university, the old question about whether something is art or not is usually reserved for professional critics and philosophers of aesthetics to answer. Within the boundaries of our topic, however, we can perhaps not only contribute to the academic discussion but also shed some light on it for non-academics by drawing attention to the variety of materials the artist has to work with—which, in the case of literature, includes all aspects of the relationship between form and content.

The study of the relationship between form and content as a vital component of literary art extends back more than two millennia, but in the modern context the revival of the inquiry is most closely associated with the Russian Formalists and members of the Prague School of Linguistics in the first half of the twentieth century and, in particular, with the work of the Russian-American linguist Roman Jakobson. A relatively new strain of work by literary critics and theorists is gaining adherents who follow rhetoric into the domain of the cognitive sciences, which (they hope) will enable them to pick out insights about cognition that can inform literary studies.[1] I'm all for this, but one of the most interesting analyses of verbal art that I know of doesn't fall neatly into any of these camps. John Robert Ross is a linguist who has done work on formal syntax, semantics, pragmatics, and poetics, and his exemplary article "Fog Cat Fog" nicely shows how much goes into—or, at any rate, can be gotten out of—even a very brief poem.[2]

I want to take the reader through Ross's article because it is so instructive about formal aspects of art in writing. Ross begins with a quotation from William Blake: "As Poetry admits not a Letter that is Insignificant, so Painting admits not a Grain of Sand or a Blade of Grass Insignificant—much less an Insignificant Blur or Mark." This he slightly recasts as a musical metaphor about poetry alone:

(10.1)   The Assumption of Total Significance (ATS)
In the musical fabric of a poem, every sound has its importance, its very own part in the melody of the poem as a whole.

It's crucial to understand that Ross is considering a poem (though it could be any type of careful writing, actually) as a physical object identifiable by the pattern of sounds that present themselves in vocal or mental recitation. You'll recall that we earlier defined a linguistic construction as a pairing of sound and sense, so in general the sounds of language can't, on our understanding, be completely pried away from their meanings. But the sounds that Ross is focusing on are often not constructions themselves, but elements or parts of constructions.

What Ross is interested in is applying the ATS to Carl Sandberg's "Fog," which we met with in chapter 7.

(7.3)   Fog
The fog comes
on little cat feet.
It sits looking
over harbor and city
on silent haunches
and then moves on.

Ross initiates the exercise by dissecting the sounds in the title, "Fog," which is pronounced with an initial fricative "f" (a consonant produced with a constant stream of air through a constricted space in the mouth; other fricatives include the "s" in "sun" and the "sh" in "shun"); and then the long vowel "o", pronounced as in the word "pod" or the word "awe" (depending on your dialect); and finally the voiced stop "g", which is a consonant produced by stopping the air stream near the back of the tongue. So: three sounds, a fricative followed by a long vowel followed by a stop.

Next Ross observes that the poem contains three clauses distributed among two sentences—the first sentence is a simple one consisting of a single clause and the second sentence consists of two clauses. Each of the three clauses is defined by a verb that carries a present tense marker: (1) "The fog *comes* / on little cat feet"; (2) "It *sits* looking / over harbor and city / on silent haunches"; (3) "and then *moves* on." The duration of the actions denoted by the verbs corresponds to the number of lines in the clauses containing the verbs:

Arrival of fog	State of being fogged in	Departure of fog
(2 lines)	(3 lines)	(1 line)
Medium duration	Longest duration	Shortest duration

The durations of the actions and the number of lines also corresponds, subjectively, to the length of the sounds in the title: the "f" is of medium duration, the "o" is of the longest duration, and the "g" is of the shortest duration. This is an interesting symmetry. Coincidence? Perhaps, but read on.

The medium-long-short pattern isn't the only one in evidence in the poem. Ross also points out that there is an ABA pattern, which we've hitherto identified as Sonata Structure. For example, the word "fog" is composed of a consonant followed by a vowel followed by a consonant, as is the word "cat." The finite verbs "comes," "sits," and "moves" denote motion, duration, and motion, respectively. There is also an ABABAB pattern— the even lines comprise three words each and the odd lines four words, making three couplets.

Perhaps more significantly, Ross finds a number of chiasms, or crossings, in the poem. First, the bisyllabic words come in alliterative pairs (little-looking, harbor-haunches, city-silent):

The fog comes

on little cat feet.

It sits looking

over harbor and city

on silent haunches

and then moves on.

Looking now at all the alliterations, Ross identifies further chiasms (fog-feet, comes-cat, little-it, sits-city):

The fog comes

on little cat feet.

It sits looking

over harbor and city

on silent haunches

and then moves on.

These chiasms emphasize the equivalence and comingling of the denotations of "cat" and "fog." Ignoring the inconsequential repetition of "on" in lines 5 and 6, we can see that all the alliterative chiasms occur in the first five lines: there is none in the last, signaling that the cat/fog is gone.

There are still more patterns. The first line and the last line each include a reversal, "fog comes" and "moves on." In the first case there is a fricative followed by a vowel followed by a stop ("fog") and this in turn precedes a stop followed by a vowel followed by a fricative ("comes"). The pattern is reversed in the final line: there is a (nasal) stop followed by a vowel followed by a fricative, which precedes a fricative followed by a vowel followed by a (nasal) stop.

Considering only the obstruents (that is, fricatives and stops), Ross notes that each line except the last contains five of them, with the first, third, and last being of the same type. (The pronunciation of "and then" is usually realized as "an' then"; hence there is no discrete "d" in the last line.)

The fog comes	th f g k z	(voiced/unvoiced)
on little cat feet.	t k t f t	(t/voiceless obstruent)
It sits looking	t s t s k	(voiceless stop/s)
over harbor and city	v h b s t	(other/voiceless fric)
on silent haunches	s t h ch z	(fricative/stop)
and then moves on.	th Ø v Øz	(voiced/unvoiced)

Admittedly, the pattern in the fourth line is not quite as striking as the patterns in the other lines, but there is an obvious harmony going on here.

OK, then, are all these patterns coincidental, a figment of Ross's imagination? I am persuaded by Ross that they're not. There are rather too many of them to be mere angels dancing on the head of a pin. If you're still not convinced, Ross offers the following. Suppose that, instead of "on little cat feet," Sandburg had written "on little cat paws," or "on small cat feet." This would destroy a number of the symmetries that Ross found, though the meaning wouldn't be much changed. If you think the quality of the poem would be unchanged with this substitution, then you perhaps wouldn't see "on little cat feet" as inevitable in context as Ross does. But if you agree that "on little cat paws" would destroy the beauty of the poem, then it would be difficult for you to argue that the patterns Ross has discovered don't play a significant role in its success. In fact, in older age, after having been asked to read "Fog" aloud to an audience innumerable times, Sandburg himself would wryly amuse them (and himself) by reciting his famous poem with changed words: "The fog comes on itti bitti kitty footsies. / He sits down on Chicago and—whamo—he's gone."[3] There can be little doubt that, to him, this changed version had an air of the ridiculous about it.

You might ask whether Sandburg had all of Ross's patterns consciously in mind when he wrote the poem. Who's to know?—but I'd guess not. I assume it was his instinct as a poet that guided him. He knew instinctively what was right, and in order to be right it had to be what it was. This brings us, in a roundabout way, back to the question of the role of the author's intention in the interpretation of a work. While my focus has been on writing, since I have advanced reading as the proximate step in acquiring writing fluency, the role of intentionality inevitably arises.

There has been much debate in literary, linguistic, and philosophical circles about intentionality.[4] It isn't my intention to joust with this literature here. However, it is important to provide at least a little context for the Sperber and Wilson Theory of Relevance. Recall the two principles that constitute this theory:

(4.16i)   The Cognitive Principle of Relevance: Human cognition tends to be geared to the maximization of relevance.

(4.16ii)   The Communicative Principle of Relevance: Every ostensive stimulus conveys a presumption of its own optimal relevance.

Together, these principles imply that every act of communication (as an "ostensive stimulus") is intended to be relevant to its audience. Well, we can be pretty certain that Sandburg intended "Fog" to be relevant to some audience, else why would he have bothered to publish it? There is also no doubt that the patterns that Ross found in "Fog" are really there, independently of whatever Sandburg intended. The question then is whether we can fill the gap by insisting that what we are saying are Sandburg's instincts count as his intentions.

If we say that no, they can't count as his intentions (because, ultimately, we can't know what was in his mind about them, if anything), then we will find ourselves snagged on the word "optimal" in Sperber and Wilson's Communicative Principle, if we believe that those patterns are contributory to the poem's optimal relevance (its beauty and significance for us), as I have been assuming (via the operation of inference). If we say that yes, the patterns were intended (even if subconsciously), then what is to prevent us from concluding that anything we find in a poem that contributes to its optimal relevance for us must have been intended? And this would put us on the slippery slope leading to the odd judgment that Keats actually had in mind one of our very own past loves when he wrote "La belle dame sans merci," despite the fact that he was born two hundred years before us.

However, we can, without contradiction, amend our conclusion to read that anything formal (i.e., the result of the operation of constructional combination) that we find in a poem that contributes to its optimal relevance for us must have been intended, even if instinctively or subconsciously, because being fluent in a language means knowing how the elements of language are put together to create sentences of that language. The patterns in "Fog," as well as the constructional structure of its elements, are formal and relevant, hence—according to this argument—intended. This comports with Relevance Theory and gets us off the slippery slope. Further, it is generally agreed that we humans all use the principles of Relevance Theory as a heuristic, an interpretive strategy, one without which we could not communicate as we do. But we also know that this heuristic does not always work, as when we misinterpret another's intentions.

With this in mind, I'd like to direct the reader's attention to the beginning of an article by the poet Adrienne Rich:

(10.2)   About the time my third child was born, I felt that I had either to consider myself a failed woman and a failed poet, or try to find some synthesis by which to understand what was happening to me. What frightened me most was the sense of drift, of being pulled along on a current which called itself my destiny, but in which I seemed to be losing touch with whoever I had been, with the girl who had experienced her own will and energy almost ecstatically at times, walking around a city or riding a train at night or typing in a student room.[5]

In this paragraph there are two sentences, and in each there are instances of a pattern Ross would call a "twoing" or "doubling." A pattern containing two elements (say, "meat and potatoes") is a twoing. A pattern containing three elements ("meat, potatoes, and broccoli") would be a threeing. The twoings in the first sentence are (i) "a failed woman" and "a failed poet" and (ii) "either to consider myself a failed woman and a failed poet" and "try to find some synthesis. . . ." In the second sentence, the twoings are (iii) "of drift" and "of being pulled . . ."; (iv) "which called itself . . ." and "in which I seemed . . ."; (v) "with whoever . . ." and "with the girl . . ."; and (vi) "will" and "energy." Rich ends the second sentence (and the paragraph) with a threeing: "walking . . .," "or riding . . .," "or typing. . . ." So we have two sentences with two twoings in the first and double that—four twoings—in the second. The only threeing, which breaks the pattern and therefore draws attention to the activities that made the author happy at an earlier time, ends the paragraph.

Looking at repetitions and alliterations, we have the "f"s of the first sentence, which figure in "felt" and "find" as well as in the two instances of "failed." We also have three "w"s—"which," "what," and "was"—at the end of the first sentence. The second sentence begins with the "w" in "What" followed by the "f" in "frightened." Now something interesting is happening here. That "f" of "frightened" is the last initial alliteration of "f" in the paragraph. It harmonizes with the four instances of "f"-alliteration in the first sentence and then, after the second word of the second sentence, the pattern is dropped. However, we have five instances of verbs with the progressive "–ing" ending in this second sentence, harmonizing with the single instance (in "happening") in the first sentence. Thus, we have a kind of chiasm going on with the "f"s and the "–ings" between the two sentences, with six more instances of "w"-alliteration occurring in the second sentence. All of this serves to bind the two sentences together neatly.

Consider now the tense, aspect, and voice structure of the verbs in the paragraph. Here follows a list of the verbs, each along with its grammatical tense, aspect, and voice. (Where the aspect and/or voice is the default value—non-progressive for aspect and active for voice I have left the space blank.)

Verb	Tense	Aspect	Voice
was born	Past		Passive
felt	Simple Past		
had	Simple Past		
to consider	Infinitive		
try	Infinitive		
to find	Infinitive		
to understand	Infinitive		
was happening	Past	Progressive	
frightened	Simple Past		
was	Simple Past		
called	Simple Past		
seemed	Simple Past		
to be losing	Infinitive	Progressive	
had been	Past Perfect		
had experienced	Past Perfect		
walking	Present Participle		
riding	Present Participle		
typing	Present Participle		

If you look at the list under "Tense," you should see a distinct pattern. The first sentence begins and ends with a marked verb (roughly, as here, a verb whose form requires two or more different degrees of description, such as past tense and progressive aspect, or past tense and passive voice). In between, there are two simple pasts and four simple infinitives, echoing the 2-4 distribution we found with the twoings. In the second sentence there are four simple pasts separated from two past perfects by another marked verb (an infinitive in the present progressive), and finally the three participles that end the paragraph. The symmetry is quite striking and unquestionably adds to the poetic effect of the writing. Whether Rich consciously intended to arrange her verbs in such a way is anyone's guess, but I don't doubt that, as a poet, she had an instinctual feel for such patterns.

I wouldn't want to suggest that the patterns here are symbolic of anything. They function to provide a rhythm, one which is reinforced and then broken with the emphatic final threeing. What is important is how the paragraph works—it flows nicely as a result of the author's word and construction choices. The contrast between the two periods of her life—one happy, one not so—is cleverly drawn.

So, is this an example of good writing? Yes, obviously, even if the grammar handbooks would fault it for the lack of infinitival parallelism in the first sentence.

To my mind, it is also literary art, or literature, which I think amounts to the same thing. What makes it art for me is not simply that it displays superfluency. One can be superfluent without, so to speak, plumbing the depths. This is probably what those who distinguish belles-lettres from literature have in mind. And it is almost certainly what Updike was talking about in his criticism of Tom Wolfe (whose novel, according to Updike, "amounts to entertainment, not literature, even literature in a modest aspirant form"), which we discussed in the prologue. In fact, my definition of fluency sets the bar separating those who write with craft from everyone else even lower: I would urge that journalists who report well (if not profoundly) display craft, even if they will never write as well as either Tom Wolfe or John Updike.

Nor is the piece from which I extracted Rich's paragraph art beyond craft just because it is shot through with formal technique (though that is important). It's true that the more in the way of formal technique I find, the more I am tempted to say that what I have before me is art. But there is literary art that makes no use of alliteration, twoings, threeings, and so forth, just as there are great paintings that make no use of chiaroscuro, perspective, etc. I suppose that what clinches the case for me that Rich's piece is art has a good deal to do with what Rich is aspiring to—it's an "aspirant" form of superfluent writing, to use Updike's word: Rich obviously aspires to contribute to an existing literature of autobiography, revelation, and social argument. Keats, I believe, called this willingness to engage with the profoundest of human thought "intensity." This, too, can be seen to devolve to relevance at its most subjective, and should therefore be fair game for the person who takes the Constructionist perspective.

I would leave this discussion of the difference between art and craft with this thought. Although for professional purposes we may want to look to critics and philosophers to tell us how to decide what art is, the word "art," like any other word, is defined by the collection of the judgments of all English speakers about what it means. And like any abstract concept, there is considerable difference of opinion about what that is. Insofar as it is possible to determine the market value of the objects produced by a craftsperson over the span of his or her lifetime, you can roughly judge the size of the audience that might just consider that person an artist, on the common understanding. It's likely that, by this crude criterion and at this time, Dan Brown would come out considerably ahead of Tom Wolfe and John Updike, with Adrienne Rich nowhere in the picture. But *de gustibus non est disputandum*—there's no disputing tastes—as the Romans used to say, and fifty years from now the tables might be entirely turned. You never know.

Conclusion

FOR THE NORMAL college composition student whose writing is significantly deficient (however assessed), no current writing program can match the potential of an intensive reading program. Anyone who wants to become a fluent writer and who isn't one now must read avidly and independently. This isn't to say that writing programs can't be useful for other reasons, such as nurturing inchoate motivations and providing direction and feedback. But it does mean that the aspiring writer with multiple serious writing deficits shouldn't expect to become a fluent writer merely by taking a few writing classes—nor should universities encourage the idea that they can.

One should start by reading what interests her or him—and then go on from there. The reading should be increasingly challenging, introducing new vocabulary, new constructions, because it is through continuous exposure to and internalization of new forms and patterns that one develops linguistic fluency. But it is imperative that the reader feel the need and desire to participate actively in the discourse that he or she has chosen—as well as the curiosity to continue reading. If reading feels like a chore and is easily abandoned, then it won't work.

As mentioned in chapter 2, there is a substantial literature on reading motivation in a writing program, and I have very little to add to it. A good place to start for someone unacquainted with this literature is L. Flower, V. Stein, J. Ackerman, M. J. Kantz, K. McCormick, and W. C. Peck, *Reading-to-Write: Exploring a Cognitive and Social Process* (New York: Oxford University Press, 1990).

You might think of language as a gift to us humans that has to be nurtured by our own urge to communicate. Without that urge, we could not receive from it all or even most of what it has to offer. This especially applies to written language, which isn't something everyone automatically acquires facility with. The pleasure that it supplies is the lubricant that makes reading easy to swallow. The more good reading you do, the more your writing will improve. If you want a simple rule of good writing, that's it.

Epilogue

OUR INQUIRY INTO the nature of good writing began with the observation that, whatever it was, it couldn't be reliably scored. We have learned to embrace this subjectivity, because, in fact, we have no other option. Writing something entails that there be someone that it is written for, just as speaking entails that there be someone who is being spoken to (disregarding the odd fellows one occasionally meets on the subway). Since no imagined audience is identical to the actual receiving one (that is, no communicator can know exactly what's in others' minds, though it's important to try to guess), and since no receiving audience of more than one person is homogeneous in every respect, there cannot help but be differences in the reception of any given communication. This subjectivity is built into the system and cannot be overcome, even if we all use the principles of relevance to guide us.

But even if there are no absolutes in good writing, we have our own internal standards by which we judge writing. We have seen that spoken and written fluency can be validly assessed if we use the thumbs-up-or-down test. But although we can count how many different constructions (including vocabulary items) a person uses in a given stretch of writing or understands on a written test, unless we add in subjective judgments of various audiences about fluency we won't even get to the validity we want.

Aspiring writers can and do learn how to write well by devoting time and energy to the task. Much reading of good literature, a good deal of practice writing, and a commitment to revising are no doubt essential. This is pretty much how I'd interpret Ben Jonson's aphorism cited in the first chapter: "For a man to write well, there are required three necessaries: to read the best authors, observe the best speakers, and much exercise of his own style." An editor or teacher who provides feedback to the writer can be very valuable, but only if the writer is sufficiently motivated and engaged with her reading.

It's unlikely that there are many aspiring writers who will overestimate the devotion to literary study that this entails (especially if their goal is to write great or even very good literature). I certainly don't know of many of whom it may be claimed that they read or wanted to read *too much*. One who did, perhaps, is Samuel Taylor Coleridge, who said in a letter dated April 1797, when he was 24:

> I should not think of devoting less than 20 years to an Epic Poem. Ten to collect materials and warm my mind with universal science. I would be a tolerable Mathematician. I would thoroughly know Mechanics, Hydrostatics, Optics, and Astronomy, Botany, Metallurgy, Fossilism, Chemistry, Geology, Anatomy, Medicine—then the mind of man—then the minds of men—in all Travels, Voyages, and Histories. So I would spend ten years—the next five to the composition of the poem—and the five last to the correction of it.[1]

With this as his guide, it's not surprising that Coleridge, who died in 1834 after years of ill health probably aggravated by his addiction to opium, never managed to write an epic poem, or the "Magnum Opus" that he talked frequently of. But he did write "Kubla Khan," "Rime of the Ancient Mariner," and "Cristabel," three of the most celebrated shorter poems in the English language. He was precocious and, at Cambridge, a literary enthusiast.

Whether or not one's ambition is to pen an epic poem as Coleridge envisioned it, the ticket to good writing continues to be to warm the mind by reading and studying "the minds of men—in all Travels, Voyages, and Histories." As another great writer, William Faulkner advised, "Read, read, read. Read everything—trash, classics, good and bad, and see how they do it."[2]

Notes

1. Fulkerson 2005, pp. 680–81.
2. See Huck and Goldsmith 1995.
3. CEEB 2004.
4. For those unfamiliar with it, the classical critique of the relativist stance goes something like this: Consider the statement "The truth of all statements, including this one, is contingent (on the situation, beliefs, biases, etc. of the person judging their truth)." Now, is the truth of *that* statement contingent? If so, then it makes no more of an enduring claim than its negative. If not, then the relativist is caught in a contradiction. A perhaps more vivid depiction of this problem for relativists is attributed to William James: If you are committed to the belief that the world rides on the back of a turtle, then it's going to have to be turtles all the way down. (Thanks to John Robert Ross for drawing the attention of linguists to this anecdote back in 1967.) Of course, relativists have supplied a spirited defense against such critiques. A more technical critique of the postmodern approach to speech acts can be found in Searle 1977. Jacques Derrida has responded to Searle in Derrida 1988.
5. See Huck forthcoming *b*.
6. For a perspective from composition studies, see Haswell 2005.
7. Williams 2005.
8. Thomas and Turner 1994, p. 6.
9. A linguistic approach is implicit in the work of Greek and Roman Stoics, of the Modistae in the middle ages, and, in the modern era, of linguists of varying stripes. See, for example, the articles in Sebeok 1960. The lifetime work of M. A. K. Halliday needs to be mentioned for its influence in the area of stylistics. More recent work in cognitive linguistics and cognitive stylistics seems to me particularly promising and is close to my conception of how and why linguistics

can inform the recognition of good writing. See especially Turner (1991) and Chametzky (1996) and the references cited therein. The concepts in Part II are fairly standard in stylistic analysis, see, e.g., V. Tobin 2009, Fahy 2000, Aviram 1998, Kingwell 1980, though I hope the particular relevance-theoretic approach I adopt sheds some light on them.

10. I understand the term *disfluency* to denote immediately recognizable departures from a fluent writer's or native speaker's best efforts. But disfluency need not be pathological—e.g., all normal children and adults are regularly disfluent to some degree. For me, *dysfluency* denotes a pathological abnormality. See Wingate 1984.

11. See especially Krashen 2010 and 2011. Krashen also cites Frank Smith (1972) and Kenneth S. Goodman (in Flurkey and Xu 2003), each of whom had previously and independently come to the conclusion that we learn to write by reading.

12. Krashen 2004, p. 18.

13. Pinker 2014. The quotation below is from p. 11.

PROLOGUE

1. Koretz et al. 1992.

2. Interrater reliability for the chosen pieces expressed as a Spearman correlation coefficient was .35 in Grade 4 and .42 in Grade 8, where agreement scores of .70 to .90 are often claimed on standardized tests (Cherry and Meyer 1993).

3. "It is well known that careful training of raters can improve interrater reliabilities" (Cherry and Meyer 1993, 109–41). Indeed, in the extreme, you can train unreliability away. See the discussion in chapters 1 and 2.

4. Daniel, Mittag, and Bornmann (n.d.) report interrater reliability coefficients of between .12 and .40 on recommendations for acceptance or rejection of 562 papers in ten journals using Cohen's kappa.

5. McGurl 2009, p. 93.

6. O'Connor 1970.

7. <http://www.uiowa.edu/~iww/about.htm.>

8. Updike 1998.

9. DeVoto 1936.

10. Menand 2000; Gopnik 2008; Wolfe 2000.

CHAPTER I

1. During the Renaissance, of course, the classics were in Latin and Greek. For example, Edward Lynch describes the *Ratio studiorum* of 1599 (see S. J. Lynch 1968 in Abbott 2001): "The one orator used in daily prelections is Cicero; among historians, Caesar, Sallust, Livy, Curtius, and others like them.; among the poets, Virgil . . . as well as Horace's Odes and elegies, epigrams, and other works of classic poets. . . . Cicero may be supplemented by Aristotle and Quintilian. Style is to be formed on Cicero, though help may be drawn from approved historians and poets."

2. For a brief but illuminating account of the recent history of intention as understood in literary criticism, see Patterson 1995. A more technical and philosophically oriented account can be found in Zunshine 2006, but see chapter 8.

3. Aristotle, *Poetics* XXII:1, trans. S. H. Butcher, 1895; rev. 1911; Horace, *Ars Poetica*, trans. Edward Henry Blakeney; Thomas of Erfurt, *Grammatica Speculativa*, ed. M. F. Garcia, 1902, in Robins 1967; Ben Jonson, *Timber*, published posthumously, 1640; Jonathan Swift, "Letter to a young gentleman lately entered into holy orders," January 9, 1721; Orwell 1946.

4. See J. Lynch 2009, which provides a very knowledgeable and readable history of the prescriptivist penchant going back to Horace (despite the subtitle). As Lynch notes, Swift did dilate a bit on his preferences, in this letter and in Swift 1710: no "Hard Words," no terms "Mean and Paultry . . . much less Slovenly and Indecent," no "flat, unnecessary Epithets," no "old threadbare Phrases," no "Affectation."

5. Marshall Kremers (1983) traces this tradition in America to Samuel Phillips Newman.

6. Strunk and White 1972, p. vii.

7. If evidence for either or both of these propositions is desired, consider comparing Shakespeare's First Folio with any student writing exercise from which any expressions that would be offensive to Strunk and White have been purged or corrected. Strunk and White were themselves aware of this:

> Style rules of this sort are, of course, somewhat a matter of individual preference, and even the established rules of grammar are open to challenge. Professor Strunk, although one of the most inflexible and choosy of men, was quick to acknowledge the fallacy of inflexibility and the danger of doctrine. "It is an old observation," he wrote, "that the best writers sometimes disregard the rules of rhetoric. When they do, however, the reader will usually find in the sentence some compensating merit, attained at the cost of the violation. Unless he is certain of doing as well, he will probably do best to follow the rules."

I more or less agree with this, although it gets us no closer to a definition of good writing.

8. For example, at the undergraduate College of the University of Chicago in the 1940s, essay writing exercises were not required. "[F]or the most part, all important examinations consisted of machine-scored multiple-choice questions" (W. H. McNeill 1991, p. 141).

9. For an excellent overview of the interpretation of validity and reliability, see Dunbar, Koretz, and Hoover 1991 and the references contained there. Some researchers have tried to get around the conflict between validity and reliability by settling on rubrics that graders agree on as constituting community standards, and then creating conditions under which graders gravitate to similar conclusions, see Elliott, Briller, and Joshi 2007 for a particularly interesting approach to the problem. Elliott and his colleagues concluded that, over a period of seven years, their graders were "evolving as a community." But when the graders were chosen from different disciplines, the same degree of unanimity was not achieved, suggesting that the observed effect was a consequence of grading to the instruction in a different guise. The judgment of a community is closer to what I regard as the best arbiter of fluency, as I'll indicate later. However, to the extent that raters are trained to replace their individual untrained intuitions with such standards, those end up being just another form of rubric. The issue of community standards is also relevant to the assessment of the effectiveness of post-secondary writing centers or writing labs. Writing centers or labs differ from writing programs in that the former generally offer only one-on-one tutoring rather than the composition courses and classes that writing programs mount. Determining whether a writing center helps students to improve their writing is thus a slightly

different task from determining whether a writing program does. Since writing centers conduct no courses, there is no "teaching to the test" or "grading to the instruction," strictly speaking, to worry about. Nevertheless, when it comes to assessing the success of a writing center, the same problems of validity and reliability apply. For example, Jones 2001 surveyed the literature on the effectiveness of writing centers from the 1970s onward and found that "only a handful of researchers have attempted to evaluate the performance of writing centers in enhancing student writing skills through the use of empirical study designs. Furthermore, even these studies are of suspect validity and limited reliability." Nor have the years since 2001 produced research on writing centers that meets strong criteria of validity and reliability, see, for example, Niiler 2005 for an interesting attempt that nonetheless falls short in this regard (Niiler found reliability problems without strong rater training); see also Lerner 2003 and Gofine 2012 for reviews of the literature.

10. See Moss 1994, who argues that for nonstandardized assessments like writing portfolio assessments, reliability should be discounted and that "hermeneutic" alternatives should be considered.

11. Fulkerson doesn't actually use this term, preferring instead "rhetorical axiology."

12. Fulkerson 1990, pp. 409–10.

13. For this, see especially Allen 2002.

14. D. M. Murray 1972, reprinted in Villanueva 2003, p. 4.

15. Murphy 1996, p. 194; Olson 1999.

16. However, the emphasis for advocates of this strategy has been on theory rather than practice. Sidney Dobrin (1999) concludes his essay: "I am not going to suggest ways in which pedagogies can or should be developed in order to accomplish the goals of these theories. I am not sure if translations to practice are possible yet."

17. CWPA, NCTE, and NWP 2011. <http://wpacouncil.org/files/framework-for-success-postsecondary-writing.pdf>.

18. See Pullum 2010 for an engaging criticism of prescriptive pomposity. For an earlier but still insightful argument against prescriptivism, see Nunberg 1983. See also Wallace 2001 for a rather less satisfying treatment of the subject.

19. Looking at prescriptive rules as merely "rules of thumb" doesn't make them any less prescriptive; it merely allows the prescriptivist to hedge. One then wants to know when to observe the rule of thumb and when not to. A definitive answer is again prescriptive, while any other answer is an admission that the rules of thumb don't work.

20. See Rezaei and Lovorn 2010.

21. Wolfe 1965*b*. Most of the literary extracts in this book are from the openings of essays or stories or novels. The rationale for this is that openings presume little in the way of context and obviously don't depend for their impact on prior content.

22. Joyce 1922.

23. Stein 1914.

24. Actually, in the case of White, we don't have to guess. White, in Guth (1976, p. 551), describes Wolfe as "a rider . . . sitting very high in the saddle these days and very sure of his mount." Of an article Wolfe wrote about the *New Yorker* editor William Shawn, White said, "it sets some sort of record for journalistic delinquency" (ibid., p. 531). White's opinion of Joyce was no more generous: "Once, when my head was pretty bad, I picked up *Ulysses* and gave it a go but found out that it was simply making me horribly nervous" (ibid., p. 551). Of Stein: "I never

understood why the slightest fuss was made over G. Stein, whose contribution to letters strikes me as very close to zero" (ibid., p. 551).

25. See Gee 1992, 2001.

26. See J. Miller 2006; Chafe and Tannen 1987; Nunberg 1990.

27. From Corpus of Spoken Professional English untagged, at <http://athel.com/index.php?cPath=24&osCsid=c7ec4d802851d71c08060cf791d03f95>.

28. Myers may have rehearsed before the press conference, but the conversational markers referred to earlier make it obvious that her speech was not wholly memorized.

29. Carkeet 1979.

30. <http://www.yourdictionary.com/library/mispron.html>.

31. <http://vodpod.com/watch/3100338-rush-limbaugh-obama-using-the-black-dialect-in-speech-to-national-governors-association>.

32. Mark Twain, *Adventures of Huckleberry Finn*. Harold Bloom (1994) says of these lines that they constitute "the most beautiful prose paragraph yet written by any American."

CHAPTER 2

1. Graham 2006; Case, Speece, and Molloy 2003.

2. Graham and Perin 2007.

3. Graham and Sandmel 2011. See also Rogers and Graham 2008.

4. Graham and Sandmel 2011, p. 403.

5. Graham and Perin 2007, p. 467.

6. Graham and Sandmel 2011, p. 398.

7. Jonsson and Svingby 2007, p. 137.

8. Graham and Perin 2007, p. 467.

9. Graham and Perin 2007, p. 448. They point out that "only 46% of the studies described procedures for training teachers/instructors and just 27% measured whether the experimental treatment was implemented as intended. . . . Although teachers/instructors may have received training and experimental treatments may have been implemented with fidelity, the researchers did not report the former or verify the latter."

10. See Clark and Lappin 2011.

11. Elbow 2004; see also Elbow 1993. For a dissenting opinion, see Salvatori 1996.

12. Elbow 2004, p. 14.

13. "E. L. Doctorow, The Art of Fiction, No. 94." Interviewed by George Plimpton. *The Paris Review* 101 (Winter 1986). Available online at <http://www.theparisreview.org/interviews/2718/the-art-of-fiction-no-94-e-l-doctorow>. Of course, it's hardly credible that he had written nothing at all before that age.

14. That is, writing is essentially different from speaking a language in that every person in normal circumstances develops the ability to speak a language fluently during childhood, while not everyone learns to write fluently or otherwise. Thus, we say that everyone is genetically predisposed to speak a language just as they are to, say, form groups and crave sex. It is conceivable that a society of homo sapiens could exist in which written language would serve as a native language, but this would require that the members of that society be incapable of acquiring spoken or sign languages and that what would count as normal language in that society only be written, a scenario that is highly unlikely.

15. Kellogg 2008.

16. Tomasello 2008, p. 123.

17. Ibid., p. 163.

18. Troia, Shankland, and Wolbers 2012. See also Hidi and Boscolo 2006.

19. L. Tobin 1989, p. 448.

20. MacDonald 1994.

21. Labov 1963.

22. <http://www.hmhbooks.com/hmh/site/hmhbooks/bookdetails?isbn=9780547041018>; <http://www.houghtonmifflinbooks.com/epub/ahd4.shtml>.

23. Johnson and Munakata 2005; Karmiloff-Smith 1998; Thomas and Karmiloff-Smith 2002.

24. See Thomas and Karmiloff-Smith 2002.

25. Coltheart 2002.

26. Thomas and Karmiloff-Smith 2002.

27. Newport and Meier 1985.

28. MacSweeney et al. 2002.

29. Corina and Knapp 2006.

30. Segaert et al. 2012.

31. Buchweitz et al. 2009.

32. Sirois et al. 2008.

33. Katanoda, Yoshikawa, and Sugishita 2001.

34. Beeson et al. 2003; Scott and Johnsrude 2003; Tettamanti et al. 2009; Purcell, Shea, and Rapp 2014; Sheldon, Malcolm, and Barton 2008; Rapin et al. 1977.

35. Gaillard et al. 2003.

36. Schild, Roder, and Friedrich 2011.

37. In particular, care must be taken not to infer too much from imaging data. Max Coltheart (2004, p. 21) has suggested that "facts about the brain do not constrain the possible natures of mental information-processing systems. No amount of knowledge about the hardware of a computer will tell you anything serious about the nature of the software that the computer runs. In the same way, no facts about the activity of the brain could be used to confirm or refute some information-processing model of cognition." However, Coltheart's argument does not prevent us from drawing conclusions about cognitive systems from behavior. In such a case, imaging evidence can serve as just one more bit of evidence in support of the conclusions.

CHAPTER 3

1. See Braddock, Lloyd-Jones, and Schoer 1963: "[T]he teaching of formal grammar has a negligible or, because it usually displaces some instruction and practice in composition, even a harmful effect on improvement in writing." Also, "direct methods of instruction, focusing on writing activities and the structuring of ideas, are more efficient in teaching sentence structure, usage, punctuation, and other related factors than are such methods such as nomenclature drill, diagramming, and rote memorization of grammatical rules" (Strom 1960). And "the thrust of current research and theory is to take power from the teacher and give that power to the learner. At no point in the English curriculum is the question of power more blatantly posed than in the issue of formal grammar instruction. It is time that we, as teachers, formulate theories of

language and literacy and let those theories guide our teaching, and it is time we, as researchers, move on to more interesting areas of inquiry" (Hartwell 1985). The quotations from Braddock et al. and Strom can be found in Hartwell's article.

However, there is an opposing perspective that suggests teachers should promote awareness of grammatical structure among their students. See, e.g., Hunston 1995: "The learner should be aware that from the mass of language in our daily experience generalisations can be made about the ways words behave; that some words share behaviours and others contrast and that names can be given to these word-groups and these behaviours." For a general introduction to this perspective, see Hawkins 1987.

2. See Goldberg 1995, 2006; Michaelis 2006.

3. Goldberg 2006, p. 6.

4. Snyder and Stromswold 1995.

5. Adapted from Goldberg 1995, p. 11. See Levin 1993 for a comprehensive list of English verbs and the patterns in which they participate.

6. From Random Word Generator at <http://www.wordswarm.net/>. The asterisk at the beginning of the sentence here and elsewhere indicates that I detect a problem with the sentence that is explained in the text.

7. For a similar view, see Pullum 2006. The issue of whether the mind is more like a standard computer operating with algorithms or a parallel distributed processor is contentious in linguistics and cognitive science and one on which I take no position in this book.

8. See Chametzky 1992 and Wilson 1992 for an insightful discussion of explanation and prediction in the context of Relevance Theory.

9. There has in fact been much written about theories of performance—Chomsky 1965 contains a seminal discussion. See also Sag and Wasow n.d. and Schutze 1996.

10. Morgan 1973; McCawley 1988, p. 4.

11. Updike 1996, p. 148.

12. Quoted in Pullum 2010, p. 56.

13. Example i is from Carson 1998; iii is from Pullum 2010; iv is from Huddleston and Pullum 2002, p. 611; vii is from Fitzgerald 1922, pp. 150–51; viii is from Ian Kerr (Canada Research Chair in Ethics, Law, and Technology and Professor in the Faculties of Law and Medicine and in the Department of Philosophy at the University of Ottawa), Evidence from 39th Parliament, 1st Session, Standing Committee on Access to Information, Privacy and Ethics, Monday, December 11, 2006, <http://www2.parl.gc.ca/HousePublications/Publication.aspx?DocId=2600931&Language=E&Mode=1#T1545>.

14. Woolf 1925, p. 47.

15. For a technical linguistic discussion, see Reinhart 1983, from which these sentences are taken. For a less technical discussion, see Huddleston and Pullum 2002, chapter 17.

16. For some technical approaches to this problem within the CG framework, see Kay 1994; Van Hoek 1995; Fillmore et al. 2007.

17. Dennett 1991, p. 76. See also Dennett 1987, p. 17, and Dennett 1971.

18. For a more technical analysis of Constructional Conflation and other generalizations about analogical relations in CG that will be introduced in the next few sections, see Huck (forthcoming *a*).

19. Acts 4:10 "Let it be known to all of you and to all the people of Israel" Philippians 4:5 "Let your moderation be known unto all men."

20. The difference is that in the first, the agent that is to make the information known is not specified, whereas in the second, the agent is assumed to be "we."

21. For those who are interested, the answers are as follows: (i) I learned the art of parking cars at a young age + I have been parking cars from a young age → *I learned the art of parking cars from a young age.

(ii) I'm happy to know you're coming + I'm grateful that you're coming → *I'm grateful to know you're coming. Of course, this *could* really mean that the speaker is grateful to know you're coming. But that means something different from *I'm grateful that you're coming.*

(iii) hope to capitalize on + hope to profit from → *hope to capitalize from; more likely the person who wrote this meant "I hope to profit when its potential is realized."

(iv) goes on in students' minds + goes through students' minds → *goes on through students' minds. This example is from the "Letters" section of the *New York Times*: <http://thechoice.blogs.nytimes.com/2009/12/29/test-scores-college/?apage=2#comment-35267>.

(v) dispense with + dispose of → *dispense of.

22. See, e.g., Messenger et al. 2009.

23. See Huck and Goldsmith 1995.

24. See Ferreira, Christianson, and Hollingworth 2001.

25. Example from Ross 1967, pp. 106–7. For a Constructionist account of island constraints, see Goldberg 2006, chapter 7.

26. Examples 3.29–3.32 are from Huck 2005.

27. Chomsky 1965, among many other books and articles by Chomsky.

28. Daiute 1981.

29. Bever, Carroll, and Hurtig 1976.

30. Overlap and Conflict can in fact be analyzed as two aspects of the same phenomenon; see Huck (forthcoming *a*).

31. Rosch and Mervis 1975.

32. Subordinate-level categories are also abstractions, of course; but the more subordinate you get, the closer you come to naming a concept that identifies a unique individual, object, or idea.

33. Carson 1951, p. 199.

34. Hurston 1928.

35. Hart and Risley 1995; see also <http://www.lenababy.com/Study.aspx>; <http://www.gsa.gov/graphics/pbs/The_Early_Catastrophe_30_Million_Word_Gap_by_Age_3.pdf>.

36. "Harold Brodkey, The Art of Fiction, No. 126." Interviewed by James Linville. *The Paris Review* 121 (Winter 1991). Available online at <http://www.theparisreview.org/interviews/2128/the-art-of-fiction-no-126-harold-brodkey>.

37. Coleridge 1956–61, vol. 1, pp. 347–48.

38. Warwick 1989.

39. Dockrell and Messer 2004.

40. Dockrell, Lindsay, and Connelly 2009.

41. Stanovich 1986.

42. Smiley 2005, pp. 32–33.

43. Nagy and Anderson 1984. See also Dockrell and Messer 2004.

44. Nation 2001*a*.

45. Liberman 2006, accessed October 5, 2010.

46. Nagy and Anderson 1984, p. 328.

47. Leech and Garside 1991.

48. Goldberg 2006, p. 79. See also Hills et al. 2010.

49. See Arnon and Snider 2009. See also Dockrell and Messer 2004, p. 45: "Initial word exposures provide the basis for developing a semantic representation of a term but input is often insufficient to establish meaning and learning is not inevitable." Also Dockrell, Braisby, and Best 2007. But even multiple exposures are sometimes insufficient. Every adult has presumably had the uncomfortable experience of realizing at some point that she or he had misconstrued the meaning of a word and had been using it for years in ways that probably puzzled her or his audience.

50. Curtiss 1977.

51. Anderson, Fielding, and Wilson 1988; Stanovich 1986; Taylor, Frye, and Maruyama 1990; Wahlberg and Tsai 1985.

52. McKool 2007. See also Massaro 2012.

53. Cornell et al. 2010.

54. Niven 1991.

55. Knight 2007.

56. Chomsky 1965 and many publications since, including especially Chomsky 1972 and Chomsky 1986.

57. Newport 1990.

58. Carroll 1999.

59. Maratsos 1983.

60. D. McNeill 1966, p. 68.

61. Tomasello 2003, p. 176.

62. See, e.g., Pinker 1989.

63. For some suggestive evidence that at least some brain physiology in the language area is specialized, see Kanwisher 2010; Fedorenko and Kanwisher 2009; Rips, Bloomfield, and Asmuth 2008; Gallistel and King 2009. A careful study of the innateness issue, which concludes that the case for it is unpersuasive, can be found in Clark and Lappin 2011.

64. There is an abundant literature on unsupervised learning strategies. For a linguistic perspective, see Tomasello and Bates 2001, especially the paper in that volume by Jeffrey L. Elman, as well as Elman et al. 1996; Goldsmith and Xanthos 2009; and Goldsmith 2010. For evidence particularly associated with CG, see Goldberg 2006, Part II, pp. 69–126.

65. E. Clark 1987; Bates and MacWhinney 1987; Brooks and Tomasello 1999.

66. Goldberg 2006, p. 96.

67. Tomasello's characterization is slightly more complex: "When an organism does something in the same way successfully enough times, that way of doing it becomes habitual and it is very difficult for another way of doing that same thing to enter into the picture. . . . If someone communicates to me using Form X, rather than Form Y, there was a reason for that choice related to the speaker's specific communicative intention. This motivates the listener to search for that reason and so to distinguish the two forms and their appropriate communicative contexts." Tomasello 2003, p. 300.

68. For additional support for the strategy in (3.53), sometimes called "entrenchment and preemption," see Brooks and Tomasello 1999; Brooks et al. 1999.

69. See Bruton 2009; Chandler 2003; Ferris 2004; Shin 2008; Truscott and Hsu 2008; Truscott 1996*a*, 1996*b*, 1999, 2007, 2010.

70. Chandler 2003.

71. P. Bloom 2000, p. 192. Bloom cites Miller 1996 for the 100,000 words figure.

72. Currently the best approximations are dictionaries like the *Collins Cobuild Dictionary* and the *Oxford Collocations Dictionary*.

73. For some recent discussion, see Shermis and Hamner 2012; Perelman 2012; and Deane 2013.

74. For example, Mark D. Sharmis and Ben Hamner 2012 describe the Lexile AES as follows: Through a research study to examine the relationship between text complexity, text features, and writing ability, a parsimonious set of significant predictors emerged—predictors consistent with the hypothesis that selected kinds of composition surface text features may be proxies for a degree of executive functioning and working memory capacity and efficiency. The resulting combination consisted of lexical representations alone—without syntax signifiers. Specifically, a combination of a small number of variables—degree of diverse use of vocabulary and greater vocabulary density, controlling for production fluency—predicted 90% of the true variance in rater judgments of essays.

CHAPTER 4

1. Grice 1975. In what follows, I will continue to talk about the information that is conveyed in a text or discourse or dialogue, although by "information" I mean more than mere facts. Following Austin 1965, I assume that every utterance or sentence of text has a locutionary force (the meaning or denotation of the words as combined in the utterance), an illocutionary force (the sort of speech act the speaker is engaging in by uttering the sentence, such as asking a question, issuing a command, announcing a verdict, etc.), and a perlocutionary force (the effect on the audience that uttering the sentence is intended to produce). On my understanding, the information that the sentence conveys includes all three. Thus, if a writer is intending to be ironic, that irony is part of the information the writer is intending to convey. James Paul Gee (2011, p. 7) says, "Since, when we use language, social goods and their distribution are always at stake, language is always 'political,' in the deep sense." I entirely agree.

2. Nor are these ethical standards or imperatives categorical or otherwise.

3. See <http://www.imdb.com/title/tt0093779/quotes>.

4. From the *New York Times*, April 13, 1995. <http://www.nytimes.com/ref/opinion/20110417_opclassic.html?scp=58&sq=andre%20aciman&st=cse>.

5. The principle of accommodation has received much attention in the philosophical literature. See von Fintel 2000, 2008; Stalnaker 1998; Thomason 1990; Lewis 1979. For a nice discussion of the definite article *the*, see Huddleston and Pullum 2002, pp. 368–71.

6. Hemingway 1929; Brookner 1984; Z. Smith 2000.

7. Bellow 1957.

8. Walker 1983.

9. Carver 1981.

10. Morrison 1998.

11. It's often said that what literary critics do is to criticize a book for not being exactly the book they would have written for themselves if they had written it—which they wouldn't and probably couldn't have done even had they wanted to. I suppose the appropriate conclusion is that it's difficult to find a book that exactly matches the needs of any reader. However, the farther from the reader's interests an author strays, the less likely will the reader be to keep reading.

12. There are exceptions: codes, private letters, and so on. See Patterson 1995 on the treatment of authorial intention in literary theory.

13. Levi 1974.

14. Grice 1975, p. 47.

15. See Fulkerson 2005 for a nice summary.

16. Fulkerson 2005.

17. Sperber and Wilson 1995; Wilson and Sperber 2012.

18. Wilson and Sperber 2005, p. 608.

19. Sperber and Wilson 2012, p. 102.

20. Wilson and Sperber 2005, p. 609.

21. Sperber and Wilson 1995, p. 32.

22. Sperber, Cara, and Girotta 1995, p. 75.

23. Wałaszewska 2011.

24. Jay 2003, p. 370.

25. See Lakoff and Johnson 1980.

26. Tomasello 2008. On p. 327 of this book, Tomasello summarizes his three hypotheses: "(1) human cooperative communication evolved initially in the gestural domain pointing and pantomiming; (2) this evolution was potentiated by skills and motivations for shared intentionality, themselves originally evolved in the context of collaborative activities; and (3) it is only in the context of inherently meaningful collaborative activities, coordinated by 'natural' forms of communication such as pointing and pantomiming, that totally arbitrary linguistic conventions could have come into existence."

27. Ede and Lunsford 1984, p. 168.

28. Wilson and Sperber 2012, p. 264.

29. Kasper 1997.

30. Bardovi-Harlig and Mahan-Taylor 2003; Bardovi-Harlig 1999, 2001; Kasper and Rose 1999; Bouton 1996.

31. Kasper 1997.

32. Schmidt 1990; N. Murray 2010; Nakatani 2005.

33. Douglas 2010. See also Ingram 2007, chapter 16, for a nice summary of research on the neurolinguistics of discourse processing.

34. Douglas 2010, p. 379.

35. Wade et al. 2010. See also Ylvisaker 2006.

36. See especially Wong, Murdoch, and Whelan 2010.

37. Ingram 2007.

38. Pickard, McAllister, and Horton 2010.

39. Eaton, Marshall, and Pring 2010.

CHAPTER 5

1. See Booth, Colomb, and Williams 1995.

2. In composition studies, narrative planning has been discussed by a number of researchers, including Flower and Hayes 1981; Flower 1985; Bizzell 1986.

3. In other words, Discourse Analysis is just a particular way of doing linguistics. But I find its methods and vocabulary especially useful for pedagogical purposes in the study of narrative.

According to Johnstone (2008, p. 3), discourse analysts "tend … to be interested in what happens when people draw on the knowledge they have about language, knowledge based on their memories of things they have said, heard, seen, or written before, to do things in the world: exchange information, express feelings, make things happen, create beauty, entertain themselves and others, and so on." There's nothing that discourse analysts do that isn't compatible with Construction Grammar or Relevance Theory, but its focus on practical exchange should help to illuminate some of the issues I want to raise about narrative.

4. Chafe 1994, p. 279.

5. Stubbs 1983.

6. Givón 1995.

7. Smith et al. 2005.

8. Ondaatje 1992.

9. I would like to thank John Goldsmith for useful discussion regarding the issues in this and the preceding paragraph.

10. Woolf 1927.

11. Lane 2000.

12. Mailer 1948.

13. Beattie 1978.

14. Fitzgerald 1925.

15. Gould 1987.

16. Updike 1964.

17. White 1941.

18. Oakley 2009, p. 139.

19. For basic work on cognitive blends, see Fauconnier and Turner 2002; Coulson 2000; Coulson and Oakley 2000.

CHAPTER 6

1. For an intriguing experiment that showed that raters tend to give more weight to spelling, punctuation, and grammatical structure than to whether the writer has adequately addressed the essay question even when raters are given a rubric, see Rezaei and Lovorn 2010.

2. Truss 2003.

3. Deck and Herson 2010.

4. Fabb 2010.

5. Nunberg 1990, pp. 32, 41, 66.

6. Hall 1999.

CHAPTER 7

1. Longinus, *On the Sublime*, chapter 32; James Boswell, 1791, *The Life of Samuel Johnson*, chapter 41.

2. Seitz 1991, pp. 291–92.

3. Lakoff and Johnson 1980, p. 2.

4. Wilson and Sperber 2012, p. 97.

5. Seitz 1991, p. 296.

6. Stevens 1923.

7. Hall 1973.

8. Seitz 1991, p. 297.

9. Stevens 1966.

10. Wilson and Sperber 2012, pp. 121–22.

CHAPTER 8

1. Chabon 1988.

2. Brown 2003.

3. Pullum 2004. See also Liberman 2006.

4. And yet, Brown boasts on his website that there are 200 million copies of his books in print, though that is not exactly the same thing as saying that 200 million copies have actually been sold or read. As of 2005 two years after its publication, *Time Magazine* claimed sales of *The Da Vinci Code* topped 25 million copies, and in 2010 it was voted one of the 100 best books of all time in a survey by the *Perth West Australian*, besting *Persuasion* by Jane Austen, *The Road* by Cormac McCarthy, *Atonement* by Ian McEwan, and *1984* by George Orwell. James Joyce didn't make the list. Of course, popularity doesn't guarantee good writing. Or does it? Can 25 million readers be wrong about whether Dan Brown's book is a good read and, therefore, presumably, well written?

5. Salinger 1951.

6. Shakespeare, *Othello* III, iii, 331.

7. Hemingway 1929.

8. Wolfe 1965*a*.

9. Orwell 1936.

10. White 1928.

11. Actually, the verb *say* does not express an intention. In philosophical language, it is not a "propositional attitude," and thus does not give rise to intentionality, embedded or otherwise. Verbs of saying can be used in a linguistically complex sentence (i.e., one containing one or more subordinate clauses), but that is not the same thing as a sentence with embedded intentionality. See, for example, the *Stanford Encyclopedia of Philosophy*, online at <http://plato.stanford.edu/entries/prop-attitude-reports/>.

12. See Bever 1970; Jurafsky and Martin 2009; Gibson 1991, 1998; Ferreira and Dell 2000; Mitchell et al. 2010.

13. "[H]umble humans live in the twilight of partial predictability and partial uncertainty. In this challenging world, a principal way to cope with the rampant uncertainty we face is to simplify, that is, to ignore much of the available information and use fast and frugal heuristics" (Todd and Gigerenzer 2012, p. 16). See also Goldstein and Gigerenzer 2002; Hochman, Ayal, and Glockner 2010.

CHAPTER 9

1. See especially Richardson 2010; Lodge 2002; Turner 1991; Zunshine 2006.

2. Ross 1991.

3. Niven 1991.

4. See Dennett 1987; Searle 1983; Wimsatt and Beardsley 1946; Zunshine 2006; Herman 2008; H. Clark 1996; Booth [1961] 1983.

5. Rich 1972.

EPILOGUE

1. Letter to Joseph Cottle, April 1797; quoted in Bate 1987, p. 46. Bate surmises that Coleridge "was not completely joking." It's worth noting that *Paradise Lost* probably occupied Milton for twenty-five years from conception to completion (although he did work on other things during that period).

2. Meriwether and Millgate 1968, p. 55.

Bibliography

Abbott, Don Paul. 2001. "Rhetoric and Writing in the Renaissance." In *A Short History of Writing Instruction*, 2d ed., edited by James J. Murphy, 165. New York: Routledge.

Allen, Guy. 2002. "The 'Good Enough' Teacher and the Authentic Student." In *A Pedagogy of Becoming*, edited by John Mills, 141–76. Amsterdam: Rodopi.

Anderson, R., L. Fielding, and P. Wilson. 1988. "Growth in Reading and How Children Spend Their Time outside School." *Language Research Quarterly* 23: 285–303.

Arnon, Inbal, and Neal Snider. 2009. "More than Words: Frequency Effects for Multi-Word Phrases." *Journal of Memory and Language* 62, no. 1: 67–82.

Austin, J. L. 1965. *How to Do Things with Words*. Oxford: Oxford University Press.

Aviram, A. F. 1998. "Literariness, Markedness, and Surprise in Poetry." In *Codes and Consequences: Choosing Linguistic Varieties*, edited by Carol Myers-Scotton, 101–23. New York: Oxford University Press.

Bardovi-Harlig, Kathleen. 1999. "The Interlanguage of Interlanguage Pragmatics: A Research Agenda of Acquisitional Pragmatics." *Language Learning* 49: 677–713.

———. 2001. "Evaluating the Empirical Evidence: Grounds for Instruction in Pragmatics?" In *Pragmatics in Language Teaching*, edited by Kenneth R. Rose and Gabriela Kasper, 13–32. Cambridge: Cambridge University Press.

Bardovi-Harlig, Kathleen, and R. Mahan-Taylor. 2003. "Introduction." In *Teaching Pragmatics*, edited by Kathleen Bardovi-Harlig and R. Mahan-Taylor, 2–4. Washington, DC: United States Department of State.

Bate, W. Jackson. 1987. *Coleridge*. Cambridge, MA: Harvard University Press.

Bates, Elizabeth, and Brian MacWhinney. 1987. "Competition, Variation, and Language Learning." In *Mechanisms of Language Acquisition*, edited by Brian MacWhinney, 157–94. Hillsdale, NJ: Lawrence Erlbaum.

Beattie, Ann. 1978. "Weekend." In *Secrets and Surprises*, by Ann Beattie. New York: Random House.

Beeson, Pelagie M., et al. 2003. "The Neural Substrates of Writing: A Functional Magnetic Resonance Imaging Study." *Aphasiology* 17, no. 6/7: 647–65.

Bellow, Saul. 1957. "Leaving the Yellow House." In *Mosby's Memoirs and Other Stories*, by Saul Bellow. New York: Viking.

Bever, Thomas G. 1970. "Cognition and the Development of Language." In *The Cognitive Basis for Linguistic Structure*, edited by J. R. Hayes, 279–362. New York: Wiley.

Bever, Thomas G., J. M. Carroll, and R. Hurtig. 1976. "Analogy or Ungrammatical Sequences that are Utterable and Comprehensible Are the Origins of New Grammars in Language Acquisition and Linguistic Evolution." In *An Integrated Theory of Language Behavior*, edited by Thomas G. Bever, J. J. Katz and D. Terence Langendoen, 149–82. New York: Crowell.

Bizzell, Patricia. 1986. "On the Possibility of a Unified Theory of Composition and Literature." *Rhetoric Review* 4, no. 2: 174–80.

Bloom, Harold. 1994. *The Western Canon*. New York: Harcourt.

Bloom, Paul. 2000. *How Children Learn the Meaning of Words*. Cambridge, MA: MIT Press.

Booth, Wayne C. [1961] 1983. *The Rhetoric of Fiction*. Chicago: University of Chicago Press.

Booth, Wayne C., Gregory G. Colomb, and Joseph M. Williams. 1995. *The Craft of Research*. Chicago: University of Chicago Press.

Bouton, L. 1996. *Pragmatics and Language Learning*. Monograph Series 7, in Pragmatics and Language Learning, 1–20. Urbana-Champaign, IL: Division of English as an International Language, University of Illinois.

Braddock, Richard, Richard Lloyd-Jones, and Lowell Schoer. 1963. *Research in Written Composition*. Urbana, IL: National Council of Teachers of English.

Brookner, Anita. 1984. *Hotel du Lac*. London: Jonathan Cape.

Brooks, Patricia J., and Michael Tomasello. 1999. "How Young Children Constrain Their Argument Structure Constructions." *Language* 75: 720–38.

Brooks, Patricia J., Michael Tomasello, W. Lewis, and K. Dodson. 1999. "Children's Tendency to Overgeneralize Their Argument Structure Constructions: The Entrenchment Hypothesis." *Child Development* 70: 1325–37.

Brown, Dan. 2003. *The Da Vinci Code*. New York: Doubleday.

Bruton, Anthony. 2009. "Designing Research into the Effect of Error Correction in L2 Writing: Not So Straightforward." *Journal of Second Language Writing* 18: 136–40.

Buchweitz, Augusto, Robert Mason, Leda M. B. Tomitch, and Marcel Adam Just. 2009. "Brain Activation for Reading and Listening Comprehension: An fMRI Study of Modality Effects and Individual Differences in Language Comprehension." *Psychology and Neuroscience* 2, no. 2: 111–23.

Carkeet, David. 1979. "The Dialects in Huckleberry Finn." *American Literature* 51, no. 3: 315–32.

Carroll, Susanne E. 1999. "Adults' Sensitivity to Different Sorts of Input." *Language Learning* 49: 37–92.

Carson, Rachel. 1951. *The Sea around Us*. Oxford: Oxford University Press.

———. 1998. *Lost Woods: The Discovered Writings of Rachel Carson*. Edited by Linda Lear. Boston: Beacon.

Carver, Raymond. 1981. "Gazebo." In *What We Talk about When We Talk about Love*. New York: Knopf.

Case, Lisa P., Deborah L. Speece, and Dawn E. Molloy. 2003. "The Validity of a Response-to-Instruction Paradigm to Identify Reading Disabilities: A Longitudinal Analysis of Individual Differences and Contextual Factors." *School Psychology Review* 32: 557–82.

CEEB (College Entrance Examination Board). 2004. "Writing: A Ticket to Work . . . or a Ticket out?"

Chabon, Michael. 1988. *The Mysteries of Pittsburgh*. New York: Morrow.

Chafe, Wallace. 1994. *Discourse, Consciousness, and Time: The Flow and Displacement of Conscious Experience in Speaking and Writing*. Chicago: University of Chicago Press.

Chafe, Wallace, and Deborah Tannen. 1987. "The Relation between Spoken and Written English." *Annual Review of Anthropology* 16: 383–407.

Chametzky, Robert. 1992. "Pragmatics, Prediction, and Relevance." *Journal of Pragmatics* 17: 73–77.

————. 1996. "Finding Language in the Language Arts: Towards 'Cognitive Language Arts.'" Educational Resources Information Center.

Chandler, J. 2003. "The Efficacy of Various Kinds of Error Feedback for Improvement in the Accuracy and Fluency of L2 Student Writing." *Journal of Second Language Writing* 12: 267–96.

Cherry, Roger D., and Paul R. Meyer. 1993. "Reliability Issues in Holistic Assessment." In *Validating Holistic Scoring for Writing Assessment: Theoretical and Empirical Foundations*, edited by M. M. Williamson and Brian A. Huot, 109–41. Cresskill, NJ: Hampton Press.

Chomsky, Noam. 1965. *Aspects of the Theory of Syntax*. Cambridge, MA: MIT Press.

————. 1972. *Language and Mind*. Enlarged ed. New York: Harcourt Brace.

————. 1986. *Knowledge of Language: Its Nature, Origin, and Use*. New York: Praeger.

Clark, Alexander, and Sholem Lappin. 2011. *Linguistic Nativism and the Poverty of the Stimulus*. Malden, MA: Wiley-Blackwell.

Clark, Eve. 1987. "The Principle of Contrast." In *Mechanisms of Language Acquisition*, edited by Brian MacWhinney, 1–33. Hillsdale, NJ: Lawrence Erlbaum.

Clark, Herbert H. 1996. *Using Language*. Cambridge: Cambridge University Press.

Coleridge, Samuel Taylor. 1956–61. *Collected Letters of Samuel Taylor Coleridge*, edited by Earl Leslie Griggs. Oxford: Clarendon Press.

Coltheart, Max. 2002. "Cognitive Neuropsychology." In *Methodology in Cognitive Psychology*, edited by Max Coltheart, 139–74. Hoboken, NJ: Wiley.

————. 2004. "Brain Imaging, Connectionism and Cognitive Neuropsychology." *Cognitive Neuropsychology* 2: 21–25.

Corina, D. P., and H. Knapp. 2006. "Sign Language Processing and Mirror Neuron System." *Cortex* 42, no. 4: 529–39.

Cornell, Nate, Alan D. Castel, Teal S. Eich, and Robert A. Bjork. 2010. "Spacing as the Friend of Both Memory and Induction in Young and Older Adults." *Psychology and Aging* 25, no. 2: 498–503.

Coulson, Seana. 2000. *Semantic Leaps: Frame-Shifting and Conceptual Blending in Meaning Construction*. Cambridge: Cambridge University Press.

Coulson, Seana, and Todd Oakley. 2000. "Blending Basics." *Cognitive Linguistics* 11, no. 3/4: 175–96.

Curtiss, Susan. 1977. *Genie: A Psycholinguistic Study of a Modern-Day "Wild Child."* Boston: Academic Press.

CWPA, Council of Writing Program Administrators, National Council of Teachers of English NCTE, and National Writing Project NWP. 2011. "Framework for Success in Postsecondary Writing." WPA Council.

Daiute, Colette A. 1981. "Psycholinguistic Foundations of the Writing Process." *Research in the Teaching of English* 15, no. 1: 5–22.

Daniel, Hans-Dieter, Sandra Mittag, and Lutz Bornmann. 2007. "The Potential and Problems of Peer Evaluation in Higher Education and Research." In *Quality Assessment for Higher Education in Europe*, edited by A. Cavalli, 71–82. London: Portland Press.

Deane, Paul. 2013. "On the Relation between Automated Essay Scoring and Modern Views of the Writing Construct." *Assessing Writing* 18, no. 1: 7–24.

Deck, Jeff, and Benjamin D. Herson. 2010. *The Great Typo Hunt: Two Friends Changing the World, One Correction at a Time.* New York: Crown.

Dennett, Daniel. 1971. "Intentional Systems." *Journal of Philosophy* 8: 87–106.

———. 1987. *The Intentional Stance.* Cambridge, MA: MIT Press.

———. 1991. *Consciousness Explained.* New York: Back Bay Books.

Derrida, Jacques. 1988. *Limited Inc.* Evanston, IL: Northwestern University Press.

DeVoto, Bernard. 1936. "Genius Is Not Enough." *Saturday Review of Literature*, April 25.

Dobrin, Sidney I. 1999. "Paralogic Hermeneutic Theories, Power, and the Possibility for Liberating Pedagogies." In *Post-Process Theory: Beyond the Writing-Process Paradigm*, edited by Thomas Kent, 132–47. Carbondale, IL: Southern Illinois University Press.

Dockrell, Julie E., and David Messer. 2004. "Lexical Acquisition in the Early School Years." In *Language Development across Childhood and Adolescence*, edited by Ruth A. Berman, 35–52. Amsterdam: John Benjamins.

Dockrell, Julie E., Nick Braisby, and Rachel M. Best. 2007. "Children's Acquisition of Science Terms: Simple Exposure is Insufficient." *Learning and Instruction* 17: 577–94.

Dockrell, Julie E., Geoff Lindsay, and Vincent Connelly. 2009. "The Impact of Specific Language Impairment on Adolescents' Written Text." *Exceptional Children* 75: 427–46.

Douglas, Jacinta. 2010. "Relation of Executive Functioning to Pragmatic Outcome Following Severe Traumatic Brain Injury." *Journal of Speech, Language & Hearing Research* 53, no. 2: 365–82.

Dunbar, S., Daniel Koretz, and H. D. Hoover. 1991. "Quality Control in the Development and Use of Performance Assessment." *Applied Measurement in Education* 4, no. 4: 289–303.

Eaton, Emma, Jane Marshall, and Tim Pring. 2010. "'Like Deja Vu All Over Again': Patterns of Preservation in Two People with Jargon Aphasia." *Aphasiology* 24, no. 9: 1017–31.

Ede, Lisa, and Andrea Lunsford. 1984. "Audience Addressed/Audience Invoked: The Role of Audience in Composition Pedagogy." *College Composition and Communication* 35, no. 2: 155–71.

Elbow, Peter. 1993. "The War between Reading and Writing: And How to End It." *Rhetoric Review* 12, no. 1: 12.

———. 2004. "Write First: Putting Writing Before Reading Is an Effective Approach to Teaching and Learning." *Educational Leadership* 62, no. 2: 10–14.

Elliott, Norbert, Vladimir Briller, and Kamal Joshi. 2007. "Portfolio Assessment: Quantification and Community." *Journal of Writing Assessment* 3: 5–30.

Elman, Jeffrey. 2001. "Connectionism and Language Acquisition." In *Essential Readings in Language Development*, edited by Michael Tomasello and Elizabeth Bates. Oxford: Basil Blackwell.

Elman, Jeffrey, Elizabeth A. Bates, Mark H. Johnson, Annette Karmiloff-Smith, Domenico Parisi, and Kim Plunkett. 1996. *Rethinking Innateness: A Connectionist Perspective on Development*. Cambridge, MA: MIT Press.

Fabb, Nigel. 2010. "Is Literary Language a Development of Ordinary Language?" *Lingua: International Review of General Linguistics* 120, no. 5: 1219–32.

Fahy, T. 2000. "Iteration as a Form of Narrative Control in Gertrude Stein's 'The Good Anna.'" *Style: A Quarterly Journal of Aesthetics, Poetics, Stylistics, and Literary Criticism* 34, no. 1: 25–35.

Fauconnier, Gilles, and Mark Turner. 2002. *The Way We Think: Conceptual Blending and the Mind's Hidden Complexities*. New York: Basic Books.

Fedorenko, Evalina, and Nancy Kanwisher. 2009. "Neuroimaging of Language: Why Hasn't a Clearer Picture Emerged?" *Language and Linguistics Compass* 3/4: 839–65.

Ferreira, Fernando, Kiel Christianson, and Andrew Hollingworth. 2001. "Misinterpretations of Garden-Path Sentences: Implications for Models of Sentence Processing and Reanalysis." *Journal of Psycholinguistic Research* 30, no. 1: 3–20.

Ferreira, V. S., and F. S. Dell. 2000. "Effect of Ambiguity and Lexical Availability on Syntactic and Lexical Production." *Cognitive Psychology* 40, no. 4: 296–340.

Ferris, Dana R. 2004. "The 'Grammar Correction' Debate in L2 Writing: Where Are We, and Where Do We Go from Here?" *Journal of Second Language Writing* 13: 49–62.

Fillmore, Charles, Paul Kay, Laura Michaelis, and Ivan Sag. 2007. "Implicit Signs." <http://lingo.stanford.edu/sag/SBCG/6.pdf>.

Fitzgerald, F. Scott. 1922. *Babylon Revisited and Other Stories*. Edited by Matthew J. Bruccoli. New York: Scribner.

———. 1925. *The Great Gatsby*. New York: Scribner.

Flower, Linda S. 1985. *Problem-Solving Strategies for Writing*. New York: Harcourt Brace.

Flower, Linda S., and John R. Hayes. 1981. "A Cognitive Process Theory of Writing." *College Composition and Communication* 32: 365–87.

Flurkey, A. & J. Xu, eds. 2003. *On the Revolution in Reading: The Selected Writings of Kenneth S. Goodman*. Portsmouth, NH: Heinemann.

Fulkerson, Richard. 1990. "Composition Theory in the Eighties: Axiological Consensus and Paradigmatic Diversity." *College Composition and Communication* 41, no. 4: 409–29.

———. 2005. "Summary and Critique: Composition at the Turn of the Twenty-first Century." *College Composition and Communication* 56, no. 4: 654–87.

Gaillard, W. D., L. M. Balsamo, Z. Ibrahim, B. C. Sachs, and B. Xu. 2003. "fMRI Identifies Regional Specialization of Neural Networks for Reading in Young Children." *Neurology* 60, no. 1: 94–100.

Gallistel, C. R., and A. P. King. 2009. *Memory and the Computational Brain: Why Cognitive Science Will Transform Neuroscience*. New York: Wiley/Blackwell.

Gee, James Paul. 1992. "What Is Literacy?" *Journal of Education* 171: 5–25.

———. 2001. "A Sociocultural Perspective on Early Literacy Development." In *Handbook of Early Literacy Research*, edited by S. B. Neuman and D. K. Dickinson, 30–42. New York: Guilford Press.

———. 2011. *An Introduction to Discourse Analysis: Theory and Method*. Oxford: Oxford University Press.

Gibson, E. 1991. "A Computational Theory of Human Linguistic Processing: Memory Limitations and Processing Breakdown." Dissertation, Carnegie Mellon University.

———. 1998. "Linguistic Complexity: Locality of Syntactic Dependencies." *Cognition* 68, no. 1: 1–76.

Givón, Talmy. 1995. "Coherence in Text vs. Coherence in Mind." In *Coherence in Spontaneous Text*, Typological Studies in Language 31, 59–115. Amsterdam: Benjamins.

Gofine, Miriam. 2012. "How Are We Doing? A Review of Assessments within Writing Centers." *The Writing Center Journal* 32: 39–49.

Goldberg, Adele E. 1995. *Constructions: A Construction Grammar Approach to Argument Structure*. Chicago: University of Chicago Press.

———. 2006. *Constructions at Work: The Nature of Generalization in Language*. Oxford: Oxford University Press.

Goldsmith, John A. 2010. "Segmentation and Morphology." In *Handbook of Computational Linguistics and Natural Language Processing*, edited by Alex Clark, Chris Fox, and Shalom Lappin, 364–93. Oxford: Blackwell.

Goldsmith, John A., and Aris Xanthos. 2009. "Learning Phonological Categories." *Language* 85, no. 1: 4–38.

Goldstein, D. G., and Gerd Gigerenzer. 2002. "Models of Ecological Rationality: The Recognition Heuristic." *Psychological Review* 109: 75–90.

Gopnik, Adam. 2008. "A Fan's Notes." *Humanities*, May/June.

Gould, Stephen Jay. 1987. "The Terrifying Normalcy of AIDS." *New York Times*, April 19.

Graham, Steve. 2006. "Strategy Instruction and the Teaching of Writing: A Meta-Analysis." In *Handbook of Writing Research*, edited by Charles A. MacArthur, Steve Graham, and Jill Fitzgerald, 187–207. New York: Guilford.

Graham, Steve, and Delores Perin. 2007. "A Meta-Analysis of Writing Instruction for Adolescent Students." *Journal of Educational Psychology* 99, no. 3: 445–76.

Graham, Steve, and Karin Sandmel. 2011. "The Process Writing Approach: A Meta-Analysis." *Journal of Educational Research* 104, no. 6: 396–407.

Grice, H. Paul. 1975. *Logic and Conversation*. Vol. 3, in *Syntax and Semantics: Speech Acts*, edited by Peter Cole and Jerry Morgan, 41–58. New York: Academic Press.

Guth, Dorothy Lobrano, ed. 1976. *The Letters of E. B. White*. New York: Harper & Row.

Hall, Nigel. 1999. "Young Children's Use of Graphic Punctuation." *Language and Education* 13, no. 3: 178–93.

Hall, Robert A., Jr. 1973. "The Transferred Epithet in P. G. Wodehouse." *Linguistic Inquiry* 4, no. 1: 92–94.

Hart, Betty, and Todd Risley. 1995. *Meaningful Differences in the Everyday Experiences of Young American Children*. Baltimore, MD: Brookes Publishing.

Hartwell, Patrick. 1985. "Grammar, Grammars, and the Teaching of Grammar." *College English* 47, no. 2: 105–27.

Haswell, Richard. 2005. "NCTE/CCCE's Recent War on Scholarship." *Written Communication* 22, no. 2: 198–223.

Hawkins, Eric. 1987. *Awareness of Language*. Cambridge: Cambridge University Press.

Hemingway, Ernest. 1929. *A Farewell to Arms*. New York: Scribner.

Herman, David. 2008. "Narrative Theory and the Intentional Stance." *Partial Answers: Journal of Literature and the History of Ideas* 6, no. 2: 233–60.

Hidi, Suzanne, and Pietro Boscolo. 2006. "Motivation and Writing." In *Handbook of Writing Research*, edited by Charles A. MacArthur, Steve Graham, and Jill Fitzgerald, 144–57. New York: Guilford.

Hills, Thomas T., Josita Maouene, Brian Riordan, and Linda B. Smith. 2010. "The Associative Structure of Language: Contextual Diversity in Early Word Learning." *Journal of Memory and Language* 63, no. 3: 259–73.

Hochman, Guy, Shahar Ayal, and Andreas Glockner. 2010. "Physiological Arousal in Processing Recognition Information: Ignoring or Integrating Cognitive Cues." *Judgment and Decision Making* 5, no. 4 (July): 285–99.

Huck, Geoffrey J. 2005. "Gerundive Modifiers in English and Korean." In *Polymorphous Linguistics*, edited by Salikoko S. Mufwene, Elaine Francis, and Rebecca S. Wheeler, 183–201. Cambridge, MA: MIT Press.

———. Forthcoming *a*. "Semi-Unacceptable Expressions, Meta-Grammatical Acceptability, and the Issue of Memory Limitations in Construction Grammar." Writing Department, York University, Toronto, ON Canada M4E 3M5.

———. Forthcoming *b*. "The Effect on Writing Skill of Participation in a Reading Group: Proposal and Rational for an Experiment." Writing Department, York University, Toronto, ON Canada M4E 3M5. For presentation at the Conference on College Composition and Communication Annual Conference, Tampa, FL, March 18, 2015.

Huck, Geoffrey J., and John A. Goldsmith. 1995. *Ideology and Linguistic Theory: Noam Chomsky and the Deep Structure Debates*. London: Routledge.

Huddleston, Rodney, and Geoffrey Pullum. 2002. *The Cambridge Grammar of the English Language*. Cambridge: Cambridge University Press.

Hunston, Susan. 1995. "Grammar in Teacher Education: The Role of a Corpus." *Language Awareness* 4, no. 1: 15–31.

Hurston, Zora Neale. 1928. "How It Feels to Be Colored Me." *The World Tomorrow*, May. Reprinted in *I Love Myself When I Am Laughing: A Zora Neale Hurston Reader*, edited by Alice Walker. New York: Feminist Press, 1979.

Ingram, John C. L. 2007. *Neurolinguistics: An Introduction to Spoken Language Processing and Its Disorders*. Cambridge: Cambridge University Press.

Jay, Timothy. 2003. *The Psychology of Language*. Upper Saddle River, NJ: Pearson Education.

Johnson, M. H., and Y. Munakata. 2005. "Processes of Change in Brain and Cognitive Development." *Trends in Cognitive Sciences* 9: 152–58.

Johnstone, Barbara. 2008. *Discourse Analysis*. Malden, MA: Wiley-Blackwell.

Jones, Casey. 2001. "The Relationship between Writing Centers and Improvement in Writing Ability: An Assessment of the Literature." *Education* 122: 3–20.

Jonsson, Anders, and Gunilla Svingby. 2007. "The Use of Scoring Rubrics: Reliability, Validity and Educational Consequences." *Educational Research Review* 2: 130–44.

Joyce, James. 1922. *Ulysses*. Paris: Shakespeare & Company.

Jurafsky, D., and J. H. Martin. 2009. *Speech and Language Processing: An Introduction to Natural Language Processing, Computational Linguistics, and Speech Recognition*. Upper Saddle River, NJ: Pearson Education.

Kanwisher, Nancy. 2010. "Functional Specificity in the Human Brain: A Window into the Functional Architecture of the Mind." *Proceedings of the National Academy of Sciences* 107(25): 11163–11170

Karmiloff-Smith, Annette. 1998. "Development Itself is the Key to Understanding Developmental Disorders." *Trends in Cognitive Sciences* 2, no. 10: 389–98.

Kasper, Gabriela. 1997. *Can Pragmatic Competence Be Taught?* Honolulu: University of Hawai'i Second Language Teaching & Curriculum Center.

Kasper, Gabriela, and Peter R. Rose. 1999. "Pragmatics and SLA." *Annual Review of Applied Linguistics* 19: 81–104.

Katanoda, Kota, Kohki Yoshikawa, and Morihiro Sugishita. 2001. "A Functional MRI Study on the Neural Substrates for Writing." *Human Brain Mapping* 13: 34–42.

Kay, Paul. 1994. "Anaphoric Binding in Construction Grammar." *Proceedings of the Berkeley Linguistic Society*. Berkeley, CA: Berkeley Linguistic Society.

Kellogg, Ronald T. 2008. "Training Writing Skills: A Cognitive Developmental Perspective." *Journal of Writing Research* 1, no. 1: 1–26.

Kingwell, G. 1980. *Repetition, Confusion, and Surprise: A Stylistics Based Approach to Teaching Poetry in EFL Classrooms*. London: Institute of Education, London University.

Knight, Lania. 2007. "A Conversation with David Sedaris." *The Missouri Review*, 72–89.

Koretz, Daniel, Daniel McCaffrey, Stephen Klein, Robert Bell, and Brian Stecher. 1992. "The Reliability of Scores from the 1992 Vermont Portfolio Assessment Program: Interim Report." Santa Monica, CA: RAND Corporation.

Krashen, Stephen D. 1993. *The Power of Reading: Insights from the Research*. Englewood, CO: Libraries Unlimited.

———. 2004. *The Power of Reading: Insights from the Research, Second Edition*. Portsmouth, NH: Heinemann.

———. 2010. "The Goodman-Smith Hypothesis, the Input Hypothesis, the Comprehension Hypothesis, and the (Even Stronger) Case for Free Voluntary Reading." In *Defying Convention, Inventing the Future in Literacy Research and Practice: Essays in Tribute to Ken and Yetta Goodman*, edited by P. Anders, 49–60. New York: Routledge. 2010.

———. 2011. *Free Voluntary Reading*. Santa Barbara, CA: Libraries Unlimited.

Kremers, Marshall. 1983. "Samuel Newman and the Reduction of Rhetoric in the Early Nineteenth-Century College." *Rhetoric Society Quarterly* 13, no. 3/4: 185–92.

Labov, William. 1963. "The Social Motivation of a Sound Change." *Word* 19: 273–309.

Lakoff, George, and Mark Johnson. 1980. *Metaphors We Live By*. Chicago: University of Chicago Press.

Lane, Anthony. 2000. "The Maria Problem." *The New Yorker*, February 14. Reprinted in Anthony Lane, *Nobody's Perfect: Writings from the New Yorker*. New York: Knopf, 2002.

Leech, Geoffrey, and Roger Garside. 1991. "Running a Grammar Factory: The Production of Syntactically Analysed Corpora or 'Treebanks.'" In *English Computer Corpora: Selected Papers and Research Guide*, edited by Stig Johansson and Anna-Brita Stenstrom, 15–31. Berlin: Mouton De Gruyter.

Lerner, Neal. 2003. "Writing Center Assessment: Searching for the 'Proof' of Our Effectiveness." In, *The Center Will Hold: Critical Perspectives on Writing Center Scholarship*, edited by Michael A. Pemberton and Joyce Kinkead. Logan: Utah State University Press: 58–73.

Levi, Judith N. 1974. "On the Alleged Idiosyncrasy of Nonpredicate NPs." In *Papers from the Tenth Regional Meeting*, edited by M. W. LaGaly, R. A. Fox, and A. Bruck, 402–15. Chicago: Chicago Linguistic Society.

Levin, Beth. 1993. *English Verb Classes and Alternations*. Chicago: University of Chicago Press.

Lewis, D. 1979. "Scorekeeping in a Language Game." *Journal of Philosophical Logic* 8: 339–59.

Liberman, Mark. 2006. "An Apology to Our Readers." Language Log. <http://itre.cis.upenn.edu/~myl/languagelog/archives/003147.html>.

Lodge, David. 2002. *Consciousness and the Novel: Connected Essays*. Cambridge, MA: Harvard University Press.

Lynch, E. J. 1968. "The Origin and Development of Rhetoric in the Plan of Studies of 1599 of the Society of Jesus." Ph.D. dissertation, Northwestern University.

Lynch, Jack. 2009. *The Lexicographer's Dilemma: The Evolution of "Proper" English, from Shakespeare to South Park*. New York: Walker & Company.

MacDonald, Susan Peck. 1994. *Professional Academic Writing in the Humanities and Social Sciences*. Carbondale, IL: Southern Illinois University Press.

MacSweeney, Malread, et al. 2002. "Neural Systems Underlying British Sign Language and Audio-Visual English Processing in Native Users." *Brain* 125, no. 7 (July): 1583–93.

Mailer, Norman. 1948. *The Naked and the Dead*. New York: Rinehart.

Maratsos, Michael. 1983. "Some Current Issues in the Study of Acquisition and Grammar." In *Handbook of Child Psychology*, Vol. 3: *Cognitive Development*, edited by P. Mussen, 707–86. New York: Wiley.

Massaro, Dominic W. 2012. "Acquiring Literacy Naturally: Behavioral Science and Technology Could Empower Preschool Children to Learn to Read Naturally Without Instruction." *American Scientist* 100: 324–33.

McCawley, James D. 1988. *The Syntactic Phenomena of English*. Chicago: University of Chicago Press.

McGurl, Mark. 2009. *The Program Era*. Cambridge, MA: Harvard University Press.

McKool, Sharon S. 2007. "Factors That Influence the Decision to Read: An Investigation of Fifth Grade Students' Out of School Reading Habits." *Reading Improvement* 44, no. 3: 111–31.

McNeill, David. 1966. "Developmental Psycholinguistics." In *The Genesis of Language: A Psycholinguistic Approach*, edited by F. Smith and George Miller, 15–84. Cambridge, MA: MIT Press.

McNeill, William H. 1991. *Hutchins' University: A Memoir of the University of Chicago 1929–1950*. Chicago: University of Chicago Press.

Menand, Louis. 2000. "In a Strange Land." *The New Yorker*, November 6, 95.

Meriwether, James B., and Michael Millgate. 1968. *Lion in the Garden: Interviews with William Faulkner, 1926–1962*. New York: Random House.

Messenger, William E., Jan de Bruyn, Judy Brown, and Ramona Montagnes. 2009. *The Canadian Writer's Handbook*. 5th ed. Oxford: Oxford University Press.

Michaelis, Laura A. 2006. "Construction Grammar." In *The Encyclopedia of Language and Linguistics*, 2nd ed., edited by K. Brown, 3: 73–84. Oxford: Elsevier.

Miller, George A. 1996. *The Science of Words*. New York: Freeman.

Miller, Jim. 2006. "Spoken and Written English." In *The Handbook of English Linguistics*, edited by Bas Aarts and April McMahon, 670–91. Malden, MA: Wiley-Blackwell.

Mitchell, J., M. Lapata, V. Demberg, and F. Keller. 2010. "Semantic and Semantic Factors in Processing Difficulty: An Integrated Measure." *Proceedings of the 48th Annual Meeting of the Association for Computational Linguistics*, 196–206. Stroudsburg, PA: Association for Computational Linguistics.

Morgan, Jerry L. 1973. "Sentence Fragments and the Notion 'Sentence'." In *Papers in Honor of Henry and Renee Kahane*, edited by Braj Kachru, 719–51. Urbana and Chicago: University of Illinois Press.

Morrison, Toni. 1998. "Strangers." In *A Kind of Rapture*, edited by Robert Bergman. New York: Pantheon.

Moss, Pamela A. 1994."Can There Be Validity without Reliability?" *Educational Researcher* 23, no. 4: 5–12.

Murphy, Christina. 1996. "Process." In *Key Words in Composition Studies*, edited by Paul Heilker and Peter Vandenberg, 192–95. Portsmouth, NH: Boynton/Cook Heinemann.

Murray, Donald M. 1972. "Teach Writing as a Process Not a Product." The Leaflet (The New England Association of Teachers of English).

Murray, Neil. 2010. "Pragmatics, Awareness Raising, and the Cooperative Principle." *ELT Journal* 64, no. 3: 293–301.

Nagy, William E., and Richard C. Anderson. 1984. "How Many Words Are There in Printed School English." *Reading Research Quarterly* 19, no. 3: 304–30.

Nakatani, Yasuo. 2005. "The Effects of Awareness-Raising on Oral Communication Strategy Use." *Modern Language Journal* 89, no. 1: 76–91.

Nation, I. S. P. 2001a. "How Large a Vocabulary Is Needed for Reading and Listening?" *Canadian Modern Language Review* 63, no. 1: 59–82.

———. 2001b. *Learning Vocabulary in Another Language*. Cambridge: Cambridge University Press.

Newport, Elissa L. 1990. "Maturational Constraints on Language Learning." *Cognitive Science* 14: 11–28.

Newport, Elissa L., and R. P. Meier. 1985. *The Acquisition of American Sign Language*. Hillsdale, NJ: Lawrence Erlbaum Associates.

Niiler, Luke. 2005. "'The Numbers Speak' Again: A Continued Statistical Analysis of Writing Center Outcomes." *Writing Lab Newsletter* 29: 13–15.

Niven, Penelope. 1991. *Carl Sandburg: A Biography*. New York: Scribner.

Nunberg, Geoffrey. 1983. "The Decline of Grammar." *The Atlantic*, December, 31–46.

———. 1990. *The Linguistics of Punctuation*. Stanford, CA: Center for the Study of Language and Information.

Oakley, Todd. 2009. *From Attention to Meaning: Explorations in Semiotics, Linguistics, and Rhetoric*. Bern: Peter Lang.

O'Connor, Flannery. 1970. *Mystery and Manners*. New York: Farrar, Straus and Giroux.

Olson, Gary A. 1999. "Toward a Post-Process Composition: Abandoning the Rhetoric of Assertion." In *Post-Process Theory: Beyond the Writing-Process Paradigm*, edited by Thomas Kent, 7–15. Carbondale: Southern Illinois University Press.

Ondaatje, Michael. 1992. *The English Patient*. Toronto: McClelland and Stewart.

Orwell, George. 1946. "Why I Write." *Gangrel*, Summer.

———. 1936. "Shooting an Elephant." *New Writing*, 1936. Published in George Orwell, *Shooting an Elephant and Other Essays*. New York: Harcourt, 1950.

Patterson, Annabel. 1995. "Intention." In *Critical Terms for Literary Study*, 2d ed., by Frank Lentricchia and Thomas McLaughlin, 139–46. Chicago: University of Chicago Press.

Perelman, Les. 2012. "Construct Validity, Length, Score, and Time in Holistically Graded Writing Assessments: The Case Against Automated Essay Scoring (AES)." In *International*

Advances in Writing Research: Culture, Places, Measures, edited by C. Bazerman et al., 121–32. Fort Collins, CO: Parlor Press.

Pickard, Richard, Jan McAllister, and Simon Horton. 2010. "Spontaneous Recovery of Writing After Stroke: A Case Study of the First 100 Days." *Aphasiology* 24, no. 10: 1223–41.

Pinker, Steven. 1989. *Learnability and Cognition*. Cambridge, MA: Harvard University Press.

———. 2014. *The Sense of Style: The Thinking Person's Guide to Writing in the 21ˢᵗ Century*. New York: Viking.

Pullum, Geoffrey. 2004. "The Dan Brown Code." Language Log. May 1. <http://itre.cis.upenn/~myl/languagelog/archives/000844.html>.

———. 2006. "Ideology, Power, and Linguistic Theory." <http://www.lel.ed.ac.uk/~gpullum/MLA2004.pdf>.

———. 2010. "These 'Rules' Are Already Broken." *Times Higher Education Supplement*, November 11, 56.

Purcell, J. J., J. Shea, and B. Rapp. 2014. "Beyond the Visual Word Form Area: The Orthography-Semantics Interface in Spelling and Reading." *Cognitive Neuropsychology* 16: 1–29.

Rapin, I., S. Mattis, A. J. Rowan, and G. G. Golden. 1977. "Verbal Auditory Agnosia in Children." *Developmental Medicine & Child Neurology* 19: 197–207.

Reinhart, Tanya. 1983. *Anaphora and Semantic Interpretation*. Chicago: University of Chicago Press.

Rezaei, Ali Reza, and Michael Lovorn. 2010. "Reliability and Validity Rubrics for Assessment through Writing." *Assessing Writing* 15, no. 1: 18–39.

Rich, Adrienne. 1972. "When We Dead Awaken: Writing as Re-Vision." *College English* 34: 18–30.

Richardson, Alan. 2010. *The Neural Sublime: Cognitive Theories and Romantic Texts*. Baltimore, MD: Johns Hopkins University Press.

Rips, Lance J., Amber Bloomfield, and Jennifer Asmuth. 2008. "From Numerical Concepts to Concepts of Number." *Behavioral and Brain Sciences* 31, no. 6: 623–42.

Robins, R. H. 1967. *A Short History of Linguistics*. Bloomington: Indiana University Press.

Rogers, L. A., and Steve Graham. 2008. "A Meta-Analysis of Single Subject Design Writing Intervention Research." *Journal of Educational Psychology* 100, no. 4: 879–906.

Rosch, Eleanor, and Carolyn B. Mervis. 1975. "Family Resemblances: Studies in the Internal Structure of Categories." *Cognitive Psychology* 7, no. 4: 573–605.

Rose, Debra J., Edward M. Heath, and Donald M. Megale. 1990. Development of a Diagnostic Instrument for Evaluating Tennis Serving Performance. *Perceptual and Motor Skills* 71: 355–63.

Ross, John Robert. 1967. "Constraints on Variables in Syntax." Dissertation, Massachusetts Institute of Technology.

———. 1991. "Fog Cat Fog." In *Cognition and the Symbolic Processes: Applied and Ecological Perspectives*, edited by Robert Hoffman and David Palermo, 187–205. Hillsdale, NJ: Lawrence Erlbaum.

Sag, Ivan, and Thomas Wasow. n.d. "A Performance Compatible Competence Grammar." <http://www.stanford.edu/~wasow/procpap2.pdf>.

Salinger, J. D. 1951. *The Catcher in the Rye*. Boston: Little Brown.

Salvatori, Mariolina. 1996. "Conversations with Texts: Reading the Teaching of Composition." *College English* 58: 440–54.

Schild, Ulrike, Brigitte Roder, and Claudia K. Friedrich. 2011. "Learning to Read Shapes: The Activation of Neural Lexical Representations in the Speech Recognition Pathway." *Developmental Cognitive Neuroscience* 1, no. 2: 163–74.

Schmidt, Richard W. 1990. "The Role of Consciousness in Second Language Learning." *Applied Linguistics* 11, no. 2: 129–58.

Schutze, Carson. 1996. *The Empirical Base of Linguistics: Grammaticality Judgments and Linguistic Methodology*. Chicago: University of Chicago Press.

Scott, Sophie, and Ingrid Johnsrude. 2003. "The Neuroanatomical and Functional Organization of Speech Perception." *Trends in Neurosciences* 26, no. 2: 100–106.

Searle, John R. 1977. "Reiterating the Differences: A Reply to Derrida." *Glyph* 1: 172–208.

———. 1983. *Intentionality: An Essay in the Philosophy of Mind*. Cambridge: Cambridge University Press.

Sebeok, Thomas A., ed. 1960. *Style in Language*. Cambridge, MA: MIT Press.

Segaert, Katrien, Laura Menenti, Kirsten Weber, Karl Magnus Petersson, and Peter Hagoort. 2012. "Shared Syntax in Language Production and Language Comprehension: An fMRI Study." *Cerebral Cortex* 22 (July): 1662–70.

Seitz, James. 1991. "Composition's Misunderstandings of Metaphor." *College Composition and Communication* 42, no. 3: 291–92.

Sheldon, C. A., G. L. Malcolm, and J. J. Barton. 2008. "Alexia with and without Agraphia: An Assessment of Two Classical Syndromes." *Canadian Journal of Neurological Science* 35: 616–24.

Shermis, Mark D., and Ben Hamner. 2012. "Contrasting State-of-the-Art Automated Scoring of Essays: Analysis." <http://www.scoreright.org/NCME_2012_Paper3_29_12.pdf>.

Shin, Sang-Keun. 2008. "'Fire Your Proofreader!' Grammar Correction in the Classroom." *ELT Journal* 62: 358–65.

Sirois, Sylvain, Michael Spratling, Michael S. C. Thomas, Gert Westermann, Denis Mareschal, and Mark H. Johnson. 2008. "Précis of Neuroconstructivism: How the Brain Constructs Cognition." *Behavioral and Brain Sciences* 31, no. 3: 321–31.

Smiley, Jane. 2005. *Thirteen Ways of Looking at the Novel*. New York: Anchor Books.

Smith, Frank. 1988. *Joining the Literacy Club*. Portsmouth, NH: Heinemann.

Smith, Sara W., Hiromi Pat Noda, Steven Andrews, and Andreas H. Jucker. 2005. "Setting the Stage: How Speakers Prepare Listeners for the Introduction of Referents in Dialogues and Monologues." *Journal of Pragmatics* 37, no. 11: 1865–95.

Smith, Zadie. 2000. *White Teeth*. London: Hamish Hamilton.

Sperber, Dan, and Deirdre Wilson. 1995. *Relevance: Communication and Cognition*. 2d ed. Oxford: Blackwell.

Sperber, Dan, Francesco Cara, and Vittorio Girotta. 1995. "Relevance Theory Explains the Selection Task." *Cognition* 57: 31–95.

Stalnaker, R. 1998. "On the Representation of Context." *Journal of Logic, Language, and Information* 7: 3–19.

Stanovich, Keith E. 1986. "The Matthew Effect in Reading: Some Consequences of Individual Differences in the Acquisition of Literacy." *Reading Research Quarterly* 27, no. 4: 360–407.

Stein, Gertrude. 1914. *Tender Buttons*. New York: Claire Marie.

Stevens, Wallace. 1923. "The Emperor of Ice Cream." In *Harmonium*. New York: Knopf. Also in *The Collected Poems of Wallace Stevens*. New York: Knopf, 1954.

————. 1966. *Letters of Wallace Stevens*. Selected and edited by Holly Stevens. New York: Knopf.

Strom, Ingrid M. 1960. "Research on Grammar and Usage and Its Implications for Teaching and Writing." *Bulletin of the School of Education* (Indiana University) 36: 13–14.

Stromswold, Karin, and William Snyder. 1995. "Acquisition of Datives, Particles, and Related Constructions: Evidence for a Parametric Account." *Proceedings of the 19th Annual Boston University Conference on Language Development*, edited by D. MacLaughlin and S. McEwan, 621–28. Somerville, MA: Cascadilla Press, 1995.

Strunk, William, Jr., and E. B. White. 1972. *The Elements of Style*. 2d ed. New York: Macmillan.

Stubbs, Michael. 1983. *Discourse Analysis*. Chicago: University of Chicago Press, 1983.

Swift, Jonathan. 1710. "A Proposal for Correcting English Style and on Corruptions of Style." *The Tatler*, September 26.

Taylor, B. M., B. J. Frye, and G. Maruyama. 1990. "Time Spent Reading and Reading Growth." *American Educational Research Journal* 27: 351–62.

Tettamanti, Marco, Irene Rotondi, Daniela Perani, Giuseppe Scotti, and Ferruccio Fazio. 2009. "Syntax without Language: Neurobiological Evidence for Cross-Domain Syntactic Computations." *Cortex* 45, no. 7: 825–38.

Thomas, Francis-Noel, and Mark Turner. 1994. *Clear and Simple as the Truth: Writing Classic Prose*. Princeton, NJ: Princeton University Press.

Thomas, M. S. C., and Annette Karmiloff-Smith. 2002. "Are Developmental Disorders like Cases of Adult Brain Damage? Implications for Connectionist Modelling." *Behavioral and Brain Sciences* 25, no. 6: 727–88.

Thomason, Richmond. 1990. "Accommodation, Meaning, and Implicature: Interdisciplinary Foundations for Pragmatics." In *Intentions in Communication*, edited by Philip Cohen, Jerry Morgan, and Martha Pollack, 325–63. Cambridge, MA: MIT Press.

Tobin, Lad. 1989. "Bridging Gaps: Analyzing Our Students' Metaphors for Composing." *College Composition and Communication* 40: 444–58.

Tobin, V. 2009. "Cognitive Bias and the Poetics of Surprise." *Language and Literature* 18, no. 2: 155–72.

Todd, Peter M., and Gerd Gigerenzer. 2012. *Ecological Rationality: Intelligence in the World*. New York: Oxford University Press.

Tomasello, Michael. 2003. *Constructing a Language: A Usage Based Theory of Language Acquisition*. Cambridge, MA: Harvard University Press.

————. 2008. *The Origins of Human Communication*. Cambridge, MA: MIT Press.

Tomasello, Michael, and Elizabeth Bates. 2001. *Language Development*. Oxford: Blackwell.

Troia, Gary A., Rebecca K. Shankland, and Kimberly A. Wolbers. 2012. "Motivation Research in Writing: Theoretical and Empirical Considerations." *Reading & Writing Quarterly* 28: 5–28.

Truscott, John. 1996a. "The Case against Grammar Correction in L2 Writing Classes." *Language Learning* 46, no. 2: 327–69.

————. 1996b. "What's Wrong with Oral Grammar Correction?" *Canadian Modern Language Review* 55: 437–67.

————. 1999. "The Case for the Case against Grammar Correction in L2 Writing Classes." *Language Learning* 8, no. 2: 111–22.

Truscott, John. 2007. "The Effect of Error Correction on Learners' Ability to Write Accurately." *Journal of Second Language Writing* 16: 255–72.

———. 2010. "Some Thoughts on Anthony Bruton's Critique of the Correction Debate." *System* 38: 329–35.

Truscott, John, and Angela Yi-Ping Hsu. 2008. "Error Correction, Revision, and Learning." *Journal of Second Language Writing* 17: 292–305.

Truss, Lynn. 2003. *Eats, Shoots and Leaves*. London: Profile.

Turner, Mark. 1991. *Reading Minds*. Princeton, NJ: Princeton University Press.

Updike, John. 1964. "Beer Can." *The New Yorker*, January 18. Published in John Updike, *Assorted Prose*. New York: Knopf, 1965.

———. 1996. "Review of *The New Fowler's Modern English Usage*." *The New Yorker*, December 23 and 30, 148.

———. 1998. "Awriiiiighhhhhhhhhht! Tom Wolfe Looks Hard at America." *The New Yorker*, November 9: 99–102.

Van Hoek, Karen. 1995. *Anaphora and Conceptual Structure*. Chicago: University of Chicago Press.

Villanueva, Victor, ed. 2003. *Cross-Talk in Comp Theory*. Urbana, IL: National Council of Teachers of English.

von Fintel, K. 2000. "What Is Presupposition Accommodation?" Unpublished manuscript, MIT.

———. 2008. "What Is 'Presupposition Accommodation', Again?" *Philosophical Perspectives* 22: 137–70.

Wade, Shari L., et al. 2010. "A Randomized Trial of Teen Online Problem Solving for Improving Executive Function Deficits Following Pediatric Traumatic Brain Injury." *Journal of Head Trauma Rehabilitation* 26, no. 6: 409–15.

Wahlberg, H. J., and S. L. Tsai. 1985. "Correlates of Reading Achievement and Attitude: A National Assessment Study." *Journal of Educational Research* 78, no. 3: 159–67.

Wałaszewska, Ewa. 2011. "Broadening and Narrowing Lexical Development: How Relevance Theory Can Account for Children's Overextensions and Underextensions." *Journal of Pragmatics* 43, no. 1: 314–26.

Walker, Alice. 1983. "Beauty: When the Other Dancer Is the Self." In *In Search of Our Mother's Gardens: Womanist Prose*, by Alice Walker. New York: Harcourt Brace.

Wallace, David Foster. 2001. "Tense Present: Democracy, English, and the Wars over Usage." *Harper's Magazine*, April, 39–58.

Warwick, Elley B. 1989. "Vocabulary Acquisition from Listening to Stories." *Reading Research Quarterly* 24: 174–86.

White, E. B. 1928. "Potter's Field." *The New Yorker*, May 5. Published in *The Fun of It: Stories from the Talk of the Town: The New Yorker*, edited by Lillian Ross. New York: The Modern Library, 2001.

———. 1941. "Once More to the Lake." In *One Man's Meat*. New York: Harper & Row.

———. 1976. *Letters of E. B. White*. Collected and edited by Dorothy Lobrano Guth. New York: Harper & Row.

Williams, Joseph M. 2005. *Style: Toward Clarity and Grace*. Chicago: University of Chicago Press.

Wilson, Deirdre. 1992. "Reply to Chametzky." *Journal of Pragmatics* 17: 73–77.

Wilson, Deirdre, and Dan Sperber. 2004. "Relevance Theory." In *The Handbook of Pragmatics*, edited by Laurence R. Horn and Gregory L. Ward, 607–32. Malden, MA: Wiley/Blackwell.

———. 2012. *Meaning and Relevance*. Oxford: Oxford University Press.

Wimsatt, William K., and Monroe C. Beardsley. 1946. "The Intentional Fallacy." *The Sewanee Review* 54: 468–88.

Wingate, M. E. 1984. "Fluency, Disfluency, Dysfluency, and Stuttering." *Journal of Fluency Disorders* 9, no. 2: 163–68.

Wolfe, Tom. 1965a. "The Last American Hero." In *The Kandy-Kolored Tangerine-Flake Streamline Baby*, by Tom Wolfe. New York: Farrar, Straus & Giroux.

———. 1965b. "Las Vegas (What?) Las Vegas (Can't Hear You! Too Noisy) Las Vegas!!!!" In *The Kandy-Kolored Tangerine-Flake Streamline Baby*, by Tom Wolfe. New York: Farrar, Straus & Giroux.

———. 2000. *Hooking Up*. New York: Farrar, Straus, & Giroux.

Wong, Min Ney, Bruce Murdoch, and Brooke-Mai Whelan. 2010. "Language Disorders Subsequent to Mild Traumatic Brain Injury (MTBI): Evidence from Four Cases." *Aphasiology* 24, no. 10: 1155–69.

Woolf, Virginia. 1925. *Mrs. Dalloway*. New York: Harcourt, Brace & World.

———. 1927. *To the Lighthouse*. London: Hogarth Press.

Ylvisaker, Mark. 2006. "Self-Coaching: A Context-Sensitive, Person Centered Approach to Social Communication after Traumatic Brain Injury." *Brain Impairment* 7, no. 3: 246–58.

Zunshine, Lisa. 2006. *Why We Read Fiction: Theory of Mind and the Novel*. Columbus: Ohio State University Press.

Index

Italicized page numbers refer to a table or figure.